Designing the just learning society

A CRITICAL INQUIRY

Michael Welton

niace
promoting adult learning

Published by the National Institute of Adult Continuing Education
(England and Wales)
21 De Montfort Street, Leicester LE1 7GE
Company registration no: 2603322
Charity registration no: 1002775

First published 2005
© 2005 Michael Welton

NIACE has a broad remit to promote lifelong learning opportunities for
adults. NIACE works to develop increased participation in education and
training, particularly for those who do not have easy access because of barriers
of class, gender, age, race, language and culture, learning difficulties and
disabilities, or insufficient financial resources.

For a full catalogue of NIACE's publications, please visit

www.niace.org.uk/publications

Cataloguing in Publications Data
A CIP record for this title is available from the British Library

ISBN 1 86201 242 3

Cover design by Boldface, London
Designed and typeset by Avon DataSet, Bidford-on-Avon, Warwickshire
Printed and bound in Great Britain by Antony Rowe Limited, Chippenham

Kate Monaghan
Summer 2005

Contents

Propelled into the learning age

This book, like all texts, is the product of a particular time and place. My own intellectual biography is inescapably woven into the narrative. During the fall of 2002, one year after the planes crashed into the World Trade Center, wounding the American psyche and releasing reckless impulses, I started working on two research projects simultaneously. One was an overly ambitious attempt to imagine how one might map the contours of the Canadian learning society from the time of exploration, conquest and Amerindian wars and cultural conflict to the present. The other, in part the product of designing and teaching graduate seminars at Mount Saint Vincent University, was an attempt to gather readings and insights into the learning society paradigm that was steadily colonising the international field of adult education. This proved to be both exhausting and exhilarating. At the same time, I was reading and writing about the meaning of events in the Middle East. This caused considerable agony and, in moments, despair over the spinning wheel of suffering.

From an intensive reading of historical literature on the mental outlook in European intellectual circles in the fifteenth through seventeenth centuries, it began to dawn on me that one might be able to trace the idea of a learning, or knowledge society, to the axial time when the European imagination dreamt that men and nature could improve. Towards the end of the fifteenth century, the European imagination, fed by other non-Western cultural streams, began to break free from the idea that the world was static. Dimly perhaps, Euro-intellectuals questioned the received sacred texts as they leapt out into a concrete world of new flora, fauna and peoples. The world of men, women, animals, plants and things was no longer seen as simple illustration of sacred knowledge. Now, the book of nature and life consisted of open, blank pages, bidding

1

careful observation and recording. This monumental historical moment, it seems, made intellectuals and explorers deeply conscious that they were learning about a new world. With the appearance of the scientific revolution in the seventeenth century, European (and later many other) societies were propelled by the clash of sacred and secular ways of ordering society. But the restless spirit of inquiry, released for all time, gradually ruled the day. Human beings became conscious that they were, in fact, the authors of society and that their rational capacities could teach them how to live together more or less peacefully.

Once this spirit of inquiry broke into the West, increasingly restless to name everything in the world in order to exercise control over it, a learning dynamic was actually driving this society forward. With the beginnings of the Industrial Revolution in mid-eighteenth-century England, this restless learning spirit was harnessed by the new capitalism's desire to use nature to manufacture goods. The Age of Improvement took on palpable existence in the form of factories, machines, steam engines, schools, anti-slave societies, missionaries. Everything – nature, man, children, the poor, non-Western peoples – had the potential to improve, to develop its inner possibilities. My hypothesis is that the age of discovery set the learning society in motion, and the industrial era intensified the learning dynamics coursing through its veins. But it is in the late twentieth century, particularly, that the language of the learning society appears in textual representations.

However, most writers who adopt the discourse of the learning society, learning city, or learning organisation believe that the idea of a learning society is both something new and something inherently good. In fact, a strong argument could be made that, while the precise phrase, 'learning society' or 'learning organisation' was not used in earlier centuries, other metaphors and language sought to capture the idea itself. Writers thought of adult learning in the metaphoric frame of the ideology of improvement when they set out to convert indigenous peoples in the Americas in the sixteenth century. During the industrial era, the education of workers and agriculturalists was driven by the idea that both land and people could be something other than what existed. Indeed, adult learning in the West's colonies in the nineteenth and twentieth centuries cannot be understood apart from the arrogant assumption that the natives had to be improved through conversion to take their place as fully human alongside (rather beneath) Europeans. Having said this, it is true nonetheless that the self-conscious discourse

2

of the learning society is worth careful and critical scrutiny. What is it that our terrible and troubled global society is trying to name, to discover, to accomplish? Is the learning age rhetoric just one more desperate gasp at breathing life into the deflating notion of progress in humankind's affairs?

Terrible and troubled – these words speak of a paradox built into the talk of the learning society as something new appearing in the West. The word 'learning' often presents itself to Western consciousness as something inherently good. But clearly, humankind learns to imagine great and horrible things. We can learn to hate other peoples, races, religions, wealth. We can acquire techniques, carefully mentored or taught, to torture, maim, murder, bomb and harass. From the historian's vantage point, when we lower the discourse of the learning society into the world in which it actually exists, we discover that the language of the learning society co-exists with many horrible practices in the world. Those who celebrate the arrival of the 'information age' usually think that this age is different from all others, and is pulsing with men and women who are wiser than those forlorn creatures of bygone eras. This, as we will see, is a dubious assumption.

While I am disturbed by the growing gap between humankind's technical know-how and our moral paralysis in the face of the unmet needs of the multitudes of weak and suffering, I assume that the discourse of the learning society may contain utopian potential that is being prevented from release into the world. The idea of a just learning society, then, might be posited as an ideal that bridges our dreams of emancipation and the way the world actually has been shaped and formed within a capitalist optic and dynamic. My choice of the word design betrays a foolish hope that human beings contain the potential for doing good in the world. Our actions still flow out of our cultural perceptions of the world. Marx taught us that human beings make the world. But they do not choose the circumstances of its making.

Designing the Just Learning Society, then, is imagined as a critical inquiry into the multiple meanings and practices of the learning society as it is thought and enacted. The first chapter, 'Out of the margins', sets the stage, elaborating on the themes announced in the introduction. In Chapter Two, 'The discourse of the learning society in the twentieth century,' I trace the appearance of the learning society rhetoric, beginning with the British document, *A Design for Democracy*, published in 1919 after World War I. I provide capsule accounts of several creative attempts to realise a just learning society in Canada in the 1930s and 1940s before examining the role UNESCO played in the development of this idealistic discourse of the learning society. By the late 1990s, I argue, UNESCO ideologues had bought into the idea that human beings now inhabited an 'information society.' Chapter Three, 'From industrialism to the information society: Beautiful dreams, gritty realities', inquires sceptically into the claim that we now inhabit a radically new 'knowledge-based society.' I dispute the claims to newness and examine the paradox of ignorance in an age inundated with information. The first three chapters, then, form a coherent cluster. My intention is to unsettle our thinking that we are living in a learning age of unbounded and unparalleled opportunities to self-express and create a better and more just global community.

Chapters Four through Six also form a cluster, each engaging the extensive literature on the learning organisation. Here we move inside what Jurgen Habermas has labelled the system realm: spheres of human interaction governed by power and money. Chapter Four, 'How business organisations learn and unlearn', reviews the social science literature on organisational learning in order to determine the empirical bases for the claim that organisations can learn. Most of my attention is focused on simply understanding the idea that an organisation can learn (an idea that seems counter-intuitive). My hope is threefold: to appropriate usable concepts for the just learning society paradigm, to lay the basis for Chapters Five and Six, and to puncture the idea that the core ideas of the learning organisation paradigm (that it can actually transform its basic governing myths) can actually be realised within the core value system of the capitalist enterprise. Chapter Five, 'Inhibited learning in business organisations', explores the various ways individual and collective learning is blocked within organisations (primarily business organisations, but with implications for state and civil society associations). Without this critical inquiry, the ideal of the just learning society detaches itself from reality. I consider some organisational defensive routines, how gender and race play out in organisational learning dynamics and how powerful interests maintain organisational silence.

Chapter Six, 'Ethics and empowerment in business organisations', queries the meanings and practices of empowerment in our organisational life. I am searching for a conceptual framework that might enable practitioners to test empirically any claims made on management's part, that employees have been empowered. I argue, essentially, that empowerment is never simply granted by those above to those below and that much of the empowerment rhetoric in business (or government) circles is delusional. These chapters engage many thinkers and proceed through careful textual explication.

If Chapters Four through Six dwell primarily in the world of formal, business organisations, the final chapters move into social spaces where people are less restricted or constrained in their beliefs and actions. Chapter Seven, 'Citizenship in the age of information', attempts to clarify what we mean by active citizenship in a turbulent and confusing world by journeying into the world of political theory. I examine several thinkers who believe we inhabit a post-political world, and others who believe that the political has been reconstituted in accordance with post-modern realities. Special attention is given to Habermas's elaboration of deliberative democracy, mainly because he consciously thinks about the learning dynamics in civil society. Habermas's decisive argument was that relationships within civil society were not governed by an instrumental logic. Consequently, one could locate transformative learning potential within the interactive dynamics of civil society itself. One could also consider how the system realm could introduce distorting dynamics (and subsequent pathologies) into the communicative learning process.

Chapter Eight, 'The lifeworld curriculum: Pathologies and possibilities', argues that the lifeworld is an especially important notion because it is the ground of our learning capacities as human beings. Any damage to the lifeworld has dire consequences for human well-being. I contend that two dominant pathologies afflict the contemporary Western lifeworld: (1) the market system which measures value and worth only in terms of the production of commodities which can be exchanged on the market; and (2) the therapeutic culture which offers itself as a compelling way of interpreting suffering, pain, problems and disappointments. These pathologies, working in tandem, accentuate our sense of powerlessness. In the final section of the chapter, I articulate a framework that specifies the pre-conditions for life trajectories that are confident and open to engaging a world believed to be worth knowing and inhabiting with others. To this end, I explore the three fundamental patterns of recognition that must be in place for the human subject to be able to participate in creating a more just learning society.

The conclusion, 'A realistic utopia for the twenty-first century', summarises the core arguments of the book. I offer a modestly resilient hope that a just learning society is a realistic utopia and not just a lovely delusion of the romantic soul. I outline some of the obstacles we confront as a species, and highlight the importance of the lifeworld foundations for designing a just learning society.

In my best moments, I fancy myself as an orchestra conductor, drawing in many and varied instruments and sounds, and synthesising them into a coherent and meaningful symphony. Without all these beautiful instruments, this symphony could not have been possible.

CHAPTER ONE

Out of the margins

For much of the nineteenth and twentieth centuries, adult educators (practitioners and theorists) became accustomed to speaking on behalf of the neglected adult learner from the margins of social and intellectual space. Certainly adults have always learned in different times and places; recent studies of human evolution underscore our species' learning capacities. The human species has a rare mind whose learning capacity is extended through cultural creation and stored memory (Donald, 2001; Pinker, 1997, 2003). But at the beginning of the twenty-first century, adult learning has never been higher on the agendas of leading Western liberal democratic policy makers in government, business, and civil society.

Scandinavian countries like Finland actually hold presidential debates over the meaning and policy implications of the learning society. It is also not uncommon for the UK government to issue documents celebrating the 'Learning Age', or for high-level Canadian civil servants to produce documents hailing the learning organisation as the necessary organisation form for changed times. This is a startling reality for those who know something of the history of adult education's long struggle to gain attention and financing from the state in North America, Europe and throughout the vast reaches of the South. Indeed, startling or shocking enough to raise a sceptical eyebrow in the global adult education community, battered as it has been through the many battles to find resources for the adult learner.

Beginning in the aftermath of World War I, the language of lifelong learning and intimations of the learning society paradigm appear in a British government document, *A Design for Democracy* (Waller, 1919). In Canada, the 1930s and 1940s saw the bold active citizenship projects of the Canadian Association for Adult Education (CAAE), Moses Coady's blueprint for the co-operative learning society, Watson Thomson's socialist learning society project in Saskatchewan, and Guy Henson's vision of a learning democracy saw several innovative initiatives to design just learning societies. After World War II, the language of lifelong learning was nurtured by UNESCO in its international conferences, beginning meekly in 1949 (Elsinore), then gathering steam in each decade or so thereafter – 1960 (Montreal), 1972 (Tokyo), 1985 (Paris) – culminating in the jubilance of 1997 in Hamburg. Today the discourse of lifelong learning has expanded to embrace the learning society, the learning economy, the learning city, and the learning organisation. This discourse permeates discussions in Europe's elite circles (OECD, the European Union parliament and its bureaucracies and many other deliberative spaces). According to some educational visionaries we have arrived in the Learning Age and this is very good. Adult learning holds the key to the twenty-first century.

Exuberant proponents of the learning society believe that major transformations in global civilisation – perhaps comparable to earlier shifts from tribal to agrarian, and from agrarian to industrial society – are responsible for wrenching adult education out of the margins. Since the late 1960s many thinkers have been trying to name the newly emergent society, calling it the 'Technological Society' (Jacques Ellul), the 'Knowledge Society' (Daniel Bell), a 'technotronic era' (Zbigniew Brzezinski) and the 'Post-Industrial Society' (Alain Touraine) or even the 'Third Wave' (Alvin Toffler). More recently, a host of scholars have fastened on to the 'Information Society' (Manuel Castells) as the appellation capturing the essence of this new societal form.

All of these labels ought to peak the adult educator's attention because they place learning processes and procedures at the forefront of the social evolutionary pathway for humanity. The most crucial resource of this new society, the visionaries claim, is techno-scientific knowledge, the principal manifestation and prime mover of the new era is the invention and diffusion of information technologies, and the generation of wealth increasingly depends on an 'information economy' in which the exchange and manipulation of symbolic data matches, exceeds, or subsumes the importance of material processing. These techno-economic changes are accompanied by far-reaching social transformations, the information revolution is planetary in scale and the information revolution marks out not only a new phase in human civilisation, but also a new stage in the development of life itself. Within this vision, no doubt designed to uplift the human spirit, learning processes have to

8

be unbound and unshackled in order for the new society to be fully realised. Historical transformations have thus made possible the realisation of the vision of the learning society (Dyer-Witheford, 1999, p. 3).

These are exhilarating ideas, but they require careful critical and thoughtful engagement. This, essentially, is the major purpose of this book. Any human being who cares deeply about the 'fate of the earth' (Schell, 1982) cannot help sense that shadows lie across this new language of human emancipation and hope. Everywhere one looks, be it to our species' relationship with the natural world, our relationship with each other in the interactions of nation-states and our inability to solve global problems of inequality, one sees calamity, ignorance and desperation. Over the past few years (2001–2004), we have watched planes crash into the World Trade Center; the US pursue unilateral goals, reluctant to sign off on international treaties to protect the environment, to the dismay of the world; massive corporate scandals; the on-going inhumane and horrific treatment of Palestinians by their Israeli occupiers; and apocalyptic reports on the state of the earth and very inconclusive and indecisive outcomes from the sustainable development summit in Johannesburg in 2002. The aftermath of the US invasion of Iraq has left a bitter mess, with nothing much resolved in the febrile Middle East. Angry critics of the Bush regime even think that the US, cut loose from an ethics of limit, is ravaging the earth (Engel, 2003). Greed, fear, ill-will, and delusion appear to propel the leaders of the most powerful nation on earth.

Our species, so superbly endowed with mind and imagination, seems unable to learn many important things about living well on our shared earth with all of its teeming inhabitants, swirl of cultures and endlessly different ways of being. Adult educators as a group tend to be humanists who affirm human potential to develop their various capacities. But this humanistic commitment to nurture the developmental potential within persons and communities is difficult to enact in a world driven by the pursuit of money, power, and greed. Thus, critical engagement with the discourse of the learning society requires, minimally, that we distinguish the discourses of the learning society from the often bitter realities of the way most people actually experience the world.

We must admit into our thinking about the possibilities of designing just learning societies analyses of some of the ways that human institutions, associational practices and belief-systems actually inhibit and constrain learning processes, whereby persons and collectives become increasingly reflective, autonomous actors. There are blockages (or hindrances) to the human, collective learning process which are inherent in the structure of the institutional form as well as in the products of the human imagination and not within the person's psyche (although one can readily admit that many persons are psychically damaged, thereby hindering their learning potential). Both critical social theorists and liberal humanists (from early Renaissance humanists to the modern humanist psychology of Carl Rogers and Abraham Maslow) have affirmed that human beings have the capacity for self-reflection, communicative interaction and the unfolding of these capacities over the lifespan. But only critical theorists have insisted that structural conditions and ideological systems pre-existing the individual may prevent human beings from unfolding their capacities as speakers, doers, meaning makers, creators, and caregivers. Even this language can sound rather tame, not quite up to the task of grasping the terror and havoc and misery members of our species are capable of wreaking upon other members of their species and animals.

The German philosopher Immanuel Kant (1793) spoke of 'radical evil'. This noxious phrase captures a dimension of the human species' capacity for acting demonically, often in the grip of delusions or megalomaniacal impulses. Theorists of the just learning society must traverse inhospitable territory to arrive at insights about the possibilities of designing a just learning society. We must learn to feel comfortable with the paradoxes, conundrums and contradictions of the human species' learning pathways. We must try to think of how our imaginative and institutional worlds interact in real time and space. Sometimes it seems that the old institutional worlds refuse to bend to the new imaginaries and dream longings of our species. And then history surprises us, as an old belief-system, like 'it is morally justifiable to enslave others', collapses, and along with it, sedimented institutional practices.

Designing as metaphor of choice

The choice of the word 'design' suggests immediately the image of the architect. As David Harvey remarks in his text, *Spaces of Hope* (2000), the figure (as opposed to the person) of the architect is central to the discussions of the intricate processes of crafting and organising spaces (for learning and interacting). Architects construct in their imaginations what materialises in space. The architect shapes spaces that people can use and derive aesthetic satisfactions. The architect helps to give material form to people's longings and desires. The architect struggles to 'open spaces for new possibilities, for future forms of social life' (2000, p. 200). These spaces are opened first in the imagination. But the actual building involves an intricate dance through and amongst regulations, materials, politicians, construction workers, trade unions and so on. Writing in *Capital* (1867), Karl Marx celebrated humankind's capacity to develop its 'slumbering powers' through acting on nature. 'A spider,' he observed in a famous passage,

> conducts operations that resemble those of a weaver and a bee puts to shame many an architect in their construction of her cells. But what distinguishes the worst architect from the best of bees is this, that the architect raises his structure in imagination before he erects it in reality. At the end of every labour process we get a result that existed in the imagination of the labourer at its commencement. He not only effects a change of form in the material on which he works, but he also realizes a purpose . . . (1867, pp. 173–4)

Our imaginations have the capacity to project outside the reality we presently inhabit. We often succumb to thinking that the ideas and containers of our lives box us in, transforming us into puppets dangling from invisible strings stretching to the centres of power, and we cannot imagine any alternatives to the way it is. But this fatalistic sense of being controlled fails to understand that capitalist ventures like Enron and WorldCom were dreams before they were catastrophes. Capitalism, we must admit, has tremendous power to draw entrepreneurs, developers, artists, architects, state planners, educators, and ordinary labourers into its project of wealth creation. This system – understood as an imaginary projection of some members of the species (often in its privileged sectors) – has found extraordinary ways to make money by boldly travelling down untrod and untested pathways. Many thoughtful critics (and there are many) of this system, now an integrated global network of production and exchange that benefits the relatively few and not so many, believe that the system has closed on us, locking the door and throwing away the key. But if, in Harvey's analysis, the 'dialectic of the imaginary and its material realisation (mediated in most cases through production) locates the two sides of how capitalism replicates and changes itself', then we are surrounded by 'fictitious and imaginary elements . . . at every turn' (2000, p. 206).

11

Like other species, ours is endowed with 'specific capacities and powers' (p. 207) that we use to change our environments to sustain and reproduce ourselves. We change our environments, like other species, and adapt further to our constructions. This adaptive mode of learning is the elemental form of learning shared across all species (Donald, 2001). But the human species, in Harvey's view, has

> species-specific capacities and powers, arguably the most of important of which are our ability to alter and adapt our forms of social organisation (to create, for example, divisions of labour, class structures, and institutions), to build a long historical memory through language, to accumulate knowledge and understandings that are collectively available to us as guides for future action, to reflect on what we have done and do in ways that permit learning from experience (not only our own but also that of others), and, by virtue of our particular dexterities, to build all kinds of adjuncts (e.g. tools, technologies, organizational forms, and communication systems) to enhance capacities to see, hear and feel way beyond the physiological limitations given by our own bodily constitution. (2000, pp. 207–208)

Our species is endowed with a vivid imagination and a repertoire of resources that we have learned in different times and places. We compete and struggle for existence; we adapt and diversify into environmental niches; we produce social arrangements; we change the natural environment to meet human requirements; we order space for distinctive purpose (such as transportation or defence); and we order time. Harvey says that these six elements 'form a basic repertoire of capacities and powers handed down to us out of our evolutionary experience' (pp. 208–9). These products of the human imagination provide channels for the learning of those who follow. We never learn in the present under conditions of our own choosing. Our restless learning capacities confront the problem of how we deal with an environment that has predetermined our engagement with it, or which has shaped the very possibilities of our experience of it in the first place. We must respect the given-ness before us. Our creations, for better and worse, have an obduracy that resists our desires. Yet we also know that things solid, like Berlin walls, collapse. Neither our imaginations nor our institutions appear to be impermeable.

The products and creations of human learning in the ancient worlds engender awe. Wandering through the great museums of the world, the partially preserved ruins, we marvel at Egyptian or Mayan civilisation (pyramids, pottery, religious devotion, great bureaucratic systems). Writing his masterpiece, *The City of God*, in the fourth century A.D., Augustine marvelled at humankind's astonishing achievements in cloth-making, navigation, architecture, agriculture, ceramics, medicine, weaponry and fortification, animal husbandry, and food preparation; in mathematics, astronomy, and philosophy, as well as in language, writing, music, theatre, painting, and sculpture (Noble, 1998, pp. 11–12). The learning of early modern Europe, manifest in cartography, scientific instruments, great humanistic texts, magnificent art and architecture, vast colonising dreams of a universal culture still astounds the observer. Yet one also knows how the ancients treated their slaves, and how modernising Europe rampaged through the globe in the early modern era, subjugating everything in its pathway. We know that human creations, celebrated at the time, ended up lying in ruins, that texts thought truthful at one moment now lie dusty, discredited, unread. We also know that some ancient texts – the works of Aristotle, for example – continue to challenge and inspire us to this day.

Our learning nature seems paradoxical and contradictory. We have the imaginative capacity to create beautiful forms. Our species has cut some marvellous channels in the rock of collective existence through which flow the manifestations of human intelligence (the libraries and archives of great universities, the galleries and museums holding wond-rous treasures of imagination and spirit). Despite the emancipatory, Enlightenment spirit and results of scientific inquiry, our understanding of the purpose of science has remained resolutely instrumental from the seventeenth century until the present (science and technology in the service of the domination of nature). We have devised the most fantastic classification schemes and systems to understand nature. Yet our scientific knowledge scarcely seems able to stop the obliteration of species by the thousands.

Our telecommunications systems are hailed by techno-utopians as ushering in a new era of participatory democracy. Yet perceptions that cultures in our world are so different that they must clash, that they cannot communicate except through opposition, that cultures are not permeable, have gained the upper hand in the popular consciousness. Expert forms of knowledge about everything under the sun explode exponentially. Yet deep ignorance of many burning issues in the West and the world persists among the ordinary citizens. Our ability to splice genes and modify food products is surely dazzling (and controversial). Yet it is simply baffling that our species' learning is harnessed and directed down certain pathways (let us say in producing weapons of destruction and systems of surveillance), while millions of our fellow and sister human beings have nothing much to eat, existing outside the charmed circles of comfort. Indeed, Thomas Homer-Dixon in *The Ingenuity Gap* (2000) wonders if human beings have the collective intelligence to grapple with the complexity of the problems facing them.

Challenging our arrogance and hubris

All societies in human history can be usefully described as learning societies. It is both silly, and arrogant, to think that our own time has a superior learning system. In the twenty-first century, cultural pessimism pervades all of our domains (environment, science, and art, our forms of economy, work organisation and governance, our systems of education and health care, moral learning as manifest in our indifferent response to suffering). Indeed, narratives of decline define our own disenchanted time (Bennett, 2001). But it does make historical sense to speak of an intensification of human learning processes that broke into human history in the sixteenth and seventeenth centuries, releasing a restless, insatiable learning dynamic into global cultural, political and economic processes. The primitive Christian Church did not believe that progress was possible. Under the curse of sinfulness, humankind could only await Christ's redemption at the end of time. Humanists like Erasmus (1469–1536) and Pico della Mirandella (1433–1494) were aware of living in a new age. Even they did not ascribe to the idea of entering into a better future. Rather, they looked backward to the ancient world to find a model suitable to emulate in the present.

Descartes (1696–1650), Galileo (1571–1630) and Bacon (1651–1626), exemplars of the new scientific attitude to nature, articulated the new rational perception of nature. This radical opening up of nature to discover its laws freed learning from the tutelage of the ancients and the Church. Until the Church could no longer keep nature, society and history under wraps, the developmental potential of the cosmos could be neither revealed nor opened out practically. Hans Blumenburg (*The Legitimacy of the Modern Age* (1985)) argues that the study of astronomy undermined the idea that truth was a kind of once-and-for-all

14

revelation. We cannot underestimate the shock to the early modern sensibility when people grasped that their knowledge of heavenly bodies had been false for centuries. Once those rational principles (manifest in the natural sciences) were transferred to history, humanity was inescapably laying the groundwork for another previously unimaginable idea: that human beings could make themselves in history. This developmental perspective fused the new scientific discoveries, technological developments in navigation and a secularised interpretation of prophetic biblical themes into a potent learning elixir.

By the end of the seventeenth century the 'idea of progress' (Nisbet, 1980) had expanded to include the development of humanity itself. This developmentalist perspective on the unfolding of knowledge and history was reinforced by the new ethnological knowledge gained from contacts with non-European worlds. The primitive Other – the Amerindians – could be incorporated into a European civilisation able to exercise rational sovereignty over nature in order to expand its own freedom from the domination of nature, myth and fate. This ideology of the improvement of men and things remained trapped, however, inside a messianic world orientation that drove men and women out to the new worlds to establish Christ's kingdom in the Americas of the sixteenth and seventeenth centuries. This belief that truth is revealed through time, and that humankind's story can be told as tale of progress is, in my view, at the root of the contemporary idea of the learning society.

The impulse to discover the principles underlying things, generated by the scientific revolution in the seventeenth and following centuries, was inexorably tied to the pedagogics of reform and improvement sweeping the earth in the eighteenth and nineteenth centuries. By the time that the products of scientific investigation could be tied to industrial forms of production in factory, on farm and at sea in the mid-eighteenth century, societal learning dynamics were harnessed in the service of usefulness. Marvelling at the riches opened through the 'door of nature' (William Woodsworth's felicitous phrase, penned in 1794), British elites extolled the 'march of intellect' and the great technical achievements of the eighteenth century (coal and iron technologies). In the early eighteenth century, Daniel Defoe wrote eloquently that, 'Every new view of Great Britain would require a new description . . . New discoveries in metals, mines, minerals, new undertakings in trade, inventions, engines, manufactures, in a nation producing and improving as we are: these things open new scenes very day' (cited, Briggs, 1959,

15

p. 19). 'In a sense', Asa Briggs observes in *The Age of Improvement* (1959, p. 19), 'the history of the years from 1784 to 1867 is the history of a continuing industrial revolution, which every new generation saw in different terms . . .'. Adult learning is only consciously placed on history's agenda when nature is unlocked, and scientific-technical discoveries propel the economy forward, reconfiguring social and intellectual learning systems.

Most of the British and colonial elites were brimming with confidence in their learning society. In this period, the adult educators of the day were committed to the ideology of improvement and attempted to create pedagogical spaces to engage their often less formally educated contemporaries in projects of improvement. Inspired by developments in the mother country, British colonial elites in Canada launched agricultural societies in the late eighteenth century in Nova Scotia, Upper and Lower Canada. The quest for a scientific agriculture – to improve the mind and soil – took flight in Nova Scotia in the 1780s when several agricultural societies appeared. In 1818 Nova Scotian John Young, adopting the pen name 'Agricola', fired gunshot across the bows of maritime farmers with a series of letters lambasting farmers for their ignorance about matters of soil and manure. Published in 1822 as the *Letters of Agricola*, these letters attempted to form the subject of general conversation among practical farmers. While paternalistic and elitist in style and sympathies, Young struggled to open up pedagogical space for farmers to converse about problems pertaining to their livelihoods. He advocated creating agricultural societies to institutionalise the conversational learning process. He wanted to cherish the nascent germ of improvement appearing in the life of the settlers. Other agricultural societies were created in Lower and Upper Canada in the late eighteenth and nineteenth centuries. Their appearance could not be imagined apart from the scientific revolution in agriculture and the cultural ethos of progress.

Mechanics' Institutes embodied the ethos of an age intent on improvement through pedagogical commitment to finesse the industrialisation of mind, body and emotions. These institutes, hundreds of which sprang up all over eastern Canada in the 1830s and 1840s (and spread into western Canada into the 1880s), constructed an important, if contested, public pedagogical space at a moment when Canadians were trying to put the associations of a vital civil society in place. These institutes were a central part of a learning configuration (which included the agricultural societies, common schools, museums, galleries, various media, and numerous voluntary associations, literary and scientific) designed to build the infrastructure of the industrial form of learning society. The Mechanics' Institutes were consciously constructed to open up learning space and opportunities to non-elites. Other voluntary associations and a flourishing literary culture burst into existence during this time as well. Exhibitions were pervasive in nineteenth-century Canada. Preceding the common school as a popular pedagogical form, they were saturated with the ideology of improvement. They were designed to appeal to the eye, avoiding text-based instruction, to inculcate a spirit of emulation and competitive spirit that would motivate people to be more efficient producers (Heaman, 1998). If we were transported back to this time, we might exclaim that learning was erupting everywhere. Nineteenth-century Canadians were engaged in an extensive project of building a more just learning society. This project was contested by those of the elite classes who feared the subordinate sectors and wanted to remain their tutors.

Critical humanists and religious persons worried greatly that the industrial learning society skewed the learning dynamics of the human species along the technical-instrumental axis. The British humanist, Thomas Carlyle, declared in the *Signs of the Times* (1829) that his age was a 'mechanical age'. But he thought that a healthy culture depended on advances in both the external and inner worlds. Carlyle thought that the mechanical mode of thinking had colonised cultural and political discourse; the question of freedom, for instance, had been reduced to 'arrangement, institutions and constitutions.' 'Mechanism' had produced enormous power and wealth; but, for Carlyle, in 'whatever respects the pure moral nature, in true dignity of soul and character, we are perhaps inferior to most civilised ages.' The Romantic rebellion in England was, in part, a reaction to an industrialism which, in William Blake's acute eye, had been built upon a 'single vision for science.' His 'dark satanic mills' were only the most glaring manifestation of a culture perceived to promote a limited, mechanistic conception of human potentiality. Percy Shelley, for his part, did not think that the 'extraordinary advances in scientific, political and economic knowledge' had resulted in a 'more equitable world, but had only added to the general weight of human misery.' Shelley despaired that the 'calculating principle' had not been matched by the parallel evolution of the 'creative faculty' (Bennett, 2001, pp. 7–8).

Work is one of the fundamental learning domains of the human species. Karl Marx certainly thought that 'school of labour', the factory, was a crucial, albeit brutal, learning site. In his pioneering study of *Labour and Capital in Canada, 1650–1860* (1981) H. Clare Pentland argues, in the spirit of Marx, that the fundamental educative process at work in mid-nineteenth-century Canada was the 'transformation of Canadians' into industrialised bodies. Pentland thinks this harsh pedagogics was conduced 'largely in the school of experience with the goad of harsh impersonal penalties for failure' (p. 176). In *In the Age of the Smart Machine* (1988), Shoshana Zuboff likewise observes that workers had to 'turn their bodies into instruments, but instruments for acting-on for producing calculated effects on material and equipment' (p. 30). With the appearance of the factory as a 'pedagogic institution where the new standards of conduct and sensibility, generally referred to as "labour discipline", would be learned, the body was honed to suppress the spontaneous, instinctually gratifying behaviour of the new industrial worker' (p. 30).

For Pentland, the 'harsh but hardening school of labour' (1981, p. 176) taught the workers really useful knowledge about the nature of work, wages, contractors, where their security lay, and the rules of the game in a new capitalist labour market. The industrialisation of society – its mighty force – worked on men and women to fit them for a turbulent and incessantly changing realm of production in the industrial learning society. This relentless process has continued into the early twenty-first century, through the different phases of capitalist trans-formation. With a sceptical eye, we must avoid being seduced by contemporary corporate claims that oppression and exploitation – the perpetuation of considerable ill-being, insecurity and anxiety amongst workers – has magically disappeared in the age of the learning organisa-tion and information society. If our analytical gaze embraces the entire world, from the tyrannical factories in remote rural areas in China to the terrible factories in south-east Asia spewing our goods for the West, the abysmal working conditions documented by Marx and Engels have not vanished into cyberspace.

Salient questions

The great tradition of Critical Theory from Hegel through Marx to Habermas argued that the power of critique lies not in announcing a new vision of humankind from the rooftops far away from the reality below. Rather, critical theory works close to the ground to detect where the potential for a new, more just way of ordering our lives is breaking into being. Here, one attempts to see the embryo of the new in the womb of the old. Working in this tradition, my main task in *Designing the Just Learning Society* is to show how transformations in the global economy and social systems have created severe problems for the realisation of a just learning society and possibilities for their super-session. The just learning society, then, is both an aspiration and a reality struggling to be realised. Adult educators (and other committed citizens) are potential midwives assisting at the birth of a new imaginary that is suited to the fluid and unstable times we inhabit. The new world is coming, the old will hold on as long as it can. But the nature of this new world must be named, identified, acted into existence. Still, in the end there are no guarantees that justice will come.

Humankind's consciousness has advanced to the point where we recognise the centrality of learning processes and pedagogic procedures (in all domains of existence) to the successful management of global systems and lifeworlds. Since the birth of early modernity in the sixteenth and seventeenth centuries (and intensified with the birth of the industrial learning society in the mid-eighteenth century until our frenetic present), human beings have been conscious that the inherited scripts and routines of their forebears had either exhausted themselves or had to be carefully scrutinised. They could not take for granted any longer that the knowledge and skills of the ancestors would orient them to an ever-changing present. They had to become conscious of themselves as persons who were constantly adapting to new learning challenges in industrial societies – work, civil society, state, and the private sphere.

Karl Marx captured this new learning dynamic that broke into history in the mid-eighteenth-century England with his poignant aphorism – 'all that is solid melts into the air.' This new industrial learning dynamic was impelled by restless factory owners who designed machines to make more profits and exercise maximum control over their labour force. But, compared to today, the early stages of the industrial learning society were relatively slow moving. Today, learning has become our most precious resource, symbolising hope that if we can only find the right pedagogical procedures and suitable organisational modalities, we will be able to confront the many problems before us in our ever-shrinking world. That many corporate leaders have adopted the learning organisation paradigm signals this changed consciousness. Yet at the very moment that zealous business leaders adopt this optimistic language, their actual, daily treatment of workers, in the rich and poor nations, is often harsh, mean and disrespectful, betraying their ideals. It is clear, then, that learning that is lifelong, life wide and just has many forces arraigned against its realisation. Powerful people and organisations in our world (in economic and political systems) skew learning processes and substance in particular directions. Corporations mobilise learning resources to learn how to dominate marketplaces and not how to create well-being in their own organisations. Governments scheme and connive to maintain their power. They choose not to mobilise energy to create the suitable forms for participatory democracy, even when the technological capacities make new ways of learning citizenship possible. Some social movements try to crush other ways of thinking and acting in the world, fomenting strife and unhappiness. It is also evident to most thoughtful persons that our scientific and technological acumen is not matched by our moral and ethical achievements. The latter duality may be our most puzzling paradox.

Moreover, our species is eminently capable of refusing to act on what it knows as well as using pleasant language to obscure bitter realities. These few generalised examples indicate that human learning is not free from the entanglements of interest and power. In fact, one might argue that modern human history has been pulled along by the tug of war between the money-code and the life-code. At its most elemental, human learning can be in the service of these two codes, and one, the money-code, has in our time captured the lion's share of human motivational resources and energy (McMurtry, 1999; Habermas, 1984–1987). In spiritual language, one might argue that learning capacities can be harnessed to track along pathways motivated by greed, lust, aggressive actions, and hatred. They can also be harnessed to actions impelled by compassion and desire to alleviate the suffering of all creatures (Loy, 2002). Our species can peer over its shoulder to the twentieth century and draw the conclusion that aggression and hatred have ruled our spirits and afflicted our imagination, despite whatever other wondrous technological and artistic achievements the species, in all its cultural variants, has managed to create.

Designing the Just Learning Society, then, explores the potential of the discourse of lifelong learning and the learning society to provide educators and citizens with a realistic utopian vision for our time. I will argue that the just learning society is a collective achievement, something created intentionally in time and space by human actors deliberating with each other. It is not simply handed to us by the accidents of history. That somehow, mysteriously, the capitalist economic and cultural order gazed into a crystal ball, realised that it was an ugly frog, and decided to transform into a kindly prince. A prince who, dressed in resplendent robes, announced that a new day had begun: the millennial time of a good age, the age of the learning society.

CHAPTER TWO

The discourse of the learning society in the twentieth century

From early modernity (the age of exploration, colonisation and science) into the industrial age, those living within the orbit of European societies have been swept into a dizzying learning age. We cannot easily mark a dividing line between our own age, with its varying labels (post-industrial or postmodern), and those of early modernity and industrialism. The opening up of nature to rational scientific investigation in the seventeenth century intensified human learning processes in relation to the natural and social worlds, wrenching Euro-human beings out of more or less static worlds (and many others elsewhere). Once wrenched from largely rural and parochial contexts, human beings were forced to learn to adapt to new modes of thinking and acting.

The industrial mode of production, as Marx so powerfully argued in the mid-nineteenth century, had little interest in conservation:

> Conservation of the old modes of production in unaltered form, was, on the contrary, the first condition of existence for all earlier industrial classes. Constant revolutionising of production, uninterrupted disturbance of all social conditions, everlasting uncertainty and agitation distinguish the bourgeois epoch from all earlier ones. All fixed, fast-frozen relations, with their train of ancient and venerable prejudices and opinions, are swept away, all new-formed ones become antiquated before they can ossify. (Marx, *The Communist Manifesto* [1848], cited McLellan, 1977, p. 224)

The ease with which contemporary social theorists like Zygmunt Bauman (1999) characterise the late-twentieth-century world as an 'age of fluidity' – to set it apart from others – seems too hasty a judgment.

Intellectuals and people in different times and places use different vocabularies and metaphors to make sense of their worlds. From the age of exploration and missionary activity in the sixteenth and seventeenth centuries until the end of World War I, the 'discourse of improvement' was the dominant way European intellectuals, and colonial intellectuals in Canada, imagined the learning dynamics of their societies. Indeed, one can argue that the construction of the industrial learning society – the putting in place of a learning infrastructure encompassing the learning of youth (in formal schools) and the domains of work, state and civil society – was fuelled by heady optimism, which, in turn, released considerable energy for the not inconsiderable tasks required by this mighty act of imagination.

But it is not until the twentieth century, which we could characterise as a time when the negative consequences of the industrial learning society become more manifest, more an integral part of the consciousness of men and women, that we actually see the conscious articulation of a philosophy of lifelong learning and the learning society. Thus, by the twentieth century, a terribly catastrophic age in many ways (Hobsbawm, 1994; Habermas, 2001), theorists and practitioners of the learning society are conscious of the incomplete and often unjust nature of the industrial learning society. One might say that the seventeenth, eighteenth and nineteenth centuries set the learning society in motion, and in the twentieth century intellectuals started to think seriously about it. My purpose in this chapter, then, is threefold: (1) to understand the emergence of the discourse of the learning society; (2) to set the talk in historical context; and (3) to begin to press the idealistic rhetoric towards the muddy world below.

A Design for Democracy (1919): To fit a man for life and citizenship

In the immediate aftermath of World War I, by all estimations a terrible blow to European civilisation, the British government commissioned a study to 'consider the provision for, and possibilities of, "Adult Education (other than technical or vocational) in Great Britain, and to make recommendations"' (Waller, 1956, p. 51). The published report, *A Design for Democracy* (1919), acknowledged that 'education for the adult must proceed by different methods, in a different order, from those mostly used hitherto in the education of the young' (Waller, 1956, p. 51). The report recognised that learning occurred in 'practical life', and that effective adult education ought to 'work from his existing avocation and interests' towards the fulfilment of his aspirations. Effective learning, then, was anchored in the interests of the learner. Intentional adult education could reveal the 'reasons that underlie his daily work, the way in which that work has come to be arranged as it is, and how it can be arranged better, the relation of his work to that of others, and its place in the economics of the nation and the world' (pp. 51–2).

A Design for Democracy recognised that the workplace learning domain had considerable formative power, wherein crafts workers developed their capacities through the exercise of their craft (which led the report's authors to advocate pedagogical practices rooted in the 'practical and the realistic' (p. 53)). If their learning proceeded, in fact, from practical manipulation of objects, the report mused, perhaps the 'growing tyranny of machinery' and the 'increasing soullessness of much of our industrial conditions' could be counterbalanced. The language of the nineteenth-century romantic rebellion against the machine age is present in this report. We also can take note of the presence of a narrative of decline now creeping into the discourse of the learning society. In the utopian, early stages of the industrial revolution, technological power was celebrated. The improvers pressed their fellows and sisters to adopt technology as a means of making a better life. Science and technology are not imagined as inherently good things.

The report's recommendations have a contemporary resonance. The 'purpose of education is to fit a man for life, and therefore in a civilised community to fit him for his place as a member of that community' (p. 53). The report recognised that key institutions within civil society – the family, the school, the trade union or profession, and municipality – all played a part in the formation of the active citizen. Indeed, the 'essence of democracy' was 'active participation by all in citizenship.' The democratic learning community (coded here as 'education') must 'aim at fitting each individual progressively, not only for his personal, domestic and vocational duties but, above all, for those duties of citizenship for which these earlier states are training grounds . . .' (p. 54). This language makes explicit what was implicit in the initial phases of building a civil society (voluntary associations were learning sites).

A Design for Democracy also retains linkages with the ideology of improvement with its use of the language of human capacity. '(I)t is also a truth that there is latent in the mass of our people a capacity far beyond what was recognized, a capacity to rise to the conception of great issues

24

and to face the difficulties of fundamental problems when these can be visualized in a familiar form.' The report's authors thought, however, that there was a 'natural aristocracy' among men – those who would naturally lead their fellows and sisters, and the 'rank and file' could develop the mind-set to recognise these leaders. Here we discover a discordant note. With the Bolshevik Revolution only two years distant from the report's crafting, and all of Europe wracked with enormous labour strife and upheavals in the aftermath of World War I, the elites think once more of utilising adult education to manage and improve the minds of their fellow citizens. The report concluded with the declaration that 'adult education' was not be 'regarded as a luxury for a few exceptional persons here and there, nor as a thing which concerns only a short span of early manhood, but that adult education is a permanent national necessity, an inseparable aspect of citizenship, and therefore should be both universal and lifelong', with opportunities to learn 'spread uniformly and systematically over the whole country' (p. 55). The report's authors dreamed that adult education could be an integral part of a post-World War I learning society that was lifelong, life wide and universal.

Coady, Thomson and Henson: The Canadian learning society in action (1930–46)

By the time Canadian adult education leaders like J. Roby Kidd and Ned Corbett, stalwarts of the illustrious CAAE, had arrived at the first, epochal UNESCO-sponsored adult education global conference in 1949, Canadians had already provided the world with several innovative ventures in creating a just learning society. Moses Coady and company had launched a bold project in a peripheral and poverty-stricken part of North America to awaken hearts and minds to wrench control of the economy from the vested interests. To accomplish this task, Coady and his pioneering band of progressives had to carve out learning space within a society in order to mobilise the people for enlightenment and find ways to organise action. Their programme of study circles trans- forming themselves into cooperative initiatives swept the Maritimes and caught the imagination of many around the world searching for hope in the dark world of the 1930s (Welton, 2001).

In 1942, the CAAE leadership (particularly Ned Corbett and Watson Thomson) crafted an epochal 'Report' of the Proceedings of a Special Committee of the CAAE at a crucial moment in twentieth-century history. These intellectuals believed profoundly that a better world did not just happen; it had to be created and sustained by vigorous learning processes characterised by a 'critical examination of the social processes by which those popular aspirations for a better world might be fulfilled' (CAAE, 1942, p. 4). They believed that the collective war learning experiences of the Canadian people gave them a cultural hook for the 'immense and urgent educational task' of creating a people's peace and laying the foundation for 'permanent United Nations cooperation.' Designing a just learning society had to both realistically face the 'facts of the existing situation with all its inexorable limitations as well as its hopeful opportunities' (p. 6). This report provided the intellectual underpinnings for the Citizens' Forum initiative: a brilliant attempt to create a new public learning form (or space) in civil society for citizens to learn from one another (Welton, 1986b).

Watson Thomson had played a key role in drafting the CAAE's famous 'Manifesto' of 1943 which called upon Canadians to take a stand on the great issues of the day. In October 1944, he joined Tommy Douglas and his newly elected democratic socialist party, the Co-operative Commonwealth Federation (CCF), to launch a campaign of grassroots radical adult education to begin to build a socialist learning society. Thomson drafted a policy document, *Adult Education Theory and Policy*, to guide the new government in 1944. In Saskatchewan, adult education had two primary tasks: to support the people with relevant knowledge in their movement towards the new objectives for which the way had been opened up, whether it be co-operative farms, larger school units or new public health projects; and to awaken the people to a sense of the 'central issues of the world crisis', still unresolved, so that there would be a clear way ahead for modern society.

Three issues were clear to Thomson and his associates. First, the Saskatchewan government had to demonstrate to the farmers, workers and plain people that a provincial socialist government could effect tangible material improvements. Second, they knew that the mass of people must be mobilised and activised as rapidly as possible. Only by participating in the processes of democratic deliberation and social change would people realise that 'socialism is democracy extended' and the bogey of 'socialism as mere bureaucracy and regimentation' ludicrous. Third, Thomson and co-workers believed that the 'political consciousness' of the mass of people must be so deepened that the foundations of prairie radicalism became unshakeable. One of the brilliant legacies of the Thomson era in Saskatchewan (1944–1946) was the citizen's conference, which brought men and women together to deliberate on key themes emerging from their struggles in local communities (health, the returning veterans, childcare, building co-operative communities). These new public learning spaces extended traditional understandings of civil society and even posed a new form of democracy (citizens would engage with one another and would deliver their policy considerations to the doors of the government for reflection and implementation). All in all, the Saskatchewan experiment imagined by Thomson in the latter war years was a remarkable design and enactment of a democratic socialist learning society (Welton, 1986a).

Guy Henson launched a similar coherent project for post-war Nova Scotia. He wrote *A Report on Provincial Support for Adult Education in Nova Scotia* in 1945/6 when Henson, who had been invited to organise the second government-sponsored Division of Adult Education in Canada, took on the task of setting up the division. He believed that the very life of democracy depended on the self-worth of the populace, intelligent and critical thinking individuals who would wrestle with controversial issues of the day and collectively would organise and develop their communities. In the post-war world of Nova Scotia, Henson believed that adult education could play an axial role in revitalising society and democracy itself. What is particularly remarkable about this plainly written report is that Henson acknowledged that formal schooling did not turn out the 'finished product', and that 'work activity' and the associative life of civil society had a deep 'educational effect for the adult.' 'The newspaper, magazine and book, the radio, the film, the church, the political parties, occupational associations, social and fraternal groups form a complex of agencies which have the main part in transmitting knowledge and opinions to grown-up people' (Henson, 1946, p. 9).

Recognising that society was, in fact, a learning society, Henson asked 'to what extent can the educational movement as such be strengthened so that an increasing body of people will turn to it for knowledge without bias, for skills efficiently taught, for attitudes towards life, and for the inspiration of the arts' (p. 9). Adult education would not be 'realistic' and would not 'fulfil its task unless it [was] geared to the vital needs of life in these times and in Nova Scotia; unless it plays its full part in enabling people to use their intelligence, their skill and their finest

27

qualities for economic and social progress and for achieving a richer and happier life' (p. 10).

Henson's argument, still pertinent today, was that 'educational planning' had to 'concentrate on multiplying the means and the efficiency of continuing self-education of leaders and the average citizen' (p. 20). Henson grappled with the question of how, and to what extent, government could stimulate and support the post-school learning activities of individuals, local groups, communities, and voluntary bodies of wide scope. Grappling with this question distinguishes, in my estimation, a lifelong learning perspective centred on the individual's growth, and a learning society perspective centred on organisations and associational life (Welton and Lecky, 1997). Coady, Thomson and Henson have left us with a legacy of innovative attempts to realise variants of the just learning society.

Elsinore (1949): To cultivate an enlightened sense of world community

Three years after its formation, UNESCO chose Elsinore, home of the International People's College in Denmark, as the venue for its first international conference on adult education. When UNESCO was formed in 1946, as J. Roby Kidd (1974) tells the story, adult education was scarcely recognised as a special brand of education. The international community of 106 delegates from 27 countries, mainly from western European countries, with a smattering of representatives of the Third World (nobody came from any of the eastern European countries or the Soviet Union), were in a sombre mood as they met to grapple with adult education's role in a world that had been torn apart by savage and brutal warfare. The delegates were deeply conscious of having lived through a time of dissolution and breakdown; their minds riveted on matters of recovery and not on the great awakening about to occur in the colonised worlds. Dr Torres Bodet, the Director-General of UNESCO, declared that the purpose of the conference was to 'awaken in the consciousness of every adult, an awareness both of his personal responsibility and of his intellectual and moral fellowship with the whole of mankind' (Kidd, 1974, p. 5). Bodet thought that the presence of totalitarian regimes, who played out their devastating agendas so ruthlessly on the world scene, had succeeded in doing so, in part, because they had colonised the free time of working people, turning 'rest into meetings, amusement into hypnotism, education into propaganda and propaganda into drill' (p. 9). Thus, awakening personal responsibility was no idle matter. Once again, the adult educator as improver pops up in the guise of providing moral guidance to masses who are apparently easily duped into cheap and not uplifting entertainments.

The delegates did not succeed in conceptualising the learning dynamics of their post-war world in any coherent way. They could not define 'adult education', and a rather narrow understanding, rooted in the British tradition of liberal adult education, tended to prevail (literacy and adult basic education were not yet part of UNESCO's mandate in the late 1940s). Rather than attempting to define adult education, they chose to specify its tasks. Adult education had its starting point in 'specific situations, and current problems for which they themselves must find solutions.' Democratic education ought to 'provide individuals with the knowledge essential for the performance of their economic, social and political functions . . .'. Here we can observe that the delegates recognise faintly what Henson and Thomson brought to the forefront: that adult learning is an integral part of the life activities of people (in work, civil society, state and private life) as they interact with others to make their worlds. Adult education can only intervene in already constituted learning domains (or, conversely, create new learning zones).

But the thinking of one of four commissions ('Institutions and organizational problems'), did recognise the 'vital importance which should be granted to private institutions in the field of adult education' and affirmed that the state 'should recognize the ability of well developed organisations to assume responsibilities and to work closely with private institutions.' Delegates manifested a strong commitment to volunteerism and a deep suspicion of state domination of people's learning. Although they did not provide us with a theoretical map for thinking of the role that the state might play in constructing a just learning society, one senses that the war experiences of the delegates (some travelled through carnage to get to Denmark) had opened them to the associative vision of democracy.

The spirit of the Elsinore meeting was humanist and restorative. They wanted to stimulate a 'genuine spirit of democracy and a genuine spirit of tolerance; restore a sense of community to people who live in an age of specialization and isolation; cultivate an enlightened sense of belonging to a world community' (Kidd, 1974). But the texts we are left with from Elsinore neither reflect profoundly on the lessons to be learned from the catastrophes of the depression and war years nor provide us with the kind of penetrating analysis required to understand the pedagogical processes and learning forms necessary to develop a spirit of tolerance or reconcile East and West. Nonetheless, steps towards international co-operation were initiated at a time when the war-weary world was still coming to terms with its friends and enemies.

Montreal (1960): Survive or perish together

The second international UNESCO conference took place in Montreal on 22–31 August 1960 at McGill University. Forty-seven members, three organisations in the UN system, two non-member states, two associated states and 46 NGOs were present. This meeting was the first international meeting in which the communist countries were represented in full force. By this time, Canadians had become active participants in UNESCO, and at Eugene Bussiere's instigation the Canadian government hosted the second conference. J. Roby Kidd, director of the CAAE, presided over the meeting, propelling him into the international limelight for the next two decades. Considerable doubt and pessimism pervaded the atmosphere of this conference before the delegates even arrived. The Cold War was in deep freeze. The U-2 spy incident was still close to memory. 'The Cold War between the two camps of the USA and the USSR, . . . utterly dominated the scene in the second half of the Short Twentieth Century, . . . Entire generations grew up under the shadow of global nuclear battles which, it was widely believed, could break out at any moment, and devastate humanity' (Hobsbawm, 1994, p. 226).

This general pessimistic ethos of the Cold War penetrated into the conference's structure of feeling. The 'Declaration of the World Conference on Adult Education' (UNESCO, 1997) began with a bleak and melodramatic statement: 'The destruction of mankind and the conquest of space have both become technological possibilities to our present generation' (Sputnik had been launched by the Russians in 1957, provoking the US educational and ideological systems out of complacency). The Montreal statement was preoccupied with the new and dramatic technological and political developments. Each generation in the modern era seems to think that it is facing rapid changes unlike any other generation. The Montreal group was no different:

> New industrial methods, new means of communication are affecting
> all parts of the world, and industrialisation and urbanisation are
> overtaking areas that twenty years ago were rural and agricultural.
> Nor are the changes which are going to fashion the pattern of our
> lives during the remainder of this century only in technology. In
> great area of the world the population is increasing fast. New States
> are emerging, and much more of the world has become divided,
> within the last few years, into rival camps. Every generation has its
> own problems; in sober fact no previous generation has been faced
> with the extent and rapidity of change which faces and challenges
> us.

Thoughtful historians like Hobsbawm (1994) acknowledge that the
demographic explosion in the Third World was simply astonishing.
References to the emergence of new states signalled a massive awakening in the colonised worlds. One need think only of the independence
of India and Pakistan in 1947, the colonisation of Palestine by Israel and
imperial-backed big powers in the same year, Mao's Chinese Revolution
of 1949, Nkrumah's presumptuous move to independence in Ghana in
the mid-1950s, uprisings in the Caribbean, with Castro coming to
power in Cuba in 1959, the Nasser-led pan-Arab movement that swept
the Middle East in the 1950s, and much more.

Like a seismic shock reverberating through the Montreal meeting,
the 'Declaration' announced that their 'first problem was to survive.' This
apocalyptic sensibility boldly affirmed that humanity would either
'survive together, or we perish together.' But Hobsbawm thinks that this
manifestation of apocalypticism did not actually reflect the historical
reality of the Cold War era; there was, he claims, 'no imminent danger of
world war . . .' (1994, p. 226). The Montreal declaration insisted that
survival required that the 'countries of the world must learn to live
together in peace.' Learn was the 'operative word.' Human beings had the
capacity to learn 'mutual respect, understanding, sympathy', qualities
'destroyed by ignorance.' Here, the Montreal gathering found the
fundamental importance for 'adult education in today's divided world.'
Betraying a yes-but, divided consciousness, the declaration had some
doubt that humankind could learn to survive. Yet at the same time, it had
'opportunities for social development and personal well-being such as
have never been open to him before.'

Although the declaration is obviously not a theoretically elaborated
document, one senses that the massive movements in the 'rapidly

31

developing countries in Asia, Africa and Latin America' were creating these new possibilities for millions of men and women. There, adult education (including literacy education) was a 'need so overpowering that here and now we must help adult men and women to acquire the knowledge and skills that they need for the new patterns of community living into which they are moving.' Avoiding any critical commentary on just why the developing world might have been in such a mess with misery everywhere evident, the Montreal declaration eschewed any political analysis (or attempt to grasp the obvious fact that the uprisings in the Third World were driven by social movement learning dynamics) in favour of rather limp affirmations that the rich should help the poor. The theme of literacy thus makes its first appearance in UNESCO discourse. The declaration imagined that illiteracy could be eradicated within a few years if the UN and its agencies created a 'resolute, comprehensive and soundly planned campaign.'

Like the Elsinore deliberation, the Montreal gathering believed that adult education needed to be placed on national government agendas. It was not just in developing countries that adult education was needed, and vocational and technical training were not enough. 'Nothing less will suffice than that people everywhere should come to accept adult education as normal, and that governments should treat it as a necessary part of the educational provision of every country.' We catch just a glimmer of the learning society perspective here. We can also hear echoes of Carlyle's critique of the mechanical age in the declaration's assumption that, 'Healthy societies are composed of men and women, not of animated robots, and there is a danger, particularly in the developed countries, that the education of adults may get out of balance by emphasizing too much vocational needs and technical skills. Man is a many sided being, with many needs. They must not be met piecemeal and in adult education programmes they must all be reflected.' Mind and spirit, the declaration's authors claimed, must 'continue to find, in our changing patterns of day-to-day living, full scope for maturing and flowering in an enriched culture. This and nothing less is the goal of adult education.'

The Montreal gathering leaves us entirely in the dark regarding the economic, social and political structures that might enable this flowering of human potential. But Rene Maheu, the Secretary-General of UNESCO, told the conference that, 'Education is no longer the privilege of an elite or the concomitance of a particular age; to an increasing extent, it is reaching out to embrace the whole of society and the entire life-span of the individual. This means that it must be no longer thought of as preparation for life, but as a dimension of life.' This statement, radical in implication, moves into the orbit of learning society discourse, leaving us with many questions about what 'education' as a 'dimension of life' might actually mean. In the end, the conceptual vocabulary of the Montreal meeting seems vague, lightly humanist, non-political, not hard-headed enough, not penetrating enough. But the idea, streaming through the apocalyptic gloom, that adult education must respond to the huge issues of the day, inexorably linked learning to the upheavals and movements of the age.

Tokyo (1972): *Learning to Be*

The third international conference on adult education was held in Tokyo, from 25 July to 7 August 1972. Representatives from 83 countries, three states with observer status, five NGOs within the UN system and 37 international NGOs were present. Nations were now represented by prestigious officers from government ministries or by professors from distinguished universities. This no doubt reflected the increasing professionalisation of the field of adult education and UNESCO's own internal development into an organisation of govern-ments. Although Jo Roby Kidd (1974) thought that the Tokyo meeting lacked the exciting atmosphere of Montreal, the world at the end of the 1960s was certainly electrifying enough. Between 1960 and the Tokyo meeting, the world's population had grown by 17 per cent to 3.5 billion people. Inequalities between North and South had persisted and deepened.

Throughout the 1960s, the US had been wracked by racial and civic strife as the Vietnam war devastated the lives of millions in south-east Asia and split Americans into warring camps. On the global front, in June 1967 Israel occupied the Palestinian territories of the West Bank, East Jerusalem and Gaza (the occupation still continues), demoralised the Arab world and set the stage for endemic conflict in the Middle East. The Soviet Union invaded Czechoslovakia in 1968. The sounds of protest resounded throughout the major cities of North America and Europe from Paris to New York to San Francisco. The moon landing in July 1969 epitomised the dizzying success of science and technology, and the computer was just edging its way into public consciousness, releasing new utopian energy and dreams. However, since the publication of Rachel Carson's *The Silent Spring* in 1962, science was also linked with environmental degradation. Popular works like Jacques Ellul's *The Technological Society* (1963) and Herbert Marcuse's *One-Dimensional Man* (1968) raised old fears of the technological domination of nature and humankind. Other prophets of gloom feared that capitalism was reaching its 'limits of growth' (Meadows *et al.*, 1974) and that the 'population bomb' was about to detonate (Ehrlich, 1968).

The global political upheavals, student unrest and spectacular accomplishments of science and technology in the 1960s reverberated throughout the Canadian establishment. Educational elites and policy-makers, manifesting the schizoid consciousness of the time (gloom punctuated with either a dream-like humanism that imagined that children could be liberated in soft, caring schools (The *Hall-Dennis Report* (1968)) or a belief in the emancipatory power of science and the new communications technology), were unsettled enough to criticise existing educational practices. Plainly, the formal educational systems were failing to either solve the big problems of the day, or prepare the youth for the changing, complex world unfolding before their eyes. Alan Thomas, the director of the CAAE, consciously adopted the 'learning society' discourse in his writings and reports in the early 1960s. He would remain one of Canada's leading liberal exponents of 'learning' against 'education' throughout the twentieth century (Thomas, 1991).

In Alberta, the Worth Commission's report, *A Choice of Futures* (1972), adopted lifelong learning as its major optic, contending that 'opportunities for adult education and support for adult learning were to come from various agencies on society, both educational and "non-educational" (e.g. employers)' (Selman, 1989, p. 36). The Commission even imagined that a new agency would facilitate adult learning by various and flexible means, with an emphasis upon the use of the media and non-formal approaches. In the same year, Ontario produced *The Learning Society* (1972), named the Wright Commission. Hopping on the lifelong learning bandwagon (an idea whose time always seems ready to come), Wright sprinkled the 'learning society' throughout the report, proposing (like Alberta) an 'Open Academy of Ontario', designed to 'foster a range of flexible and non-formal learning activities provided by many agencies' (Selman, 1989, p. 37).

The 'Final Report' of the Tokyo meeting, and the UNESCO publication of *Learning to Be* (Faure *et al.*, 1972; widely known as the

Faure Report) participated in this exuberant ethos of the learning society. This marked a significant departure from the Elsinore and Montreal meetings. The leading texts produced by UNESCO elites argue strongly for a functional understanding of adult education in relation to the lives of individuals and the needs of society as a whole. Adult education was conceptualised as an important factor in the democratisation of education, in economic and social development, in cultural development and the creation of integrated educational systems in the context of lifelong education. By democratisation, the report meant primarily the participation of more people in the cultural and political life of the nation. With their eye to the Third World, the report's authors recognised that systems of land tenure and the deliberate exclusion of rural people from political decision making blocked many rural dwellers from developing their own or their community's potentials. The report's authors believed that the 'rapid increase in technological innovation, industrial and agricultural production' required that the 'working force constantly be retrained and upgraded in all occupations at all levels.'

But this recognition gave rise to the old humanist fear that the whole man would be lost. They also thought that through embracing national literacy campaigns, adult education could play a significant role in nation-building. The report embraced the notion, present in the earlier meetings, that adult education ought to be a factor in cultural development. They hoped that adult education could 'develop taste, judgment and critical sense, encourage positive attitudes by counter-acting cultural expression, whether indigenous or external, that propa-gate war, violence, racialism or domination . . .'. Finally, education had to burst its four walls, and reside everywhere there was a potential learning environment.

Learning to Be has taken its place as one of the global adult education movement's key texts of the late twentieth century. It is the first UNESCO text to use the phrase 'learning society', and attempt a sustained reflection, grounded as much as possible in empirical scientific studies, on the principles of the learning society. This text continues in the critical humanist (or romantic) tradition. In the preamble, Faure places the individual in the centre of any learning society, whose aim is the 'complete development of man, in all the richness of his personality, the complexity of his forms of expression and his various commitments' (p. vi). Echoing yet again the belief that the industrial society creates a divided consciousness within human beings (a calculating, rational spirit of efficiency and an imaginative-creative side), Faure insisted that 'lifelong education can produce the kind of complete man the need for which is increasing with the continually more stringent constraints tearing the individual asunder' (p. vi).

Yet the humanist sensibility rests uneasily with Faure's evident captivation with science and technology. 'Science and technology have never before demonstrated so strikingly the extent of their power and potential. During this "second twentieth century", knowledge is making a prodigious leap forward' (p. 87). *Learning to Be* comes close to naming the world of the 1970s as a 'knowledge society', evidently profoundly impressed with studies demonstrating the narrowing gap between discovery and application in physical science (Ginzberg, 1964). Faure believed that 'progress in electronics, coupled with the coming of computers, is the basis of a revolution comparable with the invention of writing.' Anticipating some of the writings of contemporary exponents of the information age, Faure and associates considered that the electronic revolution 'radically renewed prospects for industrial production. Innumerable scientific discoveries were having a "tumultuous impact", touching every aspect of our physical and social universe . . .' (p. 90).

Although Faure wonders if humankind's marvellous science and technology has made him any happier, he is seduced by the 'scientific frame of mind' (p. 91). He persists in imagining that humankind can achieve balance between the scientific mind and humanist concerns about the whole man.

Learning to Be offers its insights on the learning society in a short 'Epilogue II: a learning society: today and tomorrow', as well as in part three of the text, 'Towards a learning society.' The key section is 'Innovations and search for alternatives' (pp. 181–234). Faure and associates execute the shift from 'education' to 'learning' through the extension of the vocabulary of education to domains other than formal schools. 'If we admit that education is and will be more and more a primordial need for each individual, then not only must we develop, enrich, and multiply the school and the university, we must also transcend it by broadening the educational function to the dimension of society as a whole' (pp. 161–2). Thus, 'all sectors – public administration, industry, communications, transport – must take part in promoting education.' With 'man' ensconced at the centre of this philosophy, every 'institution will have to change in order to respond more effectively to man's own needs'

(p. 162). But it is not apparent that this formulation – which extends the language of education – can think of these organisations as learning organisations rather than as organisations that must assume an educational function. It is one thing to recognise that businesses train their employees (or ought to do so). It is quite another to conceptualise business through the lens of organisational learning.

The ambiguity between the two languages, of education and learning, has bedevilled the history of adult education thought and action. Faure thinks of the learning society as the 'idea of a permanent, over-all educational system, of a "learning society", not a dream for the future, but as an objective fact and social project in our time (to which educators, pedagogues, scientists, politicians and learners are already contributing, whether consciously or not . . .' (p. 177). This is perhaps one of the most fascinating statements in the document. A permanent overall education system, without conceptualising the learning dynamics of the society (production and otherwise), easily slips into being something like the more efficient co-ordination of formal education, from cradle to grave. But the notion that the learning society is both objective fact and social project astutely captures the idea that Western societies are trans-forming themselves without fully realising the consequences of this transformation for our received notions of education.

The 'principles' set forth in the section on 'Innovations and search for alternatives' posit 'lifelong education' as the 'keystone of the learning society.' Individuals must understand themselves as self-directed learners who live, move and have their being in a world offering them endless learning opportunities. Several of the principles attempt to restore the 'dimensions of living experience' (p. 182) to education by insisting that 'all kinds of existing institutions, whether designed for teaching or not, and many forms of social and economic activity, must be used for educational purposes' (p. 183). The choice of the word 'used' indicates that the many forms of social and economic activity are not concep-tualised as learning sites as such, but, rather, must become conscious of their own educational potential.

This formulation presses toward removing the veil from the actual learning dynamics of these social and economic forms, but stops short. The Faure report recognises that 'continually developing production techniques' provide formal educational institutions with little justification for defending the old ways (p. 197). But Faure cannot think of the organisation of the production process as a learning infrastructure in itself. He can only get as far as observing that 'Lifelong education, in the full sense of the term, means that business, industrial and agricultural firms will have extensive educational functions' (p. 197). When Faure argues that the 'normal culmination of the educational process is adult education' (p. 205), it appears that he has separated it from the educative functions he has been demanding that various social and economic associations take up. The argument that 'adult education . . . must be given its own proper place in educational policies and budgets' (p. 205) is an anomalous statement because it suggests that all the sectors he mentioned, like public administration and communications, are not engaged in adult education!

Hamburg (1997): Creating learning societies committed to justice

By the time UNESCO convened its fifth international gathering of officials and educators to consider adult education's role in the world in Hamburg from 14–18 July 1997, the configuration of the geo-political world and the structure of the global economy had been significantly altered. During the period from Tokyo to Hamburg, a mere quarter of a century, the world experienced the Lenin shipyards in Gdansk, festooned with posters of the Pope in August 1980; the ecstasy of 9 November 1989, when the Berlin wall was breached; Vaclav Havel's assumption of the presidency of Czechoslovakia on 29 December, 1989, heralding the 'velvet revolution.' In this miraculous year, we watched rulers lose their nerve and people gain strength to organise and assert themselves against the state. Two years later in 1991 the Soviet Union monolith disintegrated. In Eric Hobsbawm's dramatic turn of phrase, the twentieth century dissipated to its end.

In this astounding 25 years, the global economy was transformed into an integrated system, admittedly extremely unstable, driven by the revolutions in telecommunications and giving rise to the new vocabularies of the network society and the information age. This latest phase of globalisation, initiated in the late fifteenth century and continuing its foreboding course, had drastic consequences for both the inhabitants of the rich North and the poor South. International monetary policies forced drastic curtailments of state spending on already besieged governments through the Third World. Everywhere in the Western liberal democracies, the social welfare state societies began to crumble as the governmental wisdom of the day cut spending on health, education and general social welfare to facilitate economic profit-making.

The Hamburg meeting produced a flurry of documentation (produced at and for the numerous regional meetings prior to the conference). But two publications constitute significant contributions to the learning society discourse; the conference's declaration, *Adult Education: The Hamburg Declaration* (UNESCO, 1997) and 'The agenda for the future', and the Jacques Delors report, *Learning: The Treasure Within* (1996). Federico Major, the Director-General of UNESCO, announced in his closing address that the conference marked a turning point because for the 'first time in adult education discourse, productivity and democracy are seen as simultaneous requirements for human development' (UNESCO, 1997, p. 2). This was not the first appearance of these twins. The Canadian adult educator and visionary, Moses Coady, based his emancipatory project from the 1930s to the 1950s on precisely this linkage. But Major's rhetoric was riding the wave of two contradictory movements in the mid-1990s. The World Watch Institute, an organisation that monitors the world's ecology, observed that the 'growth in economic output in just three years – from 1995 to 1998 – exceeded that during the 10,000 years from the beginning of agriculture until 1990. And growth of the global economy in 1997 alone easily exceeded that during the seventeenth century' (Brown and Flavin, 1999, p. 10).

Major's words were also propelled by the collective wisdom and actions of global civil society as it congregated at Jomtien (1990: meeting basic learning needs), Rio (1992: the UN conference on environment), Vienna (1993: the world conference on human rights), Cairo (1994: international conference on population and development), Copenhagen (1995: the world summit on social development), Beijing (1995: fourth world conference on women), Istanbul (1996: UN conference on human settlements), and Rome (1996: the world food summit). Tapping into these energies, an exultant Major believed that the concerns expressed at these meetings of a nascent global civil society were coalescing into a 'project of adult learning for personal and social change (UNESCO, 1997, p. 2).'

The Hamburg declarations proposed boldly adult education as the 'key to the twenty-first century.' For the authors, adult education denoted 'the entire body of ongoing learning processes, formal or otherwise, whereby people regarded as adults by the society to which they belong develop their abilities, enrich their knowledge, and improve their technical or professional qualifications or turn them in a new direction to meet their own needs and those of their society' (p. 10). This conceptual formulation (adult education has had many over the years!) represented an advance from *Learning to Be*. While Faure had imagined that an integrated educational system would serve the individual as she moved through the life span, the Hamburg declarations placed the learning infrastructure of the society at the forefront of the analytical framework. The individual's potential for self-development is now closely tied to the social learning infrastructure. Hamburg affirmed that the 'challenge of the twenty-first century cannot be met by governments, organisations or institutions alone; the energy, imagination and genius of people and their full, free and vigorous participation in every aspect of life is needed' (p. 13).

Hamburg recognises, more than any of the other UNESCO gatherings, that civil society is the primary learning domain of our species in the twenty-first century. This radical document argued that the 'ultimate goal' of a reorganised society 'should be the creation of a learning society committed to social justice and general well-being' (p. 13). This was the first time, I think, that learning society was decisively linked with 'social justice' in the historical lexicon of adult education.

The vocabularies and concerns of this decade – 'sustainable and equitable development', 'indigenous learning systems', 'human-centred development', 'civil society', 'gender equity' – as well as the manifest concern for the marginalised expressed in most of the ten themes of the 'Agenda' clearly indicate that the Hamburg statements are children of the 1990s (the repetition of the right-sounding phrases). In the face of mounting evidence of humankind's difficulty in learning from the past, or solving its big problems (like the degradation of the environment or unemployment), the Hamburg elites affirmed the 'potential contribution' of adult education to the 'creation of an informed and tolerant citizenry, economic and social development, the promotion of literacy, the alleviation of poverty and the preservation of the environment . . .' (p. 11). If this were to actually happen (more rather than less enlightenment, with enlightenment translating into new, just structures), adult educators and policy makers had to recognise that the world faced unprecedented challenges. Since we now inhabited knowledge-based societies, 'adult and continuing education ha[d] become an imperative in the community and at the workplace. New demands from social and working life raise expectations requiring each and every individual to continue renewing knowledge and skills throughout the whole of his or her lie.' The emergence of information-based and knowledge-based societies, resulting primarily from the 'processes of globalization and technological advance, together with a new international order' has led to 'far-reaching transformations in the political, cultural and economic fields' (p. 12).

The Hamburg 'Agenda for the future' specifies a series of learning challenges for humankind (problems require a pedagogical response). Essentially, the Agenda argues that humankind will not be able to meet its many challenges unless it is able to mobilise the learning capacities and know-how of millions upon millions of those who have been excluded from a minimally good life. Those left outside of learning loops, often intentionally, like millions of women, must have the constraints preventing them from gaining access to knowledge and information and participating as full human beings in political decision-making processes. Theme 4: 'Adult learning, gender equality and equity, and the empowerment of women' adopts a truly lifelong learning perspective by arguing that girls must not be denied access to quality education, that the family must not be an arena for uncontested domestic and sexual violence, that the education of girls and women demands more than nice words, requiring an adequate legislative, financial and economic support structure for their learning, and that girls and women must be actively encouraged to participate in decision making processes and in formal structures.

The Hamburg Agenda also recognises that, along with removing the barriers to learning and citizenship for women and others (like disabled people), meeting the challenges of the twenty-first century requires the encouraging of greater recognition, participation and accountability of NGOs and local community groups. The Agenda acknowledges that NGOs play key roles in 'awareness-raising and empowerment of people.' This acknowledgement plays itself out in theme 6, 'Adult learning in relation to environment, health and population', emphasising the need to promote the 'competence and involvement of civil society in dealing with environmental and developmental issues' (p. 36).

The Delors Report to UNESCO of the International Commission on Education for the Twenty-first Century is suffused with humanist ideals and shadowed by the 'prevailing mood of disenchantment' (1996,

p. 15). In particular, the report is haunted by the mounting evidence of the global community's inability to live together. While Delors and his commissioners were writing their report, the former Yugoslavia disintegrated and turned into killing fields, Rwandans were hacking each other to death, and the Gulf War's oil fields were still smouldering. One senses the urgency of the cry: 'We must be guided by the Utopian aim of steering the world towards greater mutual understanding, a greater sense of responsibility and greater solidarity, through acceptance of our spiritual and cultural differences.' Delors highlights one of his four pillars (learning to live together) as the most salient. This humanist idealism may, in fact, be a cry of privileged Euro-elites, a cry that somehow never quite gets heard in one of the world's most torturous conflicts where the occupying power, Israel, teaches its children to despise Arabs and Palestine (and the Arabs return the animosity in terrible words and deeds). In the US, millions of right-wing Christian fundamentalists ascribe to an apocalyptic belief system that welcomes the end of the planet earth and the death of enemies. The Delors report apprehends the world in terms of tensions and contradictions. It calls on education to confront the main tensions (some of which are the tensions between the global and the local, tradition and modernity, expansion of knowledge and humans' capacity to assimilate it).

The Delors report does not really add anything new or penetrating to the propositions outlined in the Hamburg declaration and agenda. But the Delors report does equate the 'revolution in communications in the shape of multimedia systems and the spectacular expansion of information technology networks' (p. 64) with the 'learning society.' This assessment is reinforced in the box, 'Towards a learning society', at the top of p. 173. There, the emphasis is all on using computers, cable and satellite TV, virtual reality systems. Delors and his commissioners believe this revolution is not only unstoppable, but it will also influence socialisation processes and the formation of individual and collective identities. They do recognise some of the problems – the much-heralded digital divide and the possibility of info-glut (to come to grips with info-glut, they say, youth and adults must be taught a 'critical spirit in sorting and ordering information' (p. 65)). But they still affirm that 'information and communication technologies can no doubt represent for everyone a real means of contact with non-formal education, becoming one of the most important delivery systems of a learning society in which the various stages of the learning process will be radically rethought' (p. 66).

Learning: The Treasure Within believes that contemporary civilisation is knowledge-driven. The main driving force, in the commissioners' view, is the 'emergence and development of "information societies" and continued technological progress, which is a marked trend of the late twentieth century' which emphasises the 'increasingly intangible dimension of work and accentuate[s] the role played by intellectual and social skills' (p. 71). They believe that the 'next century will provide unprecedented means for communication and for the circulation and storage of information' which will

> impose on education two demands which at first sight may appear contradictory. Education must transmit, efficiently and on a massive scale, an increasing amount of constantly evolving knowledge and know-how adapted to a knowledge-driven civilization, because this forms the basis of the skills of the future. At the same time, it must find and mark the reference points that will make it possible, on the one hand, for people not to be overwhelmed by the flows of information, much of it ephemeral, that are invading the public and private domains and, on the other, to keep the development of individuals and communities as its end in view. (p. 85)

At the end of the twentieth century, then, the learning society paradigm has found its fulfilment in the information age. In the next chapter, I subject this convenient convergence to critical scrutiny. What seductive dangers await those adult educators who embrace the information age with all of its endless possibilities?

CHAPTER THREE

From industrialism to the information society: Beautiful dreams, gritty realities

Technological textures

Those of us who reside in the rich countries of the North live in profoundly technologically textured societies. Consider the way many of us begin our ordinary days. We are awakened by a technology, whether it be a clock radio or the beeping of a quartz clock. We leave our cosy beds, warmed by electric blankets or those made from acrylic or natural fibres, each subjected to technologically transformative processes. Our waking is enmeshed with complex technological texture, vast plumbing systems stretching back to the Romans, but today entailing vast water systems and metallurgical and plasticised materials. We take our breakfast in kitchens far removed from those of yesteryear, with our plethora of automatic machines, toasters, coffee makers, ovens, dishwashers, microwaves.

After awakening and eating, we exit our homes by a transportation system, our automobiles displaying their computerised and electronic instruments, alerting us to various necessary tasks such as turning out the lights, or putting on the seat-belt. Our ordinary lifeworld activities are often accompanied by other aspects of the human-technology interaction. While eating, the television may have been tuned to CNN. While driving to work, the radio informs and entertains. Travelling to work, we can discuss business on our cell phones. Once at work, we immediately plug ourselves into the wired world, gathering our e-mails, sending messages, and conducting our daily work with the computer.

At the end of the work week, men and women can head off for relaxation to one of 'nature's museums', preserved wilderness spaces (parks, hiking trails, mountains) where, if we are venturesome and risk-taking, we might climb some steep cliff faces. If we did so, we would

44

employ pitons and carabiners made of metal alloys, climbing ropes made of braided dacron, specially manufactured climbing shoes. For an overnight climb, we could easily use a lightweight, artificial-fibre tent, and exquisitely designed miniaturised cooking equipment and dehydrated foods, easily available at the local Mountain Equipment store (marvels of technology in themselves, with their colourful tents, kayaks, jackets, canoes and assorted gadgetry). Technology also shapes the way we think about even the most intimate of human interactions, our sexual practices. The existence of birth control technologies means that most contemporary persons engage in sexual activity having first thought about their existence. One takes a decision not to use a birth control technology, knowing full well that the technologies exist. The rich, Western-liberal societies simply assume that adolescents are responsible only if they prevent possible pregnancies (Ihde, 1990, pp. 2–3).

Whether it be at the micro-level of our daily lives or the macro-level of global systems, our lives are pervaded by technology. The US went to war against Iraq in March 2003, ostensibly because this outcast nation allegedly possessed nuclear weaponry and other technological instruments of mass destruction (chemical and biological warfare). Russia stopped a hostage-taking in Moscow through the use of a poisonous gas that killed hundreds of people They couldn't do that without the sciences of chemistry and micro-biology. The great problems of ecological destruction – like global warming – are the products of technological civilisation. Primitive man, so-called, did not have the know-how to poke holes in the ozone layer, let alone imagine the existence of ozone itself. The terrifying litany of environmental degradation laid out before us, endlessly it seems, all track to modes of interacting with nature mediated by powerful technologies, be they massive forestry equipment or toxic pesticides sprayed over so many fields. As human occupation of land has rolled along inexorably, animals have become the province of zoos and game preserves that use sophisticated science and technologies to protect and breed endangered species. Humankind's capacity to clone species raises fundamental ethical and spiritual questions for our reflection. In previous generations, human beings were born with certain attributes and, in some cases, disabilities, for which they had to assume responsibility. Now, with cloning, humankind can decide the genetic makeup of another being (Habermas, 2003; McKibben, 2003). We have not faced this sort of question before. Robotics, once the realm of science fiction and spooky late-night thrillers, have, thanks to

45

computer science, burst from fiction into reality. Recently, I watched an eye surgeon describe on television a new surgical method, wherein, guided by computer imaging, a robot conducts a surgical intervention into the eye. He said that preliminary trials had been successful. No surgeon can keep her hand as steady as the robot (their metal fingers exhibit not the slightest tremor). Some techno-utopians imagine that robot 'intelligence' (artificial) will surpass human 'intelligence' (natural) by the year 2050.

During the last decade, the 1990s, many business leaders, government policy makers and academics hailed the arrival of information technology (IT), associated mainly with the Internet, but including robotics, simulation and data processing. Before the IT bubble burst in 2001 amidst corporate scandals and growing global anarchy, techno-utopians hitched humankind's future to the information train and the new economy. IT was seen as a catalyst for generating economic growth and development, global co-operation and tolerance, personal freedom and individual improvement. The beautiful dreamers of the information society promised us many great and wondrous things. Techno-optimists insisted that the computer revolution would guarantee a perpetually dynamic economy. It would create unimagined wealth for many, and make life better for just about everyone. They told us that ordinary citizens now had access to unprecedented hordes of information. Society was brimming with knowledge, bottled up, spilling out, available everywhere. They could get expert advice about their health from a Website. They could do their banking without waiting in line. They could purchase goods through the Internet from companies without resources to spend on advertising.

Universities could gain access to multitudes of students who could stay at home and study online. Citizens could create new public spaces on the Internet to rejuvenate democracy. Critics of globalisation could organise their demonstrations sitting at their desks. Choices appeared to be endlessly widening: IT was offered as the great social equaliser. In their most exuberant moments, techno-utopians proclaimed the birth of a new age, an information revolution destined to change the way we lived our lives, interacted with each other and understood our place in the cosmos. In the first wave of enthusiasm for IT, few stopped to ask many hard questions.

The scepticism would not be long in coming. In this chapter, then, I want to query some of the main arguments supporting the central claim that we live in a radically new age. How do we, in fact, demarcate periods of history? How would we actually know that we, inhabitants of the Western-liberal democracies, have crossed over the line into a new form of society and self-understanding? To assess the idea that we now live in a network society or an information society requires carefully construed concepts and empirical data. More information, for instance, does not in itself signify a qualitative transformation into a new form of society. The provocative claim that computers are precipitating a 'revolution' necessarily demands that we ask just what has been overthrown. Have there been fundamental changes in the basic structure of class and property ownership in the late twentieth century? Are we working in conditions and with technologies that indicate a radical disjuncture from the early industrial era?

Have more public spaces for citizen deliberation been created? Are citizens more engaged in decision making processes than in earlier periods of history? Are we, in fact, more knowledgeable about the many crucial issues facing us every day, at home and abroad, than in times past? Are we living more peacefully and happily? The provocative claim that entry into the age of information has rendered place and geographical space less relevant than in times past also needs to be questioned. First wave enthusiasts wrote of how virtual communities would replace communities in real space and time. Our main interest with this latter claim is to understand how IT is embedded in the lifeworld. It is still a good idea to hold on to the notion that we, as humans, have bodies, self-identities, that we interact with other bodies, that our feet touch the ground as we walk, that we hold lovers in our arms, that we eat food, that we live on the earth in specific places with specific histories, before soaring too far off into the dark reaches of cyberspace. Before considering the arguments for and against a new age, let us think for a moment about humankind's ambiguous relationship with technology.

The mythic power of technology

To gain a better understanding of how the belief that the 'techno-scientific knowledge crystallised in computers, telecommunications, and bio-technologies is now unleashing an ongoing and irresistible transformation of civilization, dramatic in its consequences, unavoidably traumatic in the short term' is 'opening out onto horizons nothing short of utopian' (Dyer-Witheford, 1999, p. 15), it is useful for us to reflect briefly on the place of technology in the human imagination. Darin Barney, in *Prometheus Wired: The Hope For Democracy in the Age of Network Technology* (2000), thinks that the story of modern technology teaches us that those who do not recognise their limits are dangerous to themselves and to their gods. He explores the human desire for command and creativity in relation to the categories of space, time, matter, biological life and the capacity for consciousness. Prometheus, who tried to steal fire from the gods, is the archetype for this desire to go beyond limits.

Humankind aspired to transcend spatial limitations through inventing glass technologies, spectacles and telescopes. At first, they could only dream of unimagined expanses. Then this daydream was replaced by a burning desire to command space by travelling over long distances. The steamboat in the eighteenth century, the railway in the nineteenth, and the aeroplane and rocket ship in the twentieth enabled humans to actually master space. In the fourteenth century, the mechanical clock was introduced and time was subjected to human regulation. But it was not until the clock was used to habituate freshly urbanised labourers to the cycles of industry and commerce, that this instrument symbolised the conquest of nature itself. Humankind has always left its mark on nature (nature is always social nature). The Industrial Revolution, with its mechanised production, intensified exploitation of raw materials and harnessing of power, enabled engineers to overcome the limitations imposed by human labour.

One can draw a straight line from the steam engine to the dynamo, to the internal combustion engine, to the turbine and to the nuclear reactor (Adorno, the dysphoric thinker, also drew a line from the sling shot to the nuclear bomb). These machines had voracious appetites for fuel. The drive in our time for petroleum shapes geo-politics while generating enormous risks to human well-being. Barney thinks that the 'shift from organic animal and vegetable matter to inorganic minerals as the primary material of production is a key marker of the modern industrial age' (p. 9). By the mid-twentieth century, plastic had become the quintessential modern product (an inorganic synthetic). Wasn't everything made out of plastic? But the matter of transcending, commanding and creating the biology of life has been the most difficult for modern humanity. Humankind has dreamt for a long time about creating life from inanimate nature (Mary Shelly's story of Frankenstein appears in the early 1800s). Cryogenics (freezing a corpse with the hope of bringing it back to life) seemed the project of cranks. With the birth of the Artificial Intelligence movement (which imagines it can create a living, thinking brain from inanimate substances) and the recent successes of the Human Genome Project (which participates in the age-old dream of finding the fountain of youth), the transcending of biology seems less far-fetched.

Modern communications technologies have complemented humankind's efforts to 'transcend time, command space, and transform matter through industry' (p. 12). The birth of the printing press in the late fifteenth century smashed the monopolies on knowledge held by the clerisy (they were the keepers of the sacred texts). In so doing, this revolutionary print technology facilitated the emergence of individual consciousness (I can interpret this text for my self; I have a self that can interpret) and the birth of the nation-state. Even more significantly, print introduced a new relationship to time and space. Oral memory was fragile, easily subject to patchy recall. The printed word was more permanent than speech and relatively easy to transport and store. The communications technologies of the nineteenth century – telegraph and telephony – freed communication from the question of transport. Instantaneous conversations across vast distances were now possible. 'Son born healthy . . .' reads the faded old telegram from my mother to my father who was fighting overseas in World War II. Audio recordings and photography preserved images and sounds, rescuing memory from the tarnish of uncertainty. 'These technologies', says Barney, 'contributed to the modern perception of the unique position occupied by the individual self in both time and place' (p. 12).

But it is not until the twentieth century that 'technologies of con-sciousness' appeared that enabled the powerful interests of modernity to facilitate the manufacture of consent and needs. Broadcasting emerged as the perfect technological solution to these distinctly modern problems. By the mid-twentieth century, with individuals increasingly isolated in suburban dwellings, radio and television were 'information conduits' piping information into their homes. While these technologies were contested by some adult educators in the 1940s and 1950s (one thinks of the Canadian Citizen's Forums), they mainly assembled citizens into a great mass, 'ready to receive political instruction in the form of "news", and basic socialization in the form of "entertainment"' (p. 13).

These technologies were almost perfect instruments to stimulate consumption, educate desire, and promote the possession of consumer goods as the good life. The ultimate purpose of broadcast technologies seemed to be the creating of an audience, gathered and delivered to advertisers. Barney says that, 'It is at this point that the socialization and commercial roles of broadcast technology dovetail to evoke one of modernity's great ironies: the paradox of mass pluralism, in which millions of consumers are convinced they can assert their essential individuality by purchasing the same running shoes in the same shopping malls as millions of other people' (p. 13; see also Niedzviecki, 2004). 'Yes, we are all individuals', the adoring masses cry out to Brian, the reluctant messiah in the Monty Python movie *The Life of Brian*, as he exhorts them to express their individuality and not follow him.

With the arrival of network technology in the last two decades, breathless visionaries like the Tofflers proclaimed that 'what is happening now is nothing less than a global revolution, a quantum leap . . . we are the final generation of an old civilization and the first generation of a new one' (cited, p. 18). Bits have replaced fire; old narratives must be scrapped; new vocabularies (multi-linearity, nodes, links and networks) must displace languages of centre and hierarchy; networks are the post-modern technology. Before getting too ecstatic, however, one must acknowledge that the hallmark of modernity is the incessant celebration of change and the forgetting of that which endures. Modernity fetishises change; it eschews tradition; it deludes itself about what persists. The idea that network technology is revolutionary, in the sense that it threatens power interests, scarcely stands the test of reasonable scrutiny. If it were truly revolutionary, Barney asks, why are 'existing governmental, bureaucratic, corporate, and financial elites . . . so enthusiastic about, and so heavily invested in, the success of this technology?' (p. 19). Barney is particularly troubled that Internet revolutionaries claim that network technology is a democratic technology.

Barney turns to Marx and Heidegger to understand more deeply how and what technology tells about our collective selves. He thinks that Marx has been falsely labelled as a technological determinist ('The hand mill gives you society with the feudal lord; the steam mill, society with industrial capitalist' is the culprit aphorism so often trotted out). Marx's message is simply that technology, like the hand mill, brings something to the mode of production that enables it to determine the shape of social and political life. It is not technology that somehow carries the seeds of the social and political within its mechanisms. Marx thought that productive activity was important for two reasons. First, human beings expressed who they were through the medium of technology. Second, the form of the technology itself had a decisive effect on the essence it expressed. Marx demonstrates the practical out-working of these principles through his critical examination of the machine in modern industrial production. Machines, simply put, replaced tools with repetition and mechanisation. It was not the tech-nology itself that required the craft skills of workers be replaced. Instead, those who enjoyed economic power consciously decided to design machines to increase profits and gain control over the know-how and skill of working people. There is nothing mysterious about this design process at all. Machinery was organised as a system; modern industry stood on its own feet; factories began to construct machines by machines. Technology, then, is 'an instrument that not only facilitates the accomplishment of capitalist exploitation and alienation, but also gathers and embodies them' (p. 39). If technologies are always embedded in the mode of production, and the mode of production speaks truths about the kind of society we imagine, then one could assume that emancipa-tion from alienated forms of the capitalist mode of production would entail the invention of technologies that spoke on behalf of emancipated humanity. Put simply, technologies spring out of the human imagination.

Martin Heidegger is one of the twentieth century's most influential and controversial philosophers. He is a metaphysical thinker who invents his own philosophical vocabulary to grasp truths often thought outside our grasp. Like Marx, he wants to know what technology reveals. Our tendency in pragmatic North America is to see objects as discrete things. A sawmill to us is an enterprise that transforms inert logs into lumber for sale on the market. But Heidegger observes the sawmill as revealing the truth about more than two by fours: how humans produce things, and the relationships they enter into with each other and with nature to do so. Heidegger believes that modern technology 'enframes' nature, delineating how we approach her. He thinks that, 'The world now appears as an object open to the attacks of calculative thought, attacks that nothing is believed able any longer to resist. Nature becomes a gigantic gasoline station, an energy source for modern technology and industry' (cited, p. 43).

He speaks of 'calculative thought', which is privileged by modern technology's enframing. 'It is this reservation concerning the likelihood of calculating beings making a meditative intervention into the advance of modern technology that perhaps led Heidegger to his now-infamous observation that "only a god can save us now"' (p. 45). Heidegger thought that the greatest danger with technology is not particular instances of pollution or invasion of privacy, but, rather, in its 'propensity to enframe the condition of Being, mistakenly, as one of calculation and rootlessness' (p. 45). Technology is more a condition of our existence and not a series of problems to be solved. He wants us to be open to the mystery of what is before us, to discard hubris and 'invoke the humility proper to their essence' (p. 47).

From the end of ideology to the information society

Daniel Bell's infamous 'end of ideology' hypothesis of the 1950s sputtered amidst the flames of Vietnam and the urban ghettos of America in the 1960s. Spurred by the disintegration of international and domestic consensus, the famous Harvard sociologist fashioned a new vision of an emergent new form of society he called 'post-industrialism.' In *The Coming of Post-Industrial Society* (1973), Bell observed that scientific discovery and technical application were increasingly synchronised, making theoretical knowledge central to wealth production. Echoing the work of management guru, Philip Drucker (who had posited the birth of the 'knowledge society' in the late 1960s), Bell argued that the old industrial world of the blue-collar worker had been superseded. The economy had shifted from goods-producing to a service economy, from the predominance of manual labour to the pre-eminence of professional and technical work. The economic system had increased capacities for assessment and forecasting.

The new intellectual technologies of games theory and systems analysis (so dear to the intellectuals surrounding Kennedy) had enabled this shift of axis to a society 'organized around knowledge for the purpose of social control and the directing of innovation and change' (Bell, 1973, p. 20). Ingeniously revising Marx, Bell saw a knowledge class (engineers, scientists, administrators) as driving the society beyond industrialism towards freedom from material want, economic crisis and class conflict. Knowledge would replace both labour and capital as the main factor of production. 'If there is an erosion of the working class in post-industrial society', Bell asked, posing the question all information society theorists will subsequently hurl at Marxism, 'how can Marx's vision of social change be maintained?' (p. 40).

Post-industrial theory gained wide acclaim among academics,

government experts and corporate managers in the 1960s and 1970s. Post-industrialism was received enthusiastically in Japan (by authors like Yujiro Hayashi and Yoneji Masuda). These influential thinkers wrote about *juho shakai* (the informational society or information society), emphasising particularly computers' potential to transform industrial production through unprecedented levels of automation and the integration of office, factory and consumer. Fusing economic analysis with futurism, Masuda imagined an emergent society in which increased availability of information and free time resulted in a 'computopia' of self-actualisation, voluntary civic participation, enhanced global and ecological consciousness (Dyer–Witheford, 1999, p. 20). In the midst of its own recession in the 1970s, the anxious West turned to the 'Japanese miracle', to *juho shakai* – computerisation, robotisation, workplace organisation – to cure its woes. Japanese notions of quality circles and teamwork spread like a virus through Western management circles. In 1978, the first North American book to use 'information society' in its title appeared. In Canada, the government issued *The Information Revolution and its Implications for Canada* in 1981 (Serafini and Andrieu, 1981). There, we were told, 'Like the industrial revolution, the information revolution is unavoidable. Consequently, the objectives of public policy should be not to prevent the revolution from occurring, but rather to turn it to our advantage' (p. 13).

By the late 1970s and 1980s, the information revolution was emerging as a central category in government and corporate planning. In subsequent works, Bell wrote of an 'information explosion', and Toffler's *Third Wave* and Naisbett's *Megatrends* fed these ideas into the popular culture. Whereas post-industrialism had defined the new age as a departure from the crises of industrialism, the information society posited that industry had been succeeded by information. The old, greasy, heavy worlds of the mechanical steel mills, and railroads had been supplanted by the new, shiny, light worlds of the digital silicon chips and communication networks. This idea of an information revolution as both 'inevitable' and 'desirable' (weren't we all just swept along, subjected without much consideration to voice-mails, e-mails, computerised answering services, wired workplaces?) was certainly accompanied by sweeping, revolutionary doctrine. In its utopic phase, the information society promised to eliminate undesirable features of industrial society – meaningless work, huge impersonal organisations, rigid routines. Somehow, it had the magical power to foster scintillating cultures of individual and collective self-actualisation. Planetary in scale, the information revolution could facilitate a unified world economy. One effusive techno-utopian, Hans Moravec (*Mind Children: The Future of Robot and Human Intelligence* (1988), even imagined that computers were a potential successor species, a further stage in evolution.

Toffler's *Third Wave* (1980) greeted the appearance of a new civilisation that has moved beyond the old 'class war' predicted by Marx. The grimy worlds of alienated labour and dehumanising mechanisation could now be cast into the dustbins of the second wave industrial civilisation. 'Today,' expounded Toffler, 'it is knowledge that drives the economy, not the economy that drives knowledge' (1990, pp. 420–1). One could bid farewell to the working class as automation-liquidated labour and scads of new work appeared in high-technology, information-intensive industries (like Nortel). Indeed, theorists like Robert Blauner (1964) and Shoshana Zuboff (1988) reversed the Taylorist trajectory of the fragmentation and simplification of work. Third-wave, or computer-mediated forms of work, depended on the intellect and skills of the workforce.

Symbols in workers' heads were more important than jack hammers in their hands. Property dissolved wondrously into non-material, non-tangible, potentially infinite 'info-property'. In his provocative text, *Cyber-Marx: Cycles and Circuits in High-Technology Capitalism* (1999), Dyer-Witheford argues that 'both the "beyond capital" and the "better capital" versions of the information revolution point in the same direction: to a future in which the capitalist development of technology leads to social salvation, whether through the perfection of the market or its transcendence' (p. 30). With the collapse of the Soviet Union in the early 1990s, the futurist Francis Fukuyama (1992) could announce his 'end of history' thesis and find an eager audience. Assisted by the instrument of information technology, technological progress had once again displaced the need for reflection on the good life and political deliberation amongst its citizens.

Darin Barney cautions us not to be swept along too easily or quickly by the techno-utopians. 'We know quite a bit', he says, 'and it can't all be wrong' (2000, p. 3). Barney reminds us to think deeply about the history of modern technology. He alerts us to the human desire (captured in the myth of Prometheus) to 'command and transcend that which is given, in the hope of creating its own future' (p. 6). He thinks that we are in the midst of a shift in myth-making which runs parallel to the alleged dramatic changes in the way we work and live. This myth teaches us that change is imminent and that things will never be the same. Network technology will fundamentally alter the relations of power within the society, it will unleash an essentially revolutionary series of social, economic and political changes, it will enhance democracy and over-come the obstacles of scale. This new society, call it the information age, knowledge society or the learning society, is here and it is good. Barney suggests that network technology be viewed within the mythic patterns of the West. 'It is imperative that we subject our hopes for this technology to the sort of thoughtful consideration that, in moderating hope, befits our nature as rational beings' (p. 6).

Let us now examine critically some of the assumptions under-pinning the claims that we have entered an information age. Time moves so fast, our memories so short, that we might forget that while all this utopian talk was occurring, millions of workers were losing their jobs, the welfare state was being dismantled, and anxiety was rampant every-where. Before we could even blink, IT industries collapsed, the stock market plunged, Enron fell apart, revealing staggering levels of greed and criminality, and the World Bank and International Monetary Fund policies only seemed to increase poverty levels throughout the Third World.

The information age idea under scrutiny

In *Theories of the Information Society* (1995), Frank Webster offers a sceptical inquiry into the idea of the information age. He wants to know just how novel our time actually is, and presents his ideas and those of other sceptics (like Herbert Schiller (1989), the media theorist). In his chapter, 'Information and the idea of an information society', Frank Webster distinguishes analytically five definitions of an information society: the technological, the economic, the occupational, the spatial, and the cultural. He thinks that the 'problem of measurement, and the associated difficulty of stipulating the point on the technological scale at which a society is judged to have entered an "information age", is surely central to any acceptable definition of a distinctly new type of society' (p. 9). When does a society stop being 'industrial' and enter into the 'information' category? Webster argues that technological definitions of the information society posit that 'breakthroughs in information processing, storage and transmission have led to the application of information technologies in virtually all corners of society' (p. 7). Indeed, computers appear to be not only cheaper than they were, they are everywhere; in cars, cookers, watches, Tim Horton's coffee shops, kids' toys, offices, bedrooms, piled in hallways, waiting to be sent to the graveyard. Since they are everywhere, this must add up to something rather distinct. Why not view the dazzling developments of network technology as evidence of a new type of society? As John Naisbitt puts it (stealing from Marx): 'Computer technology is to the information age what mechanization was to the industrial revolution' (1984, p. 28).

At first sight, these new technologies do appear to be the distinguishing features of a new society. But the moment one probes more deeply, one is struck with the 'astonishing vagueness of technology' (p. 9) in the popular texts. How much IT is actually present in the society? How much IT is required to qualify us for an information society? We need measures, because as Webster accurately states, the problem of measurement is necessary to forge an acceptable definition of a distinctively new type of society. Researchers grappling with these matters encounter two difficult problems: (1) how to measure the rate of technical diffusion; and (2) how to decide when a society ceases being industrial and enters its post-phase. The problems get even more obtuse as researchers try to figure out how to measure empirically the diffusion of IT into factories and offices.

The second major objection to technological definitions of the information society, in Webster's mind, is not that technology is seen as the prime social dynamic. Rather, it is that, viewed in this way, it relegates to a separate division social, economic and political dimensions of technological innovation. These realms are subordinate to the 'premier league of technology which appears to be self-perpetuating though it leaves its impress on all aspects of society' (p. 10). But it is demonstratively not the case, now or historically, that 'technology is aloof from the social realm in this way' (p. 10). It is, in fact, an integral and constitutive part of the social. Research and development decisions (in government, business and universities) express priorities and value judgments. A vast critical literature exists as testimony to the fact that military projects received more funding than health work throughout the twentieth century (we have state-of-the-art weapons systems and rudimentary preventive health care); that architectural design bears the stamp of human desire and power; that our attitudes to the environment shape our profligate use of fossil fuels; that our suburban housing developments speak profoundly about how we understand the nature of human community; that our love of the automobile crowds out innovative commitment to public transit; and so on. Webster asks, 'How can it be acceptable to take what is regarded as an asocial phenomenon (technology) and assert that this then defines the social world?' (p. 10).

Another promising way to define the information society is to assess the size and growth of the information industries. Fritz Machlup (*The Production and Distribution of Knowledge* (1962)) pioneered studies of the information industries, attempting to establish measures of the information society in economic terms. He distinguished five industry groups: education; media of communication; information machines; information services; and other information activities. Working with these categories, Machlup tried to ascribe an economic value to each in order to account for its contribution to the gross national product (GNP). If he could identify a trend to an increased proportion of the GNP, then one might claim that an information society was emerging through time. This is precisely what Machlup did propose, calculating that 29 per cent of the US's GNP in 1958 came from the knowledge industries.

Webster informs us that the best-known study of the emergence of an information economy is the massive report from Marc Porat (*The Information Economy* (1977)). Porat echoed much of Machlup's approach (allocating industries to five categories which created new information), but he used a tripartite scheme, dividing the economy into 'primary', 'secondary', and 'non-information' sectors. Porat included in the 'primary information sector' all those 'industries which make available their information in established markets or elsewhere where an economic value can be readily ascribed (e.g. mass media, education, advertising, computer manufacture).' However, Porat tried to identify a 'secondary information sector' to allow him to include important informational activities such as research and development inside a pharmaceutical company, information produced by government departments for internal usage, and the library resources of an oil corporation. Porat concluded that 46 per cent of the US gross national product could be accounted for by the information sector. Thus, the US was an 'information society [where] the major arenas of economic activity are the information goods and service producers, and the public and private [secondary information sector] bureaucracies' (Porat, 1978, p. 11).

Webster thinks that the economics of information approach masks serious difficulties. For instance, Porat separates out the research and development dimensions of a petrochemical company from its manufacturing element. Surely these activities are blurred, with research and development intimately linking with its production wings. Any separation for mathematical purposes falsifies the data. Porat also splits every industry with the 'secondary information sector' into the informational and non-informational domains. As many adult educators and theorists know, it is very difficult to split knowing from doing. 'Where does one place the operation of computer numerical control systems or the line management functions which are an integral element of production?' (p. 12), Webster wonders. It appears that Porat's division within industries to chart the 'secondary information sector' is arbitrary. A second problem with the aggregated data is that they homogenise very disparate economic activities. It may be possible to argue that growth in the 'economic worth of advertising and television is indicative of an "information society", but one is left with an urge to distinguish between informational activities on qualitative grounds' (p. 12).

Scholars ought to differentiate between information flowing from policy research centres or corporate think tanks, or transnational finance houses from the manufacturers of 35 mm cameras, software designers and Saatchi and Saatchi copywriters. Information economists fall prey to a trend to put a price tag on everything. Once information is reduced to bits of data, how can one determine what is really valuable? This is a serious issue for just learning society proponents. Consider only that, within the quantitative conceptual frameworks of Machlup and Porat, the multi-million sales of a wretched street tabloid newspaper would be regarded as more informational than a lesser-circulating, truth-telling paper or magazine. Thus, measured by the GNP, 'informational activity is of great weight, but of little consequence in terms of the springs of economic, social and political life' (p. 13). Even based on their own quantitative measurements, how would Machlup and Porat decide what percentage of the GNP had to be dedicated to informational services to push it into an information society?

By far the most popular measure for the arrival of the information society is that focusing on occupational change. The assumption here is that we have achieved an information age when the predominance of occupations is found in information work. To understand more clearly the trajectory of this argument, consider Peter Drucker's 'The age of social transformation' (1994), published in a leading American journal of liberal opinion. Drucker anchors his belief that we inhabit a knowledge society through a sociological analysis that tracks the decline of the blue-collar worker. He thinks that this transformation has been accomplished without significant upheaval. Drucker's supporting arguments for the bold claim that the 'newly emerging dominant group is a "knowledge worker"' (p. 62) seem weak, suffering from conceptual murkiness and absence of empirical evidence. He distinguishes the new knowledge society from the old industrial one by stating (without offering proof) that the 'great majority of the new jobs require qualifications the industrial worker does not possess . . .' (p. 62).

That many of the jobs in our contemporary world require educational qualifications (certificates, diplomas, degrees) does not, however, permit us to argue that industrial work is pure behavioural action, unmediated by cognitive and lifeworld resources. Webster gives the example of the railway signalman, contrasting it with a computer repair person (the latter would, in some analyses, be classified as a knowledge worker). Although the knowledge, skill, sensibility and attitudes of the industrial worker may very well be tacit, inscribed in the sinews and fabric of mind and body, it is knowledge nonetheless. Drucker thinks that knowledge workers give the knowledge society its character and colour. He argues that the knowledge worker gains access to these jobs through formal education. However, it was in industrial societies, after all, that instituted common schooling for everyone; where the state intervened in the life of communities, layering lifeworld learning processes with formal instruction to be prepare them for the emergent industrial order.

Drucker also believes that in the knowledge society 'knowledge for the most part exists only in application' (p. 68). This is a well-known tenet of American pragmatism: knowledge is that which works. This notion hardly distinguishes pre-industrial and industrial societies from the knowledge society! Perhaps Drucker's most contentious idea is his claim that in the knowledge society the employees own the tools of production (this is yet another version of the idea that the information society vanquishes class and property ownership). The knowledge of the surgeon, he says, resides in the individual surgeon's mind. The idea that the knowledge of the surgeon, acquired through arduous educational processes and mentored experience, resides in her mind obscures the fact that knowledge does not actually rest in the mind as such. The surgeon's knowledge resides, rather, in collectively recorded sets of scientific knowledge (stored in texts) and collectively approved sets of practices (stored in organisational memory and procedures). These forms of learning are enacted in a network of institutional practices, and flow through the cognitive processes of the person through time. Drucker's idea that individuals own their own means of production is a beautiful dream. Countering this delusion, Barney argues that the 'ownership of network technology, like the ownership of most other means of power in a capitalist society, is class based and located squarely in the hands of a powerful minority' (2000, p. 120).

Webster argues that the seemingly evident dichotomy of the economy into an 'information sector' (like a university whose prime function is creating, processing and handling information) and a "production sector" (workers there create, process and handle physical goods) breaks down once we acknowledge that 'every occupation involves a significant degree of information processing and cognition' (1995, p. 15). Even the attempt to estimate the degree to which each type of occupation is informational is just that, a crude estimation. For example, the railway signalman is a premier manual worker of the industrial age. But he must have a stock of knowledge about tracks and timetables, roles and routines. He must communicate with other signalmen down the line, with station personnel and engine drives. He must keep a precise ledger of all traffic moving through his area; he doesn't need much physical strength to pull the levers.

Yet a person who comes into the office to repair the photocopier may know little about the products, work in uncomfortable circumstances, and still be classified as an information worker by Porat since she works with new age machinery. 'If one may be suspicious of the ways in which researchers conceive of information work', Webster states, 'one needs also to beware the oversimplifications which can come from allocating a wide variety of jobs to the same pigeonholes' (p. 15). Is it really sensible, Webster wonders, to include under the category of librarian, those who spend their day issuing books with someone routinely advising academics on the best sources of information for their state-of-the-art research?

One of the most controversial claims of the information society proponents is that the emergence of information networks dramatically alters both the organisation and perception of time and space. We speak easily about cyberspace. Phrases like virtual reality are part of common vocabulary. We were told, particularly in the first wave of exuberance, that distance had been put to death, and place (in physical, geographical terms) was becoming irrelevant in the wired world. These ideas certainly gained ground in the last two decades, propelled by the 'growing "infor-matisation" of the economy' (Webster, 1995, p. 18). Few commentators on the inner dynamics of the global economy would deny that the capacity to process and exchange information rapidly enabled companies to develop truly 'global strategies for the production, storage and distribution of goods and services' (p. 18). Old notions of geo-graphical boundaries were pushed back and the restrictions of time, dissolved.

Drawing on the analogy of the electricity grid, which runs through an entire society, linking household to household, information society proponents imagined a 'wired society', which operated at 'national, international and global levels to provide an "information ring main" to each home, shop or office' (Barron and Curnow, 1978, p. 19). Manuel Castells, an ardent advocate of a 'network market' (and society), emphasises the significance of the flow of information along these invisible highways. Although the mapping of cyberspace is in its primitive stage, by all estimates there does seem to be an enormous increase in the 'transborder data flows, in telecommunication facilities, in communications between computers at every level from home to transnational organisation, in exchanges between stock markets and corporate segments, in access to international data bases, in telex messages.' But we do not yet have a 'clear picture of the size, capacity and use of the networks' (Webster, 1995, p. 19).

Yet the critical question – why should 'greater volume and velocity of information flows' (p. 20) compel us to argue that this constitutes a new type of society? – must be posed. Much has been written about space/time compression: the slow-moving world of trade across distances, or the hand-written letter taking weeks to cross the space separating people from each other surpassed through the touch of a keyboard. Webster thinks that once we ask why the simple existence of networks should actually lead analysts to label societies as information economies, we encounter the definitional problem once again. When is a network a network? When two people speak to one another by telephone? When computer systems transmit vast data sets through a packet-switching exchange? When all the offices at the university, or office, are wired or when home terminals can actually communicate with local banks and retail stores? Generalisations about living in a wired or network society sweep well beyond our ethnographic knowledge of how, in fact, people actually use computers and the Internet. Miller and Slater (*The Internet: An Ethnographic Approach* (2000)) demonstrate in their study of Internet usage in Trinidad that the Internet is not a realm apart from people's lifeworld. One cannot think of it as a technical entity. Rather, it comes to life when particular communities and groups use it for specific religious, ethnic, or familial purposes. The connectivity of real people in real time and space is strengthened and extended, not displaced.

Webster wonders, as well, if networks are being defined as technological systems or whether a 'more appropriate focus' would be on information flows. 'If it is the latter', he avers, 'then it may reasonably be asked how much and why more volume and velocity of information flow should mark a new society?' (1995, p. 20). Webster's final query actually requires considerable historical reflection. He observes that 'information networks have been around for a very long time' (p. 20). In his remarkable *A Social History of Knowledge: From Gutenberg to Diderot* (2000), social historian Peter Burke cautions us that,

> We should not too quick to assume that our age is the first to take these questions seriously. The commodification of information is as old as capitalism. The use by governments of systematically collected information is, quite literally, ancient history (ancient Roman and Chinese history in particular). As for scepticism about claims to knowledge, it goes back at least as far as the ancient Greek philosopher Pyrrho of Elis. (pp. 1–2; see also Hecht, 2003)

Information networks have probably existed since ancient times. Certainly from early modernity to the present, knowledge has been produced and has travelled along bumpy roads in horse-drawn carriages and over turbulent seas in sailing ships. Indeed, all societies, from tribal learning societies to modern nation-states, have informational learning systems that enable them to survive and sustain themselves in specific times and places.

The cultural conception of an information society has captivated the thinking of many post-modernists (Mark Poster's *The Mode of Information* (1990) is exemplary). Nobody who lives in our time doubts this for a moment as they live, move and breathe in a deluge of images and signs. Television is programmed around the clock. In Capetown, South Africa in the mid-1990s, televisions were on, always, everywhere, and my host switched on the television in my room for the night before I had a chance to lay my head to rest. Televisions have been transformed from the dark old boxes with flickering black and white images to systems incorporating video, cable and satellite channels. More radio output is available than ever before; and these once-fixed household appliances have spread out, now appearing in cars, offices, wrapped round heads, everywhere. Movies are more available than ever before as the video industry proliferated, Blockbusters in every mall, movies available in little corner grocery stores, large supermarkets, everywhere. Stroll along any street, anywhere, and billboards, window displays, advertising vie for your attention. Travel by train, and the railway stations will provide one with inexpensive magazines, paperbacks (some even worth reading), CDs – the 'scale and scope without precedent' (Webster, 1995, p. 21). If you enjoy music, hip-hop or Beethoven, audiotapes, compact discs, and radio shows will provide it for you. Newspapers can still be purchased cheaply and read, crumpled in hand. Junk mail never ceases coming.

Our society is media-saturated in ways previously unknown to humankind. But a mere listing of television, radio and other media systems, Webster claims, doesn't reveal how constitutive of our psyches and outlook the informational environment actually is. We have woven previous technologies like the telephone (once considered very threatening) into our lifeworlds. We cannot organise our everyday lives without the phone. Take it away from us and we flounder, not knowing how to proceed with life (Is Mum OK? How are we going to get a babysitter? I need to cancel that doctor's appointment, and so on). With cameras (video and other), we use technology to represent who we are, and place these representations in albums, on our walls, in our video storage cabinets. Webster considers the 'informational dimensions of the clothes we wear, the styling of our hair and faces, the very ways in which nowadays we work at our image (from body shape to speech, people are intensely aware of the messages they may be projecting and how they feel about themselves in certain clothes, with a particular hairstyle, etc.)' (p. 22).

While human beings have certainly always conveyed messages of power, status and desire through body and clothing, social intercourse these days does seem more heavily laden with informational content than in times past. Western-liberal societies are intensely consumerist. The branding process has penetrated deep inside our collective psyches, etching itself on the inner walls of self and home. Now, our bodies and our living spaces are supposed to 'express ideas and ideals' (p. 22). The global design, fashion, publishing industries (scarcely distinguishable from each other), are the pedagogical agents of the good life (Martha Stewart, now tarnished, is arguably in a long line of improvers, this time of taste and sensibility, expressed in place settings, wallpaper and the cookies of choice). The vocabularies of the symbolic environment are no longer drawn primarily from sacred traditions and art.

It is precisely this acknowledgement of an 'extraordinary expansion of the informational content of modern life' (p. 22) that has led many writers to think that we have entered an information age. It is this vertiginous explosion of signification that leads, rather too easily, to the idea that our time is, well, so new. But even if it were new, postmodern gurus like Jean Baudrillard do not think this form of society is well. As Baudrillard observes, 'there is more and more information, and less and less meaning' (1983, p. 95). Under the bewildering blitz of endless signs, coming at us from all sides and at great speed, it is difficult to know just what these signs are referencing. Clothes may well have signalled a 'given status' in times past, the 'political statement a distinct philosophy, the TV news "what really happened"' (Webster, 1995, p. 23). But now they appear to be self-referential, simulations, all there is. Nihilism seeps into the pores of the intensely consumerist society as the barrage of signs, and language itself, detach from concrete reality.

Greater quantities of information do not permit us to say we have something 'radically new' (p. 24). Scholars like Herbert Schiller (1989) and David Harvey (1989), who argue for the continuity of present with past, shift our thinking away from the quantitative/qualitative binary to the need to 'differentiate between categories of information and the purposes to which it is put' (Webster, 1995, p. 24).

Information is everywhere and everywhere we are ignorant

The US National Geographic Society recently published a survey of geographic literacy. This international survey of young people in the US and eight other countries – Canada, France, Germany, Italy, Japan, Mexico, Sweden, and Britain – asked 56 questions about geography and current events. The organisation's survey discovered that about 87 per cent of Americans, aged 18 to 24, the prime age for military service, could not place Iraq on the map. On a world map, Americans could find on average only seven of 16 countries in the quiz. The Swedes could find on average 13 of the 16 countries. Only 71 per cent of the surveyed Americans could locate the Pacific Ocean, the world's largest body of water. John Fahey, president of the National Geographic Society, thought that these results reflect something deeper than lack of geographic knowledge. He referred to the 'apparent retreat of young people from a global society in an era that does not allow such luxury.'

Fahey said that this 'generation is highly skilled at what they want to block out and what they want to know.' 'Unfortunately, the things they block out seems to include knowledge of the world we all live in' (Fahey, 2002). One can also assume that the inability to locate Iraq on a world map means that these students know next to nothing about Middle Eastern culture and politics or anything much about Islam. Are we staring a giant paradox in the face? Visionaries tell us that we now live in an information age, indeed an age of info-glut. Yet the students living in the world's most powerful and lethal country do not have much of a clue about the world out there. The US invaded Iraq. Not many Americans even know where it is, let alone that their government used to support Saddam Hussein in the 1980s.

Celebrating uncritically the information age tells us little about whether we as citizens and ordinary people are, in fact, becoming more knowledgeable and skilled in the managing of our personal and collective affairs. In his prescient essay, 'Science as vocation', Max Weber wrote of the 'process of intellectualization' that had been grinding onward for thousands of years. In his view, the 'increasing intellect-ualization' did not 'indicate an increased and general knowledge of the conditions under which one lives. It means something else, namely, the knowledge or belief that if one but wished, one could learn at any time. Hence, it means that principally there are no mysterious incalculable forces that come into play, but rather that one can, in principle, master all things by calculation' (Weber, 1948, p. 139). The Stone Age savage knew more, tacitly and explicitly, about the ground of their being than we do in our deracinated world.

Information is, indeed, everywhere and everywhere we are ignorant. The reasons for our deep ignorance are many and complex. But I think that there are several lines of inquiry that may help to illuminate this paradox. With the emergence in North America (and spreading elsewhere) of a high intensity consumerist society over the last 80 years or so, we have become increasingly less self-reliant. The driving force of the high intensity consumer society (which takes the 'fetishism of commodities' to new heights) teaches its inhabitants to 'learn to consume'. All the resources of this societal form – from primary schooling to telecommunications – are marshalled in this great learning project: to undermine our self-reliance and know-how. Everything is to be provided for us; everything is to be thought for us; everything is decided for us; everything is packaged to amuse us to death.

With the spread of urbanisation, curative medicine and schooling, 'popular know-how on which self-reliance was based' is disappearing (Gorz, 1985, p. 21). We can't treat common complaints and illnesses, we have lost the art of cooking, we don't know how to make our own furniture, care for children or keep fit. It is not that there aren't hordes of improvers around willing to help us get fit. Rather, the consumer society is not at all organised to keep us healthy. The average supermarket is full of food that contributes to ill health, obesity and illness. The store owners don't place signs around their store saying, 'eat this at your own peril.' Their stores aren't designed as knowledge-intensive food emporiums. Chocolate products do not carry the warning that the cocoa beans were produced with slave labour in West Africa. Ironically, the school and health care system devalue 'the know-how and culture of the people in favour of a veneration of expert professionals whose monopoly in selling authorised goods and services necessarily assumed a monopoly in knowledge' (p. 21). The professionalisation process, alluded to earlier, may increase the collective intelligence of the society, but at the expense of the know-how and skill of the majority of people. In a society where everything is done for you, where we suffer from historical amnesia, lose the ability to see connections between what we eat and where it was produced and under what conditions, believe what is presented to us, live in a confused fog day after day, where we are subjected to endless propaganda, it is easy to see how we remain deeply ignorant in the age of information. At the same time, we can marvel at the creativity and ingenuity of the knowledge specialists whose services we purchase.

In his chilling *Postmodern Ethics* (1993), Zygmunt Bauman argues that even if we are appalled at the conditions of work that produced our aesthetically pleasing new purchases,

> We would not take gladly the suggestion that the manufactured

products which saturate our daily life, and which we have grown to consider indispensable to a life both decent and agreeable, should be withdrawn from production, or supplied in lesser quantities – just to limit the exhaustion of natural resources or the damage done to fresh air and water supplies. We all bewail the pollution and inconvenience caused by the privatization of 'transport problems' through car business, but most of us would hotly contest the abolition of private cars, which every seventh person among us derives his or her living, directly or obliquely, from the car business's prosperity . . . We want more and faster cars to drive us to the Alpine forest, only to find upon arrival that the forests are no more, eaten up by petrol fumes. (p. 205)

One gets the picture and squirms.

The consumer society is designed to separate those who consume from those who make the big decisions about the way the world runs. We, the citizenry, are supposed to allow the experts in corporate and governmental worlds to make the decisions for us as we get on with the ordinary activities of fulfilling our heart's desires in the commodity paradise. Increasingly, the role of the mass media is to massage our minds and spur our cravings for more and more. It seems to work pretty well. This system is, however, leaky and flawed. Evidence mounts that materialism does not make people very happy. The masses may well be drugged on unscientific myths and half-baked religious ideas, popular culture and uncritical patriotism. But the knowledgeable, critically engaged citizen exists in pockets here and there. The alternative media may hover on the sidelines, but it is present. In the run-up to the war on Iraq in the winter of 2003, hundreds of thousands of people took to the streets of the world's cities, small and great, shouting out their heart cry against the devastations of war. There are many brilliant people around who actually do know much about how great powers actually operate in the world (hint: it has nothing to do with morality). This may be encouraging, it seems to be, but what needs careful analysis is why it is so difficult, in the information age, to be wise about what is actually going on in the world. Clearly the simple availability of information does not make us knowledgeable. Our great cities are full of absolutely lovely writings on every crisis everywhere in the world. These drops of consciousness could make an ocean sometime. For now, however, I am boxed in with the nagging thought that thought, itself, can simply circulate through its own channels without ever having much to do with how power holders actually make decisions about which forest gets logged or which box retail store comes to the little community on Vancouver Island. I can say this all the while proclaiming almost in the same breath that our moral consciousness has its own power to stop the invasion of the barbarians.

Nor does our knowledge of what is going on in the world – there are 800 million malnourished people in the world, one half of humanity lives in poverty, one billion are illiterate, a billion and a half have no access to safe water and two billion have no electricity – necessarily result in any action to alleviate suffering. Why does this data leave the West mainly cold? Part of the answer, of course, is that powerful transnational corporations and US-dominated organisations like the World Trade Organization, World Bank and International Monetary Fund organise the global economy in an utterly hypocritical fashion that does not permit goods from the South to penetrate Northern markets. The US, for example, subsidises its own cotton industry to the tune of $4 billion per year, with devastating consequences to producers in West Africa, Burkina Faso and Mali (Elliot, 2002). The vested interests in the North do not want the global citizenry to translate this data into a knowledge frame that links power and profits to the impoverishment of the South. It is just as simple as that: the old Marxian adage that the 'ruling ideas are the ideas of the ruling class' is on target.

An even more perplexing paradox ought to trouble the conscience of those who are proposing that we live in a knowledge society, namely, the disappointing US (and Western liberal democracy allies) responses to genocide in the twentieth century. In a recent study, 'A Problem from Hell': America and the Age of Genocide, Samantha Power (2002) argues that the US has tolerated 'unspeakable atrocities, often committed in clear view' (p. 503). America, she says, has been inactive and passive in the face of mass murder in Rwanda, Cambodia and Iraq as well as Bosnia. Here is a typical passage cited by Holmes: 'The Rwandan genocide would prove to be the fastest, most efficient killing spree of the 20th century. In a hundred days, some 800,000 Tutsi and politically moderate Hutu were murdered. The United States did almost nothing to try to stop it.' Commenting on this, Stephen Holmes (2002) observes that no US troops were dispatched or UN reinforcements authorised. No US high-level governmental meetings were held to discuss non-military options. No public condemnations were uttered. No attempt was made to expel the genocidal government's representatives from the Security Council, where Rwanda held a rotating seat at the time. Power concludes that genocide is only stopped when another self-interested country invades, or a victim group manages to fight back. This dispiriting reality confronts us with (at least) three questions. To what extent does the ignorance of the Western public (however this occurs), preoccupied with fulfilling its own desires in the commodity paradise, actually permit the governing bodies to act immorally in the world? How do we understand the bitter truth that knowing can be so radically divorced from action in the information age? Have we become incapable, somehow, of actually feeling what we know?

To understand more fully the claim that we live in a knowledge society (with a knowledge-intensive economy, and so on), we need to distinguish different kinds of knowledge. Our suspicion thus far has been that the actually existing information age, or information society, privileges resolutely a calculating, quantitative mentality among its participants and its theorists. To know is to have access to more bits of information. But any reflection on the possibility of creating a just learning society needs to have a rich understanding of the forms and contexts of human knowledge creation. Our guide will now be Stephen Toulmin, the gentle and thoughtful philosopher, who has reflected on these matters in his recent work, *Return to Reason* (Harvard University Press, 2001). Here, Aristotelian categories can be helpful. Few would doubt Toulmin's central argument that Western intellectual culture has not given equal weight to the varieties of knowledge. Indeed, he argues that there is a 'systematic preference for the kinds of knowledge that are articulated in language, and most of all in the language of formal theory' (p. 177). Toulmin calls this an 'intellectualist preference', which places 'different kinds of knowledge in an honour roll, with an understanding of pure mathematics, or *episteme,* at the head of the roll' (p. 178). He says that *techne* follows closely behind. *Techne* refers to the 'techniques we master as ways of dealing with practical problems' (p. 179). These techniques are typically presented as 'sets of printed rules having a theoretical *raison d'être*' (p. 178). Lower down the honour roll we find the 'practical skills of *phronesis* embodied in the arts of clinical medicine or sailing' (p. 178). Toulmin also thinks that *phronesis* also includes 'private perceptiveness' used to 'put such techniques into practice' (p. 179). Aristotle thought that *episteme, techne,* and *phronesis* could be mobilised by *sophia* (broader wisdom).

In his *Nichomachean Ethics* Aristotle 'provided a complex account of the various sorts of knowledge and their differences: he correctly insisted that the knowledge involved in making a piece of pottery is unlike the knowledge of how to apply a law to a particular case, and that both are unlike the knowledge of the scientist' (Fay, 1987, p. 181). Aristotle assumed that 'scientific knowing (*episteme*) resulted in propositional truths; practical wisdom, or *phronesis,* resulted in 'discriminations and actions' (p. 181). *Phronesis* 'consists in knowing how to deliberate well about the ends and means appropriate for people in the situations in which they find themselves' (p. 181). Here, in the deliberation process, we are not applying routinely a propositional form of knowledge, but a 'skill which involves complex judgments specific to the particular practices and situations at hand' (p. 182).

Toulmin thinks that our present world is 'overwhelmed by an addiction to theory' (2001, p. 193). One can agree, realising the force of Wittgenstein's assertion that the skills of the field geologist – using a hammer just so to split the rock just right – does not rely on formal inferences from a scientific theory, or that many of the 'basic skills of traditional life . . . developed in parallel in different parts of the world without any particular scientific formulation' (p. 191). It is important to balance 'reason' (scientific forms of knowing) and 'reasonableness' (practical forms of knowing). Several considerations follow from this call for balance. First, the designing of the just learning society would not privilege technical-instrumental forms of reasoning to the exclusion of other forms of knowing (Habermas, 1970). Second, the 'scientific way of knowing' would be deeply respected, its spirit of critique valued for its potential to clear away the 'unfounded customary and traditional assumptions that lie in the path to true knowledge' (Tallis, 1997, p. 5).

This latter affirmation needs urgent attention. Increasingly, men and women's lives are being transformed by the applications of science (genetics, etc.) and technology at the same time as citizens are becoming less and less scientifically literate. In fact, an anti-science and anti-enlightenment sensibility actually pervades the Academy in the social sciences and humanities (Gross and Levitt, 1998). How has that come to be? Outside the Academy, aggressive and irrational forms of religion have their tight grip on the minds and hearts and emotions of millions of people, in and outside of the West. Fundamentalisms – Islam, Christian, Hindu, Jewish – are flourishing throughout the world (Armstrong, 2000). These apocalyptic belief systems close their followers' minds to rational discussion, or any discussion at all. They are based on the splitting of each from the other and mobilise aggressive, military spiritual energy oriented to destroying the not-self. Now is not the time, I would argue, to make silly and thoughtless denunciations of the global scientific enterprise. Third, the Aristotelian varieties of knowledge can enable us to consider how various societies actually function to increase our scientific literacy, enlarge the possibilities of technical mastery in all dimensions of our lives, nurture practical wisdom in our deliberations with each other, and increase our collective wisdom. Increased wisdom emerges from the considered interplay of the three primary modes of knowing. It is inconceivable, for example, that our species could solve the problem of holes in the ozone layer without the products of scientific thought and technology. But we will not even bother being concerned at all if the other forms of knowing are not given equal play in the dialogue. If all sources of wisdom, *sophia*, dry up, the baleful impulses inherent in an instrumental rationality detached from, and colonising other forms of knowing, will continue on their destructive way.

CHAPTER FOUR

How business organisations
learn and unlearn

On 18 September 2001, just one week after the hijacked planes crashed into the World Trade Center and the Pentagon, Greg Kersten wrote in *The Financial Times* that the 'world is now too complex for corporate leaders to make their decisions alone, and in the emerging barrier-free global market, where competition will be intense, a company's ability to learn faster than its rivals may be its only sustainable advantage' (2001, p. M6). Framing learning securely within the struggle for market advantage, Kersten argued that, 'To do this, companies will have to become "learning organizations" – companies that have an ingrained philosophy for anticipating, reacting and responding to change, complexity and uncertainty' (p. M6). This importunate refrain is echoed in the scholarly literature.

Gerd Schienstock, a leading contemporary Finnish work researcher, argues that 'global innovation . . . is the driving force that compels economies to undertake rapid and radical changes.' A country's 'sustainable competitiveness' will depend 'heavily on the capacity of all companies to learn and to innovate on a continuous basis. To be able to hold their own against global competitors, companies have to pay more attention to social innovation . . .' (1999, p. 9). This belief, now almost a truism in management rhetoric (if not practice), asserts that productivity is dependent on the organisation's capacity to 'generate, process and apply efficiently knowledge-based information' (Castells, cited, Schienstock and Kuusi, 1999, p. 13). The transformations within the global economy, perceived and otherwise, have converged in the last couple of decades with trends within the social sciences and learning theory to place 'learning in organisations' on the theoretical agenda.

However, this preoccupation with business organisations as learning sites, and the possibility of intervening in the organisation to influence beliefs, attitudes and behaviour, has deep roots in the industrial capitalist mode of production. In the mid-nineteenth century, on both sides of the class divide, capital and working-class advocates battled for the control of the learning dynamics of the workplace. Marx thought that the workplace was a pre-eminent school of labour. There, he forecast that immiserated workers could learn through their bodily suffering and degradation that their only hope for self-development lay with their gaining control of the productive apparatus (some form of workers' control). For their part, the owners understood well that workers' sophisticated knowledge and skill sets threatened their power. By introducing technologies, like textile factory looms, they could undermine the workers' main power base, their knowledge. The great battles of early industrial capitalism, often coded as the Luddite wars against technology, remind us that the contemporary discourse of the learning organisation is a continuing moment in the ongoing struggle over the learning content and pedagogical procedures in the capitalist work environment.

This chapter has two purposes: (1) to raise critical and cautionary questions about the emancipatory claims of learning organisation proponents; and (2) to engage with the learning organisation discourse to understand what may be required for the emancipatory claim to be authentically redeemed.

From Taylorism to action research: A cautionary historical note

By the beginning of World War I the lineaments of decisively modern work conditions appear. Capitalism entered its monopolistic or corporate phase (the age of conglomerates, cartels, administrative efficiency, advertising agencies, professionalisation and labour unrest), the labour process was radically reshaped by widespread mechanisation, incorporating scientific research in the solving of production problems (the scientisation of labour): the subdivision of labour (the deskilling thesis); the emergence of more centralised, authoritarian managerial systems (the bureaucratic control theme); and professionalisation (the elite expert appears in many areas of social life). Within the work literature, these interconnected processes are coded as Taylorism, after Frederick Winslow Taylor, the obsessed and driven American architect of scientific management.

Harry Braverman (1974) is the most influential expositor of Taylorism. He argues that the twentieth-century capitalist organisation of work inexorably breaks down job content into simple, monotonous, strictly controlled and narrowly specialised work phases, which to a very high degree are lacking in demands on professional skill, mentality activity and judgment on the part of the worker. Braverman thinks that the central organising principle of the Taylorist curricular structure is the radical separation of thinking from doing. An imaginative engineer with extensive shopfloor experience, Taylor announced his first principle in *The Principles of Scientific Management* in 1912: 'the deliberate gathering in on the part of those on the management side of all of the great mass of traditional knowledge, which in the past has been in the heads of the workmen, and in the physical skill and the knack of the workmen' (cited, Andrew, 1981, pp. 77–8). Here, the 'unity of thought and action, conception and execution, hand and mind, which capitalism threatened from its beginnings, is now attacked by a systematic dissolution employing all the resources of science and the various engineering disciplines based upon it' (Braverman, 1974, p. 171). Stripped of their subjectivity, workers have been transformed into things that can be manipulated to serve ends they have not chosen.

Scientific managers underwent their own intensive educative process as they learned how to usurp workers' knowledge and take the initiative in designing methods of production. The workers, Taylor thought, could not comprehend the 'scientific laws' inherent in their jobs. They were transformed into objects of managerial action. Tools were standardised and the 'markings of craftsmanship' removed from the workers. Class solidarity was reduced and piece rates and a premium system of payment replaced the standardised day rate. The opportunity for workers to organise their working lives and choose their working teams and production procedures and exercise leadership is eliminated (Andrew, 1981, p. 86ff). Within the Taylorised workplace, where the jobs of the shopfloor worker are simplified, learning opportunities were reduced.

The de-skilling of the skilled shopfloor worker, however, accelerates the growth of white-collar jobs (in management, clerical work, stockroom and inventory jobs, and lower administrative positions). This instrumental paradigm for workplace learning assumes that most workers have a limited capacity to learn and that self-realisation cannot occur in the realm of production. Management thought that higher wages were adequate compensation for loss of control. F.W. Taylor's infamous worker, the pig-iron loader Schmidt, stands forever as a symbol of the guiding premise of the most powerful managerial learning theory in the early twentieth century, namely that the workers are rather stupid or that their knowledge is a dangerous thing (Welton, 1991).

The two decades following World War I were fraught with intense conflict between working people and their employers and government. Political dissent was widespread. In 1919, for example, after bombs exploded in eight American cities (it was unclear just who set them off), A. Mitchell Palmer, President Woodrow Wilson's Attorney General, sent his men on raids against radicals and leftists. They smashed the offices of trade unions, and the headquarters of socialist and communist organisations. They concentrated their efforts on aliens rather than citizens, deporting over 200 men and women for alleged subversive activities. By the mid-1920s, America's industrial elite was searching for new techniques of control and ways of fostering harmony between workers and employers. The stark brutality of Taylor's methods and the use of private police forces like Pinkertons and the National Guard reserves to beat up labour organisers needed to be replaced by something softer. One of the most promising directions lay in the direction of incorporating 'social and clinical psychological approaches into an enlightened management' (Bramel and Friend, 1981, p. 868). If the workers' emotional needs could be met, so went the argument, then the manifestations of irrational hostility and the need for unions could be dispensed with.

The industrial elites found something of what they were looking for in the emergent applied social sciences. John D. Rockefeller, the ruthless capitalist and philanthropist, financed the Department of Industrial Research at Harvard's Graduate School of Business Administration (among other ventures) and expected some benefits. Elton Mayo (whose name would be indelibly associated with a famous intervention in the workplace) was a close associate of John D. Rockefeller. With his protégé Fritz Roethlisberger (1941), he became closely linked with the Hawthorne experiments. The Hawthorne Studies (Harvard Graduate School of Business collaborated with the National Research Council and the Western Hawthorne Electric Company), which began in 1927 as study of the relation between conditions of work and incidence of fatigue and monotony, made the 'epochal discovery' that when workers were treated with respect they responded favourably and were more productive. The researchers (Elton Mayo did not actually design or conduct the actual experiments; rather, he popularised them (1933; 1945)) were able to articulate an important idea: an industrial organisation was 'essentially a social system whose patterned regularities could be measured and whose behavior could be altered through appropriate interventions by management' (Friedman, 1987, p. 204).

However, under the harsh light of critical scrutiny in the decades following the Hawthorne experiments – which laid the foundation of the development of the 'human relations' approach to management – the famous epochal discovery has turned out to be a myth. Alex Carey (1967) found that the Hawthorne experiments were deeply flawed in scientific methodology. He also challenged the validity of the claim that the 'Hawthorne effect' (the attention paid to the workers by experimenters and bosses was the salient independent variable) were false. On his reading, the material, and especially financial rewards, were the principal influence on work morale and behaviour (1967, p. 403, 416). Bramel and Friend (1981) demonstrate that Elton Mayo, who had 'faith in the basic health and rationality of the capitalist system' (p. 867), suppressed empirical evidence of worker resistance to the capitalist relations of production.

From the outset, his work was biased toward whole-hearted co-operation between workers and bosses. Bramel and Friend provide compelling evidence that the Hawthorne experiments were interpreted such that the 'conflict between workers and management [was] always due to something other than a basic outgrowth of interests in the exploitative capitalist relations of production' (1981, p. 871). The Marxian idea that the conflict between workers (who receive wages) and owners (who own and deploy the means of production) is an inherently exploitative relationship is ruled out from analytical consideration by these applied social scientists. 'One could say', claim Bramel and Friend (1981, p. 874), 'that much of his persistent advocacy of "human relations in industry" found its rationale in the problem of how to manipulate workers in such a way as to harness the power of the cohesive group in the "good" direction (relay assembly) rather than have that power turned against management (bank wiring).'

Braverman (1974, p. 145) astutely observes that the Hawthorne experiments marked the collapse of the power of individualistic applied psychology as researchers discovered the power of the social group to influence worker actions. The challenge for 'human relations' advocates, in the face of this discovery, necessarily focuses on how to enlist the loyalty of workers to the aims of the organisation as a whole. But this language itself reveals a class bias: language like 'organisation as a whole' indicates that workers and bosses have the same aims (or are committed to a similar learning agenda). Bramel and Friend (1981, p. 875) also observe that class bias is manifest in 'ill-disguised contempt for workers' intelligence and rationality' expressed by writers like Roethlisberger and Dickson's (1939, pp. 256–68) discussion of worker complaints. Worker complaints were perceived to be somehow unreal, conflict as irrational and opposition to management unnatural. Thus, Bramel and Friend reluctantly admit that Mayo is a slight advance on Taylor. While the social scientists were now paying attention to worker subjectivity, they still refused 'to admit that resistance to exploitation could be rational in twentieth-century America' (1981, p. 876).

In his remarkable study of science, technology, and the rise of corporate capitalism in America (*America by Design: Science, Technology, and the Rise of Corporate Capitalism*), David F. Noble summarises the meanings of the Hawthorne experiments:

> The Hawthorne experience called into question many of the basic assumptions of scientific management, gave impetus to the infant applied sciences of industrial psychology and sociology, ushered in the new field of "human relations," and provided management educators with a wealth of case-study material. Less obviously, it reflected the extent to which the horizons of engineering had expanded as engineers strove to control the elusive human factor in every engineering problem. For it had been the corporate engineers, with the support of the large corporations of the science-based electrical industry, who had conceived the project and pushed it ahead to its unanticipated conclusion. . . . And it was not long after the experiment was over that the same engineers began to incorporate industrial sociology within the engineering curriculum, declaring Mayo's writings to be required reading for all student engineers. (1977, pp. 319–20)

Looking to the future at the dawn of the great depression and massive worker struggles to unionise, William Wickenden, in one of the most thorough studies of engineering education ever written, identified the need for schools of engineering 'to bring together the mechanical, physiological, and psychological factors in human work within the bounds of a predictable science' (cited, Noble, 1977, p. 320).

Like their counterparts in America, behavioural scientists in Europe in the 1920s had almost utopian expectations about how scientific psychology could serve to resolve problems in labour–management relations and other troublesome social and political spaces. One of the notable young experimental scholars actively participating in the experimental ethos percolating in Germany was Kurt Lewin (1890–1947), a charismatic and loquacious intellectual, whose own interest in applied psychology was clearly manifest at the end of World War I. A socialist humanist (who had taught adult education classes for workers while studying at the University of Berlin), Lewin took issue with Taylor's one-sided emphasis on the 'relentless exploitation of the individual in the service of production' (Lewin, in Gold, 1999, p. 307) in a far ranging essay, 'Socializing the Taylor system'. Lewin argued, essentially, that a 'socialist reconciliation' could be effected with applied psychology placed in the service of work that was both economical and pleasant. Reflecting some of the radical ideas present in post-war Germany, Lewin insisted that workers ought to have the right to decide on the 'introduction of changes in work methods' (p. 311) such that neither profitability nor diminution in the life value of work would occur. These ideas would recede to the background over the next decades of research in the US.

When Kurt Lewin, a refugee Jewish social psychologist from Berlin, arrived in the US in 1932, with Europe just a few years away from erupting into flames and moral degradation, he had spent the 1920s searching for a scientific theory of human behaviour and engaging in practical experimentation. Perhaps the most important influence on Lewin's world and scientific outlook was that of Gestalt Psychology (associated with Wolfgang Kohler). The Gestaltists argued that perception could be considered in terms of 'forms of organized wholes.' Wholes were not just the sum of their parts; they had a distinctive structure in themselves that determined how new mental experiences were integrated (Marrow, 1969, pp. 12–14). Lewin worked this salient idea into a 'field theory': behaviour was the function of person and the environment. One could not understand the 'life spaces' of individuals apart from the concrete social situation that shaped who they were. Lewin's intellectual project was actually very ambitious. He was driven to develop the scientific concepts, methods and theories of group life to 'permit a more intelligent management of social problems in small and large settings' (Kariel, 1956, p. 280). In his consultancy for the Harwood

Manufacturing Corporation in Virginia in 1939, for example, Lewin argued that one could not solve management's problem of inexperienced workers' slow pace of output without dealing with the workers as members of small groups rather than as individuals (Marrow, 1969, pp. 141–52). One of the dubious consequences of Lewin's advice, however, was the firing of many workers only to have them replaced by a more cohesive, experienced work group.

By 1944, Lewin was working with the Research Center for Group Dynamics at MIT. The power of the 'small group' to shape personal beliefs and actions captivated the imagination of Lewin and his associates. His theoretical foundation – co-operative research, pragmatic investigations, practical experiments – found approval in the US. The Research Center was 'devoted to the development of scientific concepts, methods, and theories of group life which should lead to a deeper understanding and permit a more intelligent management of social problems in small and large settings' (Kariel, 1956, p. 280). Everywhere the researchers looked, the small group turned up as playing a significant role in social learning. Study circles were bountiful in university and communities. Military organisations used the ten-man team. The Hawthorne Electric Company worked with teams of six persons. Wasn't the nuclear family a small group? Lewin's granite idea – which has been enormously influential in the field of adult education – was that groups were 'interactive wholes that cannot be further broken down into their individual elements without having their existence as an organic unity destroyed' (Friedman, 1987, p. 205). Groups had a life of their own (destroy the relations, the group is destroyed); they could be authoritarian or democratic. Lewin's way of studying groups was, simply, to try to change their behaviour. Rather than bringing in an outside change agent, Lewin conducted exercises that challenged the group members to 'experience themselves as acting subjects.' By acting on itself, the group became the 'relevant subject for learning.' Thus, 'true learning' involved the 'restructuring of one's relations to the world' (Friedman, 1987, p. 206). He called it action research. Such explorations of group dynamics would be carried forward by the National Training Laboratory in Group Dynamics in Bethel, Maine, organised at the end of World War II in 1947. Proponents of group dynamics in the 1940s and 1950s, an age of the idealisation the American way of life, often imagined that they held the secrets for the resolution of inter-racial strife and working class hostility to their bosses.

Today Lewin's big intellectual project, with its obsessive use of mathematical analogies and formulae, seems obscure and antiquated. Lewin's drive to find more intelligent ways of managing social problems led him to locate the problems of individual behaviour and attitudes in the group context. Whether changing family food habits or racist attitudes, one had to identify the forces determining the decisions of gatekeepers (see Gold, 1999, pp. 265–84). This core idea shifted organisation theory towards understanding the social learning dynamics of institutions. But Lewin's belief that group decision was a 'process of social management or self-management of groups' (Gold, 1999, p. 283) had lost its critical edge in a Cold War America on the prowl for anti-American sentiments. The young Lewin's socialist leanings – societies are split along class lines – disappeared in the last decade of his life. He knew that social psychologists would have to contend with an intemperate boss, now and then. But basically Lewin had accommodated himself to America's conformist ethos. His social engineering approach to social problems was easily assimilated by the ruling systems that could use his research findings to manage economic, political and social life.

To humanise the corporation: Chris Argyris's contribution to organisational learning theory

Chris Argyris (b. 1923–) had a solid body of thinking and experimentation to draw from when he began to form his vision of humanistic organisational development. Post-Mayo and Lewin humanist psychologists had helped him to understand the importance of structuring organisations so that persons could meet their own self-actualising needs. Argyris (and other organisational practitioners like the evangelistic Warren Bennis (1966)) fused these humanistic beliefs with the idea that organisations could actually learn to be 'decentralized, spontaneous, and non-hierarchical' (Friedman, 1987, p. 203). This vision, articulated in the late 1950s, 1960s, 1970s and fine-tuned ever since, was highly normative and idealistic. But it set the pace for contemporary approaches to organisational learning. It was also highly optimistic in its assumption that change agents could intervene in an organisation and precipitate reflective learning processes towards creating 'post-industrial' institutions free from 'coercive power, exploitation, and oppression' (p. 203).

Today, in the aftermath of Enron and the multiple corporate scandals, it is not so easy to be optimistic about what, and how, cutting-edge companies actually learn (Stiglitz, 2002). The last decades have also seen companies ruthlessly downsize and shift production to grimy Third World sites. How can our optimism persist in the face of overwhelming evidence that companies learn along only one trajectory? Our attention is now focused on Argyris's seminal text, *Organizational Learning: A Theory-of-Action Perspective* (1978).

Argyris acknowledges the landmark work of Kurt Lewin on group dynamics and behaviour. He recognised that groups were not reducible to individuals: they believed in action research; intervention as an approach to theory-building; and theory-building as a guide to intervention. Rather conveniently, Argyris (and the hordes of others soon unleashed on the scene) positioned himself in an advisory relationship to organisations. The idea that organisations could learn opened up many opportunities to be of service to the corporate sector. If organisations failed to learn, Argyris claimed, then we could 'arrive at the importance of interventions aimed at increasing the capacity for organizational learning' (1978, p. 320). The way was open for a new growth industry, corporate consulting.

In the late 1970s, Argyris linked the unstable economic, political and technological environment to an intensifying interest in the 'importance of organizational learning' (p. 8). The requirement for organisational learning, consequently, was not an 'occasional, sporadic phenomenon, but [was] continuous and endemic to our society' (p. 9). But while admitting the reality of constant change and endless problems, Argyris was not clear what it meant for an organisation to actually learn. Nor was it even clear how we might 'enhance the capacity of organizations to learn' (p. 9). His work was cut out for him. He needed to have a conceptual basis for his work with corporations: a way of acknowledging problems in the work domain without challenging the fundamental power relationships of corporate domination of the means of production.

Argyris identifies two main difficulties with making the conceptual shift to thinking of organisations as able to learn. The first difficulty was with the notion of learning itself. Argyris notes that we usually associate learning with change that is good. But much change is not good, and some forms of learning – viz. how a government or company learns to deceive and manipulate the public – are morally unjustifiable (and more evident than ever). The second difficulty, one that has plagued adult education theory for decades, was that organisational learning is not the same as individual learning. Argyris pursued the following paradox: 'Organizations are not merely collections of individuals, yet there is no organization without such collections. Similarly, organizational learning is not merely individual learning, yet organizations learn only through the experience and actions of individuals' (p. 9).

Argyris's solution to the paradox was to transpose an idea from cognitive psychology – viz. that 'all deliberate action had a cognitive basis' (p. 10) – to the organisational context. An ardent constructivist, Argyris moved beyond behaviourist assumptions to argue that human learning could be 'placed in the larger context of knowing' (p. 10). Within this model, organisation learning 'might be understood as the testing and restructuring of organizational theories of action and, in the organizational context as in the individual one, we might examine the impact of models of action theories upon the capacity for kinds of learning' (p. 11). But the conceptual difficulties persist. A term like organisation learning is a metaphor because organisations do not, literally, think or learn. Do organisations really act? Doesn't this seem counter-intuitive? Aren't CEOs paid millions to lead the companies down the profitable yellow-brick road? Argyris thinks that if we are to speak of organisational theories of action, we must dispel 'some of the confusion surrounding terms like organizational intelligence, memory, and action' (p. 12). We must, he says, say something about what it means for an organisation to know something. And we must spell out the metaphors of organisational memory, intelligence and learning.

Argyris argues, essentially, that the organisation's design of its task systems and particular strategies for performing the component tasks both precedes the individual's entry into the company (or workplace) and predetermines his or her work procedures. He also posits that every corporation has 'norms for performance, strategies for achieving norms and assumptions which bind strategies and norms together' (p. 15). Argyris calls this an 'instrumental theory of action' (p. 15). The organisation's instrumental theory of action includes patterns of communication and control, its ways of allocating resources to goals, rewarding and punishing individual performance, constructing career ladders, recruitment of new members and instructing them in ways of the organisation. These rules for collective decision and action may be tacit. Argyris devised his famous distinction between theory-in-use (what people actually do) and espoused theory (what people say they do) to position himself to assist managers to critically reflect on the consequences of the divergence between these two poles within corporate culture.

The linchpin in Argyris's theory of organisation learning is the idea that members of an organisation construct their own maps or representations of the organisation. These maps are 'shared descriptions of organization which individuals jointly construct and use to guide their own inquiry' (p. 17). An organisation's theory-in-use comes about through a complicated pattern whereby individuals mesh 'individual images of self and others' with those of co-workers. While these insights are exciting, the fly in the ointment is the way organisation learning theorists use a phrase like 'members of an organisation' so uncritically. Corporations are hierarchically structured, and managers have the legal right to control their workers in office and on the shopfloor. Not everyone is included equally in the communication process that underpins the creation of a collective cognitive map. Thus, the 'organisation' is not really a holistic 'family.' It is actually a complex of various, interrelating systems of status and domination (race, class, gender, age) organised to maximise profitability and greed within a ruthless global environment.

Argyris draws upon popular cybernetic metaphors to articulate his most famous distinction between different kinds of learning. Single-loop learning occurs when 'members of the organization respond to changes in the internal and external environments of the organization by detecting errors which they can then correct so as to maintain the central features of organizational theory-in-use' (p. 18). Here, workers detect errors and propose solutions 'so as to keep organizational performance within the range set by organizational norms. The norms themselves – for product quality, sales, or task performance – remain unchanged' (p. 19). Thus, normal problem solving, akin to Kuhn's 'normal science', functions within the accepted framework of the organisation. If organisational learning is to occur, 'learning agents' discoveries, inventions, and evaluations must be embedded in organisational memory' (p. 19).

The problem-solving procedures must be encoded in 'individual images and the shared maps of organizational-theory-in-use . . .' (p. 19). Individual learning is, then, a 'necessary but insufficient condition for organization learning' (p. 20). To test whether organisation learning occurred or not, requires asking certain kinds of questions. Did the results of individual error detection, inquiry, and so on become embodied in images and maps subsequently employed for purposes such as control, decision, and instruction? Were these changes regularised, and taught to new members of the organisation? The latter are good questions (and an advance from individualistic learning theories). But there is little empirical research evidence providing much help in thinking about the answers.

Double-loop learning can only happen when single-loop learning processes have proved inadequate to detect and remedy errors. Argyris claims that corporations often face the bind of conflicting requirements – growth and predictability. If corporate managers are to engage this conflict, they must undertake an inquiry process which is 'significantly different from the inquiry characteristic of single-loop learning' (p. 21). When solutions are not amenable through tried and true methods, management must undertake a learning process which may 'lead to restructuring of organizational norms, and very likely a restructuring of strategies and assumptions associated with those norms, which must then be embedded in the images and maps which encode organizational theory-in-use' (p. 22). Argyris admits that conflicts, at this stage, are bound to occur. The organisation must fight its way through the conflict. 'We will give the name "double-loop learning" to these sorts of organizational inquiry which resolve incompatible organizational norms by setting new priorities and weightings of norms, or by restructuring the norms themselves together with associated strategies and assumptions' (p. 24).

Argyris observes that it is impossible to 'cleanly separate' inquiry from the 'uses of power' (p. 24). An example might help. Wal-Mart does not countenance the forming of trade unions, pays low wages and expects employees to work overtime without pay. Wal-Mart's corporate executives determine this policy and managers, at different levels, enforce it. The workers' insistence on better wages and working conditions would challenge organisational values and norms they have had no say in creating. So growth versus predictability is not the only bind companies face. They also confront the imperative of doing justice. This could be labelled the justice-versus-profitability bind.

But single and double-loop learning do not exhaust the possibilities of organisation learning. Deutero-learning occurs when its

> members learn, too, about previous contexts for learning. They reflect on and inquire into previous contexts for learning. They reflect on and inquire into previous episodes of organization

learning, or failure to learn. They discover what they did that facilitated or inhibited learning, they invent new strategies for learning, they produce these strategies, and they evaluate and generalize what they have produced. The results become encoded in individual images and maps and are reflected in organization learning practice'. (p. 27)

Deutero-learning, then, is reflection on how we learn; essential, Argyris claims, because how else can members of an organisation carry out the 'kinds of inquiry essential to double-loop learning' (p. 28) unless they are reflecting on their learning procedures? 'Hence, if we wish to learn more about the conditions that facilitate or inhibit organization learning, we must explore the ways in which the behavioural worlds of organizations affect the capacity for inquiry into organizational theory-in-use' (p. 28). In sum, Argyris argues that organisation learning 'occurs when members of the organization act as learning agents for the organization, responding to changes in the internal and external environments of the organization by detecting and correcting errors in organizational theory-in-use, and embedding the results of their inquiry in private images and shared maps of organization' (p. 29). This requirement places a premium on the organisation as a communicative learning space. This nice language also masks the power dynamics within organisations that filter out those norms and values that are outside the taken-for-granted rules of the capitalist game.

How social science researchers understand organisation learning: Bo Hedberg and the cartography of learning in organisations

Chris Argyris articulated a prescriptive, consultancy-oriented model of organisation learning that sketched out some of the conceptual elements a theory of organisation learning required in 1978. Three years later, Bo Hedberg (1981) published a sophisticated, empirically-based scholarly discussion of how organisations learn and unlearn. Like Argyris, he wants to know if it is 'meaningful to think of organizations as having objectives, learning abilities, and memories, or do organizations only learn and remember through their current members?' (p. 3). Hedberg works within a broadly defined stimulus-response model. Organisations interact with their environments: when they observe the results of their acts, they increase their understanding of reality. He also admits, though, that those who use the stimulus-response model (March and Olsen (1976), for instance) often argue that the individual's action leads to organisational actions. Here the organisation merely provides the stage for the individual player.

Within his interactive model, Hedberg provides us with richly textured understanding of learning. He presses beyond the reactive behaviourist understanding of 'habit forming and conditioning' to embrace learning as involving 'more active responses' (1981, p. 4). He integrates essential Deweyian insights: learners can engage in trial-and-error learning in everyday life situations. Their discoveries can lead to the integration of 'new constructs into existing cognitive structures and, in the process, reconcile incongruent experiences and beliefs' (p. 4). Hedberg and other organisational learning theorists embrace the systems theory vocabulary. Thus, while learning in stable environments is like 'mental bricklaying', an unlearning process occurs when environmental discontinuities threaten an organisation's survival. When situations are too stable, there are few opportunities for learning.

Organisations, Hedberg informs us, 'do not have brains, but they have cognitive systems and memories' (p. 6). Clearly, the science of anthropology's thinking about culture has influenced Hedberg. Organisations have memories and they preserve certain behaviours, mental maps, norms and values over time. Organisational myths, sagas, and managerial cultures uphold certain norms. These phenomena 'influence individuals' learning within organisations and then transmit the learning heritage to new generations of members' (p. 6). It is also true that organisations may not know as much as their individual members. Organisations may have insufficient channel capacity, segments of the organisation may filter and distort information flows, both from below and above. It is normal, Hedberg claims, for the 'whole to be less than the sum of the parts' (p. 6). The organisation can usefully be imagined as a stage where 'repertoires of plays are performed by individual actors. The actors act, but they are directed. They are assigned roles, they are given scripts, and they become socialized into a theatre's norms, beliefs and behaviours' (p. 6). This is a beautiful metaphor. But the actors may also improvise, tear up scripts, make up their own lines, act badly.

Organisations are, then, cartographers of human interaction with each other and an ever-changing external environment. They map their environments and must identify which causal relationships operate in their environments. These maps (or myths or sagas) serve as theories of action that are refined as new situations are encountered. Their main function is to 'filter and interpret signals from the environment and the stimuli to responses' (p. 7). This is an unnerving task: environments contain more information than can be sensibly processed. As representations of reality, maps only highlight certain features of the environment. Organisations face a barrage of realities requiring 'definitions of situations' (p. 7) that necessarily simplify the buzzing facticity before them. Organisations' definition of situations determines what problems are perceived in the first place, how they are interpreted and what learning ultimately results. Thus, the organisation's cognitive maps act as perceptual filters, making observations meaningful. This requires that choices be made among perplexing alternatives. But the abstraction of this language can lull us to sleep. Think only of the 'perceptual filters' of gigantic logging companies who are searching for available forests to log. How would we characterise their cognitive maps? What pathways are not even mapped out?

Hedberg proposes a two-level stimulus-response model to understand how organisations learn, assuming that the learning cycle is complete. His model assumes that 'learning results when organizations interact with their environments: each action adds information and strengthens or weakens linkages between stimuli and response' (p. 9). This is similar to Argyris's single-loop learning. More substantial changes in the organisation–environment relationship sometimes requires that the 'old responses be deleted and sometimes replaced. This unlearning is difficult, and it takes time. Environmental changes create uncertainty, so organizations are tempted to rely on previously successful behaviors' (p. 9). But organisations often resist radical restructuring. It seems that organisational maps may become too rigid. Cognitive psychologists Festinger (1957) and Kelly (1955) offer the compelling idea that socially constructed reality and logical congruence in human brains stabilise established perceptions and beliefs. We are predisposed, as individuals and organisations, to deny any clues that do not fit into the perceptual frame. We see what we want to see; and ideological beliefs may anchor the blinkers very deeply in our psyches.

Hedberg thinks that ideal learning conditions 'fall somewhere between the extremes of environmental stability and turbulence' (1981, p. 12). Certainly rapid environment change may precipitate 'meta-learning in which the people in organizations learn to identify patterns of environmental behavior, but organizations in turbulent environments mostly find it very difficult to cope and survive' (p. 12). Two decades later, Thomas Homer-Dixon's *The Ingenuity Gap* (2001) accentuated the problem of complexity (in natural and social systems) and our bafflement before systems that resist technical-instrumental control. Indeed, Hedberg argues that 'complex, fast-moving industrial societies appear to afford bad conditions for learning' (p. 13). He thinks that in turbulent environments, 'organizations float with their surroundings, almost unable to learn and to control their development' (p. 13). If individuals' information-handling capacity is overloaded, then they cannot learn very well. Other conditions come from inner environments. Hedberg places great emphasis on how organisations manage and process information flow. He thinks that decentralisation and participative management can reduce demands on information channels, diminish individuals' cognitive workloads, improve the quality of upward communications, and stimulate innovation and learning.

Hedberg believes that 'learning is typically triggered by problems' (p. 16). Too much wealth, too much harmony or goal accomplishment breeds complacency. Problems serve as triggers, but there are different theories of why, and under what conditions, organisations initiate a search for warning signals. Cyert and March (1963) posit that both 'excess amounts of organizational slack and sharp reductions of slack trigger search and learning' (Hedberg, 1981, p. 17). Hedberg comments:

> Neither scarcity and severe problems nor affluence and benevolence provide a good climate for learning. Low levels of organizational slack may trigger search, but slack resources may be needed in order to implement new strategies. Problems and crises can force organizations to act, but problem-ridden organizations can often not afford to take risks. . . . But the dilemma of organization-slack mechanisms is that they buy tolerances and routinizing for organizational problem solving at the expense of organizational curiosity and readiness for change. (p. 17)

Hedberg also observes that organisations' members actions also trigger learning. Without a 'vivid opposition, an organization deteriorates rapidly and loses its ability to invent and implement new strategies' (p. 17). Thus, organisations must create the enabling conditions for questioning the present without predetermining answers. Removing members from the organisation may create dynamic learning conditions.

But the organisation also risks losing some of its memory along with individuals. The shattered nature of contemporary work places, battered by downsizing and re-engineering throughout the 1980s and 1990s, attest to this fact.

New maps require that learners discard knowledge in order to make way for 'new responses and mental maps' (p. 18). But how 'capable then are organizations to unlearn old behaviors and world views and to relearn when they face new situations'? (p. 18). Unlearning is difficult because unlearning in the 'human mind is a cumbersome and energy-consuming process' (p. 18). Hedberg thinks that some people are 'able to perceive reality in different terms' and can 'redefine their problems, unlearn old behaviour, and replace them with new responses almost immediately' (p. 18). These individuals cannot be formed easily in cultures (or milieu) that are highly authoritarian, didactic and dogmatic. Within the stimulus-response framework, Hedberg argues, unlearning moves through three modes of operation. First, disassembly, whereby the receiver no longer knows what is received; second, dis-confirmation of connections between stimulus and response; and third, dis-confirmation of connections between responses. The unlearning process takes time. It may be blocked so that incomplete cycles develop.

Hedberg offers his thoughts on how organisational learning is best facilitated. The first challenge is to learn more about organisational learning. He doesn't think that current knowledge provides the necessary empirical basis for understanding the 'relationships between individual and organizational learning and unlearning' (p. 20). He asks how hierarchies, status systems and perceptual filters affect organisations' abilities to learn and unlearn. He maintains that organisation learning will have to derive from a 'separately developed body of theories about how organizations learn as organizations, or from better assessments of how individual learning is modified when it occurs in organizations' (p. 20). As well, researchers need to investigate how organisations actually shift their theories of action, or myths, as they develop over time. Second, organisations need to promote experimentation. Experimental actions are crucial because organisations 'rarely master their environments so that they can develop lasting optimal responses' (p. 20). Adult education methods – role reversal, simulation, role-playing, brainstorming – can 'encourage experimentation and reframing' (p. 21).

Third, organisations must keep the entire system alert. Anticipating, perhaps, those who would embrace chaos theory in the 1990s, Hedberg advocates that, 'Instead of striving for clarity and harmony, perceptual filters should let decision makers see important properties of the real world. Crises, conflicts, dialectics, self-doubt, and hesitancy can facilitate unlearning and reframing' (p. 21). Fourth, Hedberg suggests that personnel ought to be selected 'who are able to structure problems effectively and who are less inclined to overestimate difficulties' because the 'willingness to learn and unlearn varies with the relationship between perceived problem complexity and estimated problem-solving capacity' (p. 22). Finally, a dynamic learning organisation should only rely minimally on 'consensus, contentment, affluence, faith, consistency, and rationality.' Hedberg strongly believes that 'dissatisfaction is needed to trigger action so that long-term contentment results. . . . There should be balances and counterbalances, processes and counteracting processes' (p. 22). 'To learn, unlearn, and relearn is the organizational walk: development comes to and end when one of these legs is missing' (p. 23).

Organisations learn in the hallways: Nancy Dixon on facilitating organisational learning

Nancy Dixon's *The Organizational Learning Cycle* (1999) allows us to gauge where pedagogical thinking on organisation learning has arrived by the end of the twentieth century. Dixon insists that the vague encouragement of organisation members to 'exchange their accessible meaning structures with each other' will never foster organisation learning. The 'organization', she says, 'must actively facilitate collective learning' (p. 63). To do so, the organisation must proceed through four steps. There must be a widespread generation of information, the integration of new/local information into the organisational context, collective interpretation of information, and the authority to take responsible action based on the interpreted meaning. Although this sounds simple enough, Dixon observes that 'organizations typically carry out these steps in ways that severely limit organizational learning' (p. 64). Often, the 'steps of the organizational learning cycle are disconnected' and 'collective learning is lost' (p. 64). She argues that we 'must make drastic changes in the way these four steps are undertaken as well as who accomplishes them' (p. 65).

Appropriating Kolb's famous reflective learning cycle model, Dixon transforms his individualistic heuristic to a collective orientation to focus our attention on how organisational learning ought to proceed. His model begins in 'concrete experience.' At the collective level, members engage in the practices that gather information from the external environment (customers, suppliers, conferences) and that likewise all engage in work-related experiments that produce new information. Kolb's second step is reflective observation: the individual reflects on an experience, distilling what was notable. At the collective level, everyone needs the same information that everyone else has. Here the task is one of integrating newly generated information into the organisational context. The third step in Kolb's model is abstract conceptualisation. In organisation learning, the task of interpreting information is a collective one. Organisational members come to the task with different perspectives, varied ways of interpreting the information. Dixon insists that without 'differences' learning does not occur. Finally, members must act on the collective interpretation and generate new information to continue their learning (p. 66).

Dixon scans the corporate landscape to find exemplars of the 'intentional use of learning processes . . . to continuously transform the organization in a direction that is increasingly satisfying to its stake-holders' (p. 67). Chaparral Steel fit the bill. It, she says, considers itself a 'learning lab' and uses straightforward principles to reach its competitive goals. Employees are given discretion to both identify and solve problems. The organisation designs structures to disseminate knowledge. With its strong emphasis on multi-skilling and multi-functioning, Chaparral Steel reduces 'territorial possessiveness' (p. 71). The company also integrates research and development with production. Most of the learning is conducted on the job or through cross-training, but employees still spend four hours per week in classrooms. Dixon thinks that Chaparral Steel actively searches for workers who have a curious and inquiring sensibility. They are encouraged openly to challenge the status quo. Organisation learning advocates like Dixon, however, have a limited conception of the corporate status quo.

Dixon thinks that Johnsonville Foods is another exemplary learning organisation. CEO Ralph Stayer was struck by the divergence between the vital lives his employees led outside the workplace and their apparent boredom with their work tasks. Concerned about his competition and his employees lack of vibrancy, Stayer met with his workers in groups of four, later in groups of 20 to 25 for fireside chats. But this didn't accomplish much. It dawned on Stayer that he could turn things around if he could design an organisation in which 'people were responsible for

91

their own performance' (p. 84). He realised that this would require a basic shift of mind-set, his and the employees'. His first step was to redesign the information systems so that employees could get data needed to make their decisions. Stayer imagined that the 'new performance system' had to be 'designed from the customer's perspective' (p. 85). To get continuous improvement, the information system had to be both usable by the members and tied to a reward system. His system rewarded individuals and teams, and, more controversially, personal growth and development. And twice a year, workers shared a percentage of the company's profits.

Stayer's people-centred company had to recruit the right people, developing and retraining them. He changed the Human Resource Department to Member Development. He created a fund of $100 per member of the organisation to spend as they chose, from buying books to attending a course. Still, the velvet glove hid the subtler forms of employee coercion. If a member was performing at an unacceptable level, other team members would contract with this person to improve his or her performance. Dixon comments: 'Within a well-defined process, teams monitor, correct and, if necessary, even fire their own members' (p. 87). Less sanguine than I am about the dangers inherent in employee self-monitoring, Dixon asserts that: 'Learning is seen as the acquisition of facts and knowledge, but also as the questioning of actions and behavior in ways that improve performance' (p. 87). Within her model, Stayer discovered that performance standards did not work until the employees engaged in conversation with employees. In the second step, Johnsonville Foods shifted from controlling information to identifying what the workers needed as well as the form it would take. To accomplish the third step, collectively interpreting information, Stayer restricted the size of the organisation. Unless the first three steps are traversed, the fourth, allowing workers to act on the collectively arrived at meaning, is never reached.

Dixon, who is a committed constructivist, argues compellingly that organisations could not learn if individuals did not. Since this is so, she offers the idea of three types of 'meaning structures' – private, accessible and collective. Each individual in the organisation, she argues, 'constructs meaning for themselves' (p. 44). Through informal, non-formal and formal learning processes, individuals accumulate a 'great deal of knowledge and expertise about their organization full of individuals who each possess extensive knowledge and expertise – and yet the organization may not be learning because these individuals keep private the meaning that they construct; they keep their meaning making within the walls of their private office' (pp. 44–5). Dixon defines private meaning, then, as meaning that workers keep to themselves. She acknowledges that workers may have very good reasons for keeping meaning private.

Accessible meaning, the second category, identifies the fact that individuals do share meaning with others in the organisation. Dixon considers this process 'analogous to the hallways of the organization where important exchanges take place' (p. 46). In my view, this metaphor contains important insights. 'Hallways are places where collective meaning is made – in other words, meaning is not just exchanged, it is constructed in the dialogue between organizational members' (p. 47). In the confluence of ideas, new meaning develops that none of the individuals brought into the hallway. 'It is this joint construction of meaning that is organizational learning' (p. 47). This insight is in line with the spirit of Habermas's communicative learning.

The final category, collective meaning, is simply that 'which organizational members hold in common' (p. 48). To be collective, the norms, strategies and assumptions – which specify what work is important to do and how it gets done – must reside in the minds of organisation members. Dixon says this like having a 'storeroom where the mementos of the past are kept. It is extremely important to an organization – it is its history' (pp. 48–9). She thinks that collective meaning is the glue holding the organisation together. But she admits that collective meaning can become fossilised, resisting new ideas that bump up against the old. Dixon's confidence quivers, however, when she realises that sudden shifts in the external environment can demand radical changes in collective meaning that members will be unable to negotiate because they go on reaffirming the old map.

'If organizations are going to learn they will need to construct hallways in which the learning can occur' (p. 50). This is her granite idea: organisation learning will be a lovely fiction or mere topic for business school luncheons unless they develop pedagogical processes in real hallways. These pedagogical processes must be intentional, system-wide processes organisations employ to facilitate the construction of collective meaning. Here we can identify a wide range of processes designed to serve this function – dialogue groups, network meetings, town halls, scenario planning procedures, learning maps. In other words, organisation learning remains haphazard and confused unless the organisation consciously designs the procedures and gives time to enabling 'organizational members to interact with each other, exchanging their data, conclusions, reasoning and questions with others, rather than listening to speeches or presentations' (p. 51). We only know what we know in dialogue with others. 'It is necessary', Dixon insists, 'to hold both one's own and others' perspectives in mind simultaneously to create new knowledge' (p. 52). But these lovely words seem far removed from the contentious politics of organisations in the global economy.

Dixon articulates several norms that ought to govern the collective learning process. Collective learning is 'more effective when organizational members talk with each other as equals rather than as disparate members of a hierarchy' (p. 52). Like Argyris and Hedberg, Dixon affirms that 'we can learn only when there is a discrepancy between how we are currently thinking about something and some event or data that calls our current thinking into question' (p. 53). She thinks that, if individuals can only learn when they hold two perspectives simultaneously, then organisations must also 'simultaneously contain multiple perspectives' (p. 53). But she readily admits that most organisational problems do not require more information. The problem itself needs to be re-framed. Dixon argues that organisational designers must resist placing decision-making power in the hands of technical experts. When the problems are based in human systems, then expert advice is just one of several perspectives. Dixon challenges upper levels of management's control of data and information flow. 'Hallways bring together, not reports from others, but the primary source of the data, allowing the "sense-making" process to be less inferential and more data-based' (p. 55). Four elements are critical here: the availability of organisational data; the primary source of the data being present; publishing the data; and the dialogue that constructs meaning from the data. She concludes on a utopian, upbeat note: if organisational members are able to 'generate exciting new ideas, re-frame issues in more useful ways, and act in a more egalitarian manner, they may come to think of themselves and others in a new light' (p. 56).

Dixon counsels us to realise that group decision making must be differentiated from collective meaning making. Collective meaning could result in an organisation deciding not to pursue a particular course of action. She also believes that 'experience alone does not produce learning. It is the time we spend "thinking about" or "reflecting on" those experiences that creates the new meaning for us – the time we spend in that processing space' (p. 59). Thus, organisations need to consciously design hallways – communicative learning spaces to comprise the organisation's comprehensive communicative learning infrastructure.

Organisation learning through the critical optic

By the latter decades of the twentieth century, learning theory had executed a significant shift from restricting learning to individual psychology and behavioural change to understanding how organisations learn. But there are solid reasons for believing that the organisation learning paradigm, as proposed by the likes of Argyris, Hedberg and Dixon, lacks the conceptual power to penetrate into the actual learning/action dynamics of corporate capitalism. One's suspicions emerge not only from the human relations school's unwillingness to challenge the class relations structuring work relations. Contemporary organisation learning theory has also developed in tandem with capitalism's prolonged neo-conservative phase (privatisation, de-regulation, downsizing, informatisation, re-engineering). These catastrophic developments (in both first and third worlds) have registered in organisation learning theory primarily as intensified turbulence in the external environment. Organisation learning theorists, or consultants, have not raised any fundamental questions about the Basic Value Program (McMurtry, 1999) of globalised corporate capitalism itself. Stripped down, organisation learning is offered as a possible managerial solution to the hyper-competitive, even hysterical, economic climate throughout the world.

Thus, organisation learning is both an instrumentally driven strategy to adapt to a chaotic and unpredictable world and a social scientific model to understand learning in organisational contexts. Some of the concepts – maps, double-loop learning, learning cycles, hallways – are valuable and helpful for imagining emancipatory practice. But abstract systems language empties learning of its content and wrenches it out of historical context. At their best, organisation learning concepts might serve as a normative benchmark to assess corporate learning dynamics and action. At their worst, these concepts take on an unworldly quality, pointing to a dreamscape far removed from corporate machinations. Take, for instance, an abstract concept like 're-framing' or 'collective learning.' These objective concepts certainly permit radical re-orientation within an organisation. But without acknowledging (or challenging) the historical determinants of capitalist business organisations, any re-framing of the organisation's purposes can only occur within the constraints of the Basic Value Program. McMurtry's principle one – 'There are large capitalist corporations which control production and distribution of social goods so as to maximize the money value of their stock' (1999, p. 36) – identifies what can and cannot be learned. Double-loop learning, in this sense, is a bogus concept that never actually happens.

At most, double-loop learning could reconfigure managerial strategies to find different means to maximise the money value of the company's stock. The Basic Value Program (companies' own property and goods; they have the right to define what labour does and deploy it as they wish; they have the right to fire at any whim without consequence; and they want to pay as low wages as possible and thwart trade unionism) is the taken-for-granted frame around the capitalist organisation's learning and actions. Famous and adept consultants like Chris Argyris or Peter Senge would not get in the door of any of the Fortune 500 corporations if they advocated an alternative economic order, authentic participatory democracy, or laid the blame for global troubles, unrest and unhappiness at the CEO's feet.

Existing organisation learning theories also lack realism. As theoretical models, they are not able to account for the actual way corporations learn and act in the globally competitive economy. The Basic Value Program lays the trajectory for corporate learning, propelling it along the tracks, inexorably. The historical and contemporary evidence suggests that what actually happens, is that business organisations, large and small, will, left to their own devices, do everything possible, including breaking the law, to extract profits and undermine their competitors. The learning sensors of the corporation only register what is necessary to maximise the money value of their stock. Everything else is expunged from the organisation's learning agenda. If the factory floor workers at Nike, for example, propose 'data' from their experience (namely, that their wages are too paltry), this problem identification from below will either go unnoticed or will only gain attention when the workers themselves organise seriously disruptive actions against Nike's money interests. In Nigeria, the giant oil company, Chevron, only moved outside its primary learning agenda when women occupied the Chevron Texaco oil terminal at Escravos. Their occupation led to the promise of clean water and schools. The memory of Shell's compromised role in the death of Ken Saro-Wiwa in Nigeria also lingers in the fetid air. Examples such as this are legion.

The organisation learning cycle cannot be restricted, then, to the particular business organisation's culture and practices. The circle must be widened to include the various people affected by the organisation's actions. If we want to understand how a global organisation like the International Monetary Fund (IMF) or the World Bank (WB) learns, we would need to both move inside the organisation to ascertain its leaders' actions and outside to understand the demands of the social movements' protests against the consequences of IMF or WB actions amongst the worst-off and powerless. The anti-globalisation movement is protesting against their exclusion from the organisation's learning cycle. The just learning society paradigm challenges the way the Basic Value Program of global capitalism marshals its intellectual resources to maximise profits, executive power and privilege over justice and social (and natural) development. Within this framework, what is important in organisational learning and action is whether the organisation, in interaction with its environment, is actually producing, not merely profits for shareholders, but well-being for its own members and those outside the organisation, including non-human beings. In other words, organisation learning theory cannot stand apart from moral and ethical considerations. Let's probe this matter in more detail with a provocative example.

Thousands of men and women work for US companies that manufacture military armaments. American corporate executives are mandated under US law to follow the laws, such as the US Foreign Assistance and Arms Export Control acts. The US law stipulates that any defence articles and defence services to any country shall be furnished 'solely for internal security, [or] for legitimate self-defense' (22U.S.C. 2302 and 2754). Israel's excessive and disproportionate use of force to suppress the Palestinian people and its recent offensive against Palestinian cities with US-supplied weaponry clearly exceeds the bounds of what could be considered legitimate self-defence. Therefore, it is in violation of US law. Moreover, according to US law, 'no security assistance may be provided to any country the government of which engages in a consistent pattern of gross violations of internationally recognized human rights' (22U.S.C. 2304). The US State Department has repeatedly documented in its annual reports that Israel engages in 'torture or cruel, inhuman, or degrading treatment of punishment, prolonged detention without charges and trial, causing the disappearance of persons by the abduction and clandestine detention of those persons, and other flagrant denials of the right to life, liberty, or the security of people.'

These policies should guide morally corporations in this conflict. Now, consider if you were an ordinary, reasonably well-educated worker for Caterpillar. You realise that your firm is making equipment that is used to build the illegal settlements in the West Bank, the Gaza Strip and East Jerusalem. Your corporate executives have won lucrative contracts, basically because the US requires that 75 per cent of its $2 billion aid to Israel be used to purchase US-made armaments. You, however, do not believe that this is a moral action (in fact, it may be even be a criminal act under international law). What would it take to get this matter on the learning agenda of the Caterpillar corporation? What would it take for the company to re-frame its business orientation and lucrative profit-gathering in the Middle East?

We could also travel to Lockheed Martin Aeronautics Company, which provides the fighter jets that have been used by Israel to bomb Palestinian cities that have been under military closure for 27 months (I am writing this section in January 2003). Lockheed proudly announced on 5 September 2001 from Fort Worth, Texas that Israel had decided to purchase 52 more Lockheed Martin F-16 fighter jets. This contract was reported as approximately $1.3 billion for only the aircraft. Sikorsky Aircraft Corporation, a subsidiary of United Technologies Corporation, sells Israel Black Hawk helicopters to serve the Israeli air force. Are the consequences of the use of these armaments – ruined homes, smashed up cities, obliterated human beings – part of the learning agenda of Sikorsky or Lockheed? Could you, ordinary worker, raise your voice against your company?

But corporate America's support for Israel is not restricted to military equipment suppliers. In fall 1999, Burger King opened a franchise in an illegal settlement in the West Bank. It was only closed down in response to a threatened worldwide boycott by its customers. In May 2002, Microsoft Israel put executives in an awkward position when it sponsored two large billboards on an Israeli main highway saluting Israel's armed forces at the same time as the Israeli Defence Force (IDF) was indiscriminately bombing the refugee camp of Jenin. One recalls that international observers (UN, Red Cross) maintained that Israel had committed numerous war crimes and executed many degrading acts during this siege. Only a grassroots campaign sponsored by an Israeli peace group, Gush-Shalom, forced Microsoft US to instruct their Israeli counterpart to pull them down (Bahour, 2002).

Executives of these companies make decisions in ways far removed from Nancy Dixon's transparent organisation learning cycle. They climb the corporate ladder learning all the while to make decisions far from the public gaze. They are loathe to rock the boat regarding Israel. In fact, since most of these war industries are in the southern US states, many of the workers would be Bible-believing Christians who actually believe that their god has promised Israel the land of Palestine. To get the attention of one's co-workers, let alone management, the worker would have to break through the constraints of religious ideology (which sanctioned aggressive military action against Arabs) and business practices which expel moral considerations from the realm of production. Hedberg thinks that an organisation can best survive a turbulent environment by developing a new myth. A just business learning organisation could only make the shift from retreading old myths (and calling them new) by creating an authentic myth which would open itself to learning along moral and ethical trajectories. Realistically, however, the only way this can happen is through collective action from outside the business organisation intersecting with forces inside businesses that decry anti-moral, even criminal, activity on the part of their enterprise. This latter observation contains a ray of hope. The business organisation, as a human invention, can be re-invented as new, radical myths break through into corporate consciousness. In the next chapter, we examine the way democratic learning is inhibited in business organisations. By so doing, we move from the conceptual fairyland of beautiful concepts to the real world.

CHAPTER FIVE

Inhibited learning in business organisations

Anyone who has spent time working in business or community organisations knows only too well that they don't always conform to mission statements (to do 'good in the world') or run effortlessly according to chart ('this is your role and we value your input'). People can be pretty nasty. Managers lord it over the workers. Workers don't always like one another. Some try to undercut others. Most jockey for power, status and influence. People crack up. They are greedy and get swept up into wild dreams of being the biggest and the best. There is often a yawning gap between the way organisations talk about their actions in the world and what they actually do. Managers stumble along, crisis to crisis. Workers positioned way down on the totem pole fume their way through the day. Despite paying lip service to democracy or participation, most organisations give little attention to the energy, mindfulness and commitment needed to create a democratic learning organisation.

Harnessed to the money-code, the business organisation is actually learning disabled. It is intensely pressured to learn along a single trajectory: to enhance shareholder profits and interests. It accentuates the economic at the expense of the social. It appears to be immature and resolutely stupid at learning how to care for the environment or equalise the distribution of wealth. Non-business organisations, the myriad of associations in civil society, have a better chance of becoming learning organisations. Freed from the blunt instrumental imperatives of the money-code, they are communicatively coordinated (civil society organisations can, of course, get derailed over money issues). Government organisations have more potential for communicative learning processes than businesses, but they, like business organisations, lie within

100

the system-domain. They are bureaucratic and hierarchical organisations that manage our affairs strategically. Despite difficulties, one can never rule out the hope that business organisations could, under increasing pressure from the global progressive movements, open up communicative learning space to consider their moral and ethical responsibilities. Or, that organisations within the state-apparatus could open their gates to learning influences generated from civil society.

In this chapter, I focus attention on inhibited or ineffective learning in organisations. Without a careful examination of the way individual and collective learning is blocked within organisations (business, state and civil society), the ideal of the just learning organisation detaches itself from reality. We will consider some organisational defensive routines, how gender and race play out in organisational dynamics and how organisational silence is maintained. My goal is to understand more fully how open and democratic communication procedures and processes get distorted and undermined.

Chris Argyris and organisational defensive routines

Conventional organisation theory has focused some attention on organisational defensive routines. These routines 'inhibit individuals, groups, inter-groups, and organisations from experiencing embarrassment or threat and, at the same time, prevents the actors from identifying and reducing the causes of the embarrassment or threat. Organisational defensive routines are anti-learning and overprotective' (Argyris, 1993, p. 15). The desire to look good and manage our self-presentation is rooted in our childhood formation. We want to be loved and recognised. We will, it seems, do just about anything to avoid being humiliated or losing face. We turn away from situations in our personal and working lives that are negative. Consequently, the learning potential contained in having to confront our actions (or management's) in the workplace is bypassed. We save face but lose the possibility of collective learning and creative action. We also lose the possibility of learning humility, grace and tolerance of the foibles of humankind.

Reducing embarrassment also allies itself to ego-enhancement and hubris. At its most extreme, a world leader (say George W. Bush) could, in fact, lead his country into a war primarily because he does not want to lose face after inflating the danger of Saddam Hussein to world security and mobilising vast numbers of troops (150,000) on Arab soil.

A similar process was at work when managers came together to understand 'why safety was handled in a poor way in an organisation that understood the importance of safety' (1993, p. 17) when the Challenger space shuttle exploded. Humiliated and angry, managers could not honestly air their views. Absorbed in details, they never expressed any doubts about the larger picture. Powerful leaders seldom admit they're wrong or have failed.

Argyris argues that defensive routines inhibit the detection and correction of error and problem solving and decision making. Defensive actions are often hidden in the organisation's dirty basement. Who will admit openly to deception, lying, manipulation and wilful distortion? Very few. Doing some excavation work in the dirty basements, Argyris classifies some of the actions that could be called defensive routines. People may actually take the opposite stand to the one they prefer if they believe their position will be seen as deviant. To conform is to be embraced, accepted, loved. People can ignore orders and cut corners. They can avoid taking bureaucratic or personal responsibility. They can hold ritualised meetings, going through the motions of openness, but in truth, hindering any true reflection (Argyris, 1993, p. 18). All types of organisations engage in these cover-up activities and require that individuals 'communicate inconsistent messages but act as if they are not doing so' (p. 20).

Argyris surveys the literature of educational administration for comparable examples. He observes that administrators will use arguments guised as safeguarding the profession to defeat proposed innovations that might threaten the territorial interests of teachers. They lose recommendations from working groups by referring the recommendations to other groups, hoping that they will simply disappear. They rig agendas, massage the minutes and invent consensus where consensus has not been tested. They circumvent regulations (and laws). They may even play one group off against another. These organisational tactics are well known; part of the game is that the actors must never admit they are doing these things.

Argyris comments, 'If individuals or groups use untested attributions, advocacy that curtails inquiry, and attributions which assign responsibility to individuals or cultural forces, the individuals or groups will harden their positions, develop rivalries, become mistrustful, and distance themselves from taking the responsibility for confronting process issues' (p. 23). Within Argyris's systems model, when the error-detecting process is hindered, the organisation loses its balance and organisational learning cannot occur. But covering up or bypassing are strategic moves that are not inscribed in any organisation's policies. Officially, deceit, manipulation and distorting information violate the organisation's norms and regulations. In the courtroom scene from *A Few Good Men*, Tom Cruise's character establishes that a 'Code Red' (peer punishment) occurred even though it didn't exist in any military protocol. It was not officially sanctioned and was always covered up. In the process of enactment, the actors must never admit that they are spinning language to accomplish an end hidden from its audience (Berringer, 2002).

Malcolm Gladwell (2002) argues that Enron, celebrated as an exemplary model of corporate action in the globalising economy, actually favoured the 'narcissist' style of management. 'Narcissists', he intones, 'are terrible managers. They resist accepting suggestions, thinking it will make them appear weak, and they don't believe that others have anything useful to tell them.' Enron was a narcissistic corporation – a 'company that took more credit for success than was legitimate, that did not acknowledge responsibility for its failures, that shrewdly sold the rest of us on its genius, and that substituted self-nomination for disciplined management' (p. 31). In fact, Enron believed that stars plucked from upscale MBA schools could drive its fortunes. They paid little attention to how an organisation actually got its work done consistently over good and bad times. Consultants would not get this high-octane group to a weekend retreat on 'Teamwork – the secret to organisational learning in competitive times.' Argyris speaks of 'skilled incompetence' – teams full of people who are incredibly proficient at keeping themselves from learning (cited, Senge, 1990, pp. 24–5).

Defensive routines, then, keep the organisation from learning. But to even recognise these routines – where we appear to agree but really don't – is very difficult. At an early age we learn to deny our own needs and desires so that we are not embarrassed before others. Think only of the way school children, and adults too, will nod their heads when the teacher asks if there are any questions. Like donkeys, we move our heads up and down. It is common, in societies where many have been denied access to formal education, for men and women to be too embarrassed at being singled out for mockery to take the risk and go to a class. When we move into the world of work and become full citizens, we carry our early socialisation (and often the resultant damage to our self-esteem and confidence) into our organisational cultures. Playing the defensive game becomes natural and is not even discussed. Argyris thinks that 'changing the human predisposition to produce organizational defensive routines and the organizational norms that protect these routines requires altering both individuals' master programs and organizations protective norms' (1993, p. 21).

Bypassing and covering up have had two serious consequences. 'First, feedback to the original features maintained, protected, and reinforced those features. Second, actions were taken that made it possible for the participants to explain away by-passing and covering up.' Ways of avoiding the public testing of validity claims included

> blaming others – who might have been external or internal – while avoiding a public test of the validity of the blame, expressing private dissatisfaction with the way the group dealt with difficult issues by by-passing them, expressing private doubt about the group's capacity for change, experiencing helplessness about taking initiatives to change the group, and distancing oneself from one's own causal responsibility for any counterproductive consequences. (1993, p. 45)

Breaking the chains of embarrassment requires risk. These risks, says Argyris, can 'be transformed into opportunities only if the risks or the opportunities are not associated with embarrassment or threat' (p. 45). Adult educational counsel to exhibit trust and integrity while sharing ideas or to engage in dialogue must face the difficulty of accomplishing this, given our present resources. The long range challenge for the just learning society paradigm is to become aware of what needs to be in place in the lifeworld (families, schools, communities, public spaces) for children and youth to grow up recognised, affirmed, loved and socially engaged. The alternative is pathologised life worlds and organisational cultures. These latter themes are explored in depth in chapter eight.

Organisational silence: A barrier to change in a pluralist world

Elizabeth Morrison and Frances Milliken ('Organizational silence: a barrier to change and development in a pluralistic world' (2000)) provide us with an astute scholarly analysis of the powerful forces in many organisations that cause widespread withholding of information about potential problems or issues by employees. They identify the contextual variables that create conditions conducive to silence and explore the collective sense-making dynamics that can create the shared perception that speaking up is unwise. They also discuss some of the negative consequences of systemic silence, especially for organisations' ability to change and develop in pluralistic contexts.

Imagine, they say, an organisation where the CEO has no clothes. Apparent to everyone, the employees go about their business without ever mentioning this. To his or her face, some even compliment their stunning attire. They even look askance at those who hint that the CEO's dress is less than perfect. Yet, behold, there are some employees who aren't blind. Behind closed doors, they mumble and grumble about their leader's lack of clothing. Clearly, they all know the CEO is naked, but only the foolish dare speak of it in public. 'Is this a fairy tale?', Morrison and Milliken ask. They think not: 'far too many organizations are caught in an apparent paradox in which most employees know the truth about certain issues and problems within the organization yet dare not speak that truth to their superiors' (p. 706). Although they observe that organisational thinkers like Argyris and others mention the games employees play that prevent them from saying what they know (about either technical or policy issues), they admit that few scholars have explored systematically why this situation occurs. In fact, Morrison and Milliken think that data about why employees feel compelled to be silent appears mainly in popular magazines and journals. They also claim that most of the popular accounts focus on individual-level antecedents of whistle blowing or issue selling. In contrast, they believe that examining the withholding of opinions and concerns as a collective phenomenon – organisational silence – deserves serious scholarly attention.

They are struck by the paradox that while many scholars accentuate the importance of multiple perspectives, the upward flow of information, and employee empowerment, so many employees report feeling that they cannot communicate upward. Why should this be? They insist that 'organizational silence is a potentially dangerous impediment to organizational change and development and is likely to pose a significant obstacle to the development of truly pluralistic organizations' (p. 707). A pluralist organisation, the authors claim, values and reflects divergence of viewpoint and creates the pedagogical forms to permit the articulation of difference. But when the workers do not believe they can speak, when they gag themselves, the pluralist norm is violated. One fundamental consequence of this self-censoring is that the organisation's viewpoints remain monolithic. The learning potential carried in the organisation's web of different bodies, genders, experiences, knowledge and skill is simply excised from the organisation's learning repertoire.

> Thus, we argue that in order to understand how change and development might unfold within pluralistic settings, we need to understand the organizational forces that often systematically cause employees to feel their opinions are not valued and that thereby discourage them from speaking up. It is our belief that only by tracing and understanding the cause of organizational silence can we begin to build an accurate and comprehensive understanding of the barriers to pluralism in organizations. (p. 707)

Silence, then, is systemic. There are forces that both set it in motion and reproduce it through time.

Morrison and Milliken begin by considering how organisational silence is produced. They believe that organisational silence is produced by managers' fear of negative feedback and their belief systems. They identify conditions that foster these beliefs (of senior management) and how these beliefs sustain particular types of organisational structures and policies. Like Argyris, they believe that the 'climate of silence' (Freire speaks of a 'culture of silence' in his famous text, *Pedagogy of the Oppressed* (1972)) is facilitated when top managers are afraid of receiving negative feedback from those with lower status. But they press beyond this truism to identify the set of beliefs, often implicit, that managers hold about their employees. Would workers be alarmed to learn that their bosses think that they are self-interested and untrustworthy? Research (Ghoshal and Moran, 1996; McGregor, 1960; Pfeffer, 1997) indicates that most managers believe their workers are averse to effort and can only be goaded into working hard through incentive or sanction. Morrison and Milliken link this managerial belief (or myth) to managerial practice of discouraging, implicitly or explicitly, upward communication. Following Argyris, managers espouse a theory of open communication, but their theory-in-use impels them to act otherwise.

The ideology that managers must lead, direct and control (gladiatorial corporate CEOs do not consult below or hang out with the masses) was fuelled in the 1990s before the collapse of the IT boom. In fact, if the recent popular managerial self-help literature is any indicator, managers were instructed by gurus that great and powerful managers

106

know what is best for the organisation. Morrison and Milliken claim that another unstated belief is that unity and consensus are 'signs of organizational health, whereas disagreement and dissent should be avoided' (p. 710). Critical organisation theorists Burrell and Morgan (1979) argue that this 'unitary view' contrasts sharply with the 'pluralistic view' (where dissent is regarded as normal). The pedagogical procedures within the unitary organisation (group decision making, strategy formulation, and innovation) are constrained by the idea that 'agreement is good' (Morrison and Milliken, 2000, p. 710).

What conditions foster these beliefs? To answer this, we need to know how widespread these beliefs actually are. The authors argue that these beliefs are widespread in many organisations. Studies of the system of management education in the US (Pfeffer, 1997) indicate that the idea about employee self-interest is taught. Despite the rhetoric of the flattened organisation and the end of hierarchy buzzing around the workshop circuit, scholarly evidence suggests that as people climb the company ladder they are less likely to identify with their colleagues below. They gradually absorb the prevalent managerial myths about workers. If I have been promoted for my excellence, then I must know best and deserve my new post up the pyramid. But Morrison and Milliken admit that these managerial beliefs and assumptions may be held more strongly in some organisations than others. For instance, they think that when a top management team is dominated by individuals with financial or economic backgrounds, they are more likely to treat their workers as human capital. Allowing the cleaning staff or production line workers into the charmed circle might press management to see their workers as something other than instruments eating into potential profits. They also predict that when top management shares similar functional training and experience, the more threatened they are likely to feel by dissent. Further, if the top managers have been together for a long time, their assumptions tend to blend into a shared world-view.

We can also braid other themes into this tapestry of managerial beliefs. Unity is strongly valued when the top management team comes from a collectivist culture which places a high premium on harmony. We can also expect that the more similar the demographic profile (gender, race, ethnicity, age) of the top management team, when compared to lower-level employees, the more likely the team is to be unwilling to listen to those below. Research on diversity (Cox, 1993) has shown that 'salient [racial] differences often create distrust and fear of the unknown' (cited, p. 711). Morrison and Milliken believe that organisation-level and environmental variables also constrain top management to foster silence. Organisations heavily dependent on control, predictability and efficiency reinforce negative feedback. Dissent threatens to crack the carapace covering the organisation. 'This logic', they say, 'is more likely to emerge not only in cost-focused organizations but also within highly competitive environments characterized by a diminishing resource base' (p. 711). Indeed, the cost-cutting climate of the 1990s stoked the egos of corporate engineers to 'go it alone', 'to be tough and intimidating' and to 'make the hard decisions.' Scarcely any of the celebrated managerial swashbucklers of the previous decade really believed in organisational learning. Perhaps some of the newer, volatile industries – like the Internet – were forced to draw upon workers' knowledge and skill in their relentless quest for new strategies. Perhaps . . .

They also expect that in organisations with 'tall organizational structures', top managers will be less likely to relate to lower-level employees. This gap may even be heightened if managers are brought in from the outside. They posit this proposition: 'The managerial beliefs contributing to organizational silence will be more common in organizations with many hierarchical levels and in organizations that hire senior-level managers from the outside, rather than promote from within' (p. 712). It appears to me that the outsider often symbolises both disdain for the cultural intricacies of the organisation – it has nurtured its social capital delicately over time – and a resolutely instrumental approach to management. Those of us working in universities, for instance, have watched the way university administrators are chosen for their managerial toughness, business sense, and seldom for their commitment to fostering the humane letters. The outsider, the wandering corporate cowboy who shoots up the town and moves on, has no commitment to the organisation's traditions, culture, contradictions, and ways of being. The tendency, manifest to every eye over the last two decades, to hire contingent, part-time workers also reinforces, and contributes to, organisational silence. They come in, do their job and go home. The structure and ethos of their workplaces does not permit them to become informed, attuned to the nuances and daily politics of weaving the organisation's life into something reasonably pleasing for most. Managers easily exploit this situation. Behind closed doors, they make their decisions, with little fear that anybody cares or is watching. They can also interpret employee lack of commitment to the organisation as proof positive that workers are untrustworthy. Sennett (1998) argues that one of the consequences of the temporary nature of work is that organisations, lacking trust in employees, have become more tightly controlled.

Morrison and Milliken argue that beliefs are enacted in structures, policies and managerial behaviours. This axiom has been long recognised in the organisational studies literature. In 1960, McGregor proposed his famous contrasting theories of X and Y, noting, essentially, that managerial beliefs have a powerful impact on how managers treat their employees and how they behave. He argued that if managers assume that their workers can't be trusted to do a good job, they will institute control mechanisms to prevent shirking. Once the workers realise that manage-ment is suspicious of them, searching constantly for effective means of surveillance, the workers in turn engage in various forms of opposition to this perception – from work slowdowns to outright sabotage. A vicious circle is created, worker actions feeding the mythic belief system of management. Cracking this circle of animosity requires – as Argyris, Hedberg and Dixon might say – a new founding myth, one that would never counsel the humiliation and violation of the dignity of any workers. Current transnational corporate practice is light years removed from proffering a new myth or signing a 'right to dignity at work' charter elevated to the status of the UN charter for a humane and dignified world.

Morrison and Milliken propose that when the 'unspoken yet dominant ideology' (p. 712) within the organisation is that the employees are self-interested, management knows best and disagreement is bad, then management erects structures and policies that will not encourage the upward flow of information. In other words, management beliefs will be embodied in structural features that centralise decision-making and lack any formal procedures for information to flow upward. From management's point of view, it is rational to not involve the workers in decision making. Decentralised decision making is too time consuming, not worth the effort. Certainly, there maybe a show of participatory decision making – task forces, committees, and so on – but true decision-making authority resides at the top. The authors believe that 'despite discussions of organizations becoming more decentralized, the implicit belief structure that dominates many organizations gives rise to structures that are often quite centralized in reality' (p. 713; see Foegen, 1999; Sennett, 1998). The Marxian critical theoretical tradition would invert this formulation somewhat. The Basic Value Program of corporate capitalism rules out any input from labour that would in any way challenge Capital's right to deploy labour as it so wishes. The managerial belief system nestles itself inside this basic structural feature of Capital's domination over Labour. Beliefs accommodate to underlying interest.

Within the just learning society paradigm, this fundamental structural feature of capitalism distorts the communication process. Hierarchical organisations do not intentionally design the pedagogical procedures to solicit employee feedback (before or after decisions are made). It is unlikely that Dixon's first two stages of the organisational learning cycle would be put in place. What can actually be learned from the workers about the big picture? Doesn't the open encouragement of communication foment dissent and dissatisfaction? When managers believe that workers are 'self-interested, opportunistic, and not well informed, and that agreement is preferable to disagreement, they also will tend to enact these beliefs in their day-to-day behaviour toward employees' (Morrison and Milliken, 2000, p. 713). If, for example, employees express concerns about some proposed organisational change, management's tendency is to assume that their resistance to change reflects their personal biases – 'not because they were truly concerned that the change might be bad for the organization' (p. 713). Managers discount information from workers, particularly if those views differ from their own. Conversely, trade unions are notoriously hostile to any managerial rhetoric that invites them to participate in making changes in the organisation. In the 1980s, many companies tried to convince trade unionists to use Japanese-style work teams and ideas. Workers rightly understood that what this meant was speed-up, once the rhetorical icing was removed.

Threatening and controlling managers are also reluctant to learn through the informal processes of chatting, listening, talking, keeping an ear open. They do not actively seek out corridor knowledge and, instead, spend time with those see the world in the same way. This is not intentional, just related to the all too human desire to escape embarrassment and to seek confirmation. These various managerial practices may operate at 'multiple organizational levels' (p. 714). Morrison and Milliken expect that if top management is secretive and closed to communication from below, then this attitude will trickle down to middle and lower levels in the organisation. They expect that 'consistent clues' will emerge

110

from middle and upper management. But it always possible for communication to cross-fire, with one superviser or another actively discouraging upward communication, while another located elsewhere in the company nurtures open dialogue. 'There may be widespread silence at the divisional level', say our authors, 'that does not characterize the larger organization' (p. 714).

To fully grasp how these structures and practices that impede the upward flow of information lead to organisational silence, Morrison and Milliken think that it is necessary to understand the organisation's 'climate of silence.' This latter phrase is akin to adult learning theory's 'climate of learning.' They want to understand both how a climate of silence develops and the 'collective sensemaking process (Weick, 1995) through which this climate emerges' (Morrison and Milliken, 2000, p. 714). By organisational climate, they mean the 'shared and enduring perceptions of psychologically important aspects of a particular work environment' (p. 714). A climate of silence, then, consists of two shared beliefs: (1) speaking up about problems in the organisation is not worth the effort; and (2) voicing one's opinions and concerns is dangerous. In this climate, organisational members assess what it will cost them to speak up. If the cost is high, they choose to remain silent.

The idea that meaning arises from inter-subjective interactions is widely shared amongst progressive adult educators and critical organisation theorists. This constructivist orientation (the classic statement is Berger and Luckman (1967)) posits that a shared outlook and sensibility is crafted out of the social interactions of men and women who share their experiences, perceptions with one another. They evaluate their perceptions in the light of others, triangulating on a 'single set of perceptions and meanings' (Ashforth, 1985, p. 839). Morrison and Milliken argue that the climate of silence is anchored not only in the 'objective features of the workplace', but also in the 'social interactions that contribute to a subjective process of sensemaking' (2000, p. 715). Thus, the structural features and subjective meanings do a kind of dialectical dance. When the organisation's decision making is highly centralised with few procedures for upward communication, employees embroider the words 'Employees' opinions not valued' on their common tapestry. When management opposes employees' viewpoints, brushing them aside or telling them, Yes, we will take this under consideration, employees gather to formulate the second embroidery: 'Speaking up is risky.' In oppressive managerial regimes, shared perceptions can become

111

intense, seething barely beneath the surface of daily work life.

By themselves, structural conditions do not generate shared perceptions. But common perceptions and attitudes require the right soil to flower. For one thing, workers must have the opportunity to associate with one another. Frequent and intense contact creates 'social contagion – a spreading of attitudes and perceptions from one person to another' (p. 715). Common perceptions require relatively stable work conditions, interdependence of work tasks and functions and informal social networks that are 'dense and composed of strong ties' (p. 715). Labour historians point to the important role that working class neigh- bourhoods played in generating a shared, oppositional consciousness. With the advent of suburbanisation and the consumer society in the post-World War II years, these working class communities (people lived close and shared community associations, games, public places) were gradually eroded and fragmented (Aronowitz, 1975). Morrison and Milliken claim that the strong bonds (or social capital) amongst the employees in places conducive to organisational silence increases the 'likelihood of a strong climate of silence developing' (p. 715). Under the right circumstances, these powerful bonds can generate a militant class consciousness. The workers could remain silent; they could also find their voices and begin to contest their exclusion from organisation's key learning dynamics. They conclude that, 'Hence, as employees attempt to make sense of such structural features as top-down decision making and closed feedback channels, they will be more likely to converge on and reinforce the interpretation that the organization is hostile to their input when their work necessitates regular communication, coordination, and teamwork' (p. 716).

Sense-making in hierarchical organisations that hinder upward communication gives rise to 'biased and often inaccurate perceptions as employees share and collectively interpret their observations and experiences (Ashforth, 1985)' (p. 716). Employees must construct their perceptions from second-hand information, oftentimes without testing a colleague's judgments about others. Research indicates that we give more credence to what others believe about situations than we do to our own perceptions (Nemeth, 1997). If others regard the organisation as unreceptive to voice, we assume this to be case. We silence ourselves, grumble and mumble with colleagues over drinks about an uncaring management. Looking around, we notice that others remain silent; this reinforces the perception that 'speaking up is taboo' (Morrison and

Milliken, 2000, p. 716). We can also easily exaggerate the riskiness of speaking up. One member expresses dissent, fails with the expected promotion, we assume that the employee did not receive the promotion because she spoke up. These anecdotes work their way through the grapevine, cementing perceptions about the costs of speaking up. Similarly, we assume that because one person had his suggested policy change rejected, that all input will be ignored.

Extensive research on group decision-making processes indicate that 'decision quality is enhanced when multiple perspectives and alternatives are considered' (Shaw, 1981). When top management teams have multiple and conflicting viewpoints to process, the quality of decision-making improves. Further, innovation – so highly prized by learning economy advocates – requires a context in which employees believe they can deviate from party lines. Reviewing the research, Morrison and Milliken argue that

> these research streams suggest that organizational silence will compromise the effectiveness of organizational decision making and change processes by restricting the variance in information input available to decision makers. In addition, without minority viewpoints there is less likely to be the type of critical analysis necessary for effective decision making, which may also compromise organizational change processes (Nemeth, 1985; Nemeth and Wachter, 1983; Shaw, 1981). (p. 719)

Certainly, too much employee input may overload decision-making procedures and impede 'timely and effective' communicative action (p. 719). Some radical groups have learned hard lessons about how time consuming consensual decision making can be. Bitterly, others cast doubt on the possibility of democratic decision making anywhere but the small group (Chambers, 1995). The challenge for the just learning society paradigm is to specify the meaning of democratic decision making in complex societies. But my central claim, following Morrison and Milliken, is that most organisations have too little employee voice. Energy and resources (inside organisations and outside in research institutes) are not marshalled to develop the pedagogical procedures necessary to understand how employees are affected by management's decisions. We have already seen that the organisational learning theorists insist that negative feedback must not be blocked. If this happens, corrective action cannot be taken.

To make matters worse, say Morrison and Milliken, top managers may even interpret silence as signalling widespread acceptance of policy. The hierarchical organisational structure, we must insist, operates like an invisible disciplinary presence. Employees filter out negative feedback to management because of fear, and managers filter out what they don't want to hear. Bies and Tripp (1999, p. 17) discovered that, 'Bosses, based on their observations of the employees' loyal and obedient behaviour, made inferences that led to a false consciousness and a false consensus as to the level of affection or disaffection with their leadership.' Managerial use of distorted feedback pushes the organisation off track. On the dark underside of this process, managers intentionally distort information in order to accomplish dubious goals – behind employees' and the public's back. Firms present over-optimistic analysis of stocks to the public. WorldCom falsely claimed profits exceeding $9 billion. And so on (Mokhiber and Weissman, 2002). For managers intent on either pressing closely to the legal limits of economic action, or exceeding them, they will want to be protected from upward communication that blows the whistle on their actions. When most employees collude in managerial deception, the organisation becomes corrupt, damaging humane relationships and moral action irreparably. Morrison and Milliken think that the

> negative effects of silence on organizational decision making and change processes will be intensified as the level of diversity within the organization increases. We would also propose that organizational silence will be most detrimental within rapidly changing environments. Within such environments it is virtually impossible for those at the top to have all of the information they need. (Duncan and Weiss, 1979. p. 719)

Morrison and Milliken believe strongly that organisational inhibiting of communicative learning leads to several debilitating outcomes. For one thing, studies on procedural justice indicate consistently that when these procedures allow employee input, employees value them more favourably. Lind and Tyler (1988) argue that employees view procedures allowing for their input positively. Instituting these procedures signals that employees are recognised and valued. Their 'group value model' also suggests that if employees do not have voice, they do not feel valued. The struggle for recognition is, I would argue, one of the primary motivators for adult learning and action. Workers want voice. Thwarted, the bonding form of social capital (Putnam, 2000) erodes trust and commitment to the organisation. High turnover and low worker morale are usually bound up with blockages in the communicative infrastructure of the organisation.

Evidence from the mid-nineteenth-century analyses of work in capitalist economies by Marx (Honneth, 1995, pp. 15–49) to contemporary reflections on work environments indicates strongly that individuals have a 'strong need for control over their immediate environment and over decisions that affect them (see Greenberger and Strasser, 1986; Parker, 1993; Wortman and Brehm, 1975)' (Morrison and Milliken, 2000, p. 720). One of the ways workers gain control over their environment is through articulating their preferences and viewpoints. Morrison and Milliken expect that 'when employees are surrounded by social cues that discourage speaking up, they will feel they lack sufficient control over their work environment' (p. 720). The other, perhaps more fundamental way workers gain control is through control over the design and execution of work tasks. Failing the possibility of a radical control by workers of the work processes themselves, having the opportunity to exercise voice is essential nutrient for their well-being. Without voice, workers will seek control through other means that may be destructive to the organisation. Workers themselves may exhibit pathological characteristics: stress, sickness, little motivation. Within the managerial mind-set, however, worker apathy or withdrawal may be interpreted as evidence of their hostility and willingness to contribute just enough to get by. Manager's beliefs may turn into self-fulfilling prophecies. Cut off from alternative perceptions, management risks being consumed in their own pathologies of power (hubris, crazed consumption, egomaniacal desires to dominate the market, reckless decision making, and so on).

Organisational silence is also likely to give rise to cognitive dissonance: an 'aversive state that arises when there is a discrepancy between one's beliefs and one's behaviour (Festinger 1957)' (p. 720). In this situation, individuals may well be impelled to reduce the divergence between beliefs and reality. Yet this is difficult in an organisational setting that produces silence in its normal everyday functioning. Consider a salesperson working for Wyeth, the mighty pharmaceutical company, whose mandate is to sell the hormone replacement therapy (HRT) sold by her company under the brand name Prempro. In early 2002, a US National Institutes of Health study concluded that HRT posed major health risks to millions of women in the US and around the world. The studies indicated that long-term HRT increased the risks of breast cancer, heart attack, stroke, and pulmonary embolism. For decades, Wyeth and Ayerst, the originator of HRT, had proclaimed the benefits of the long-term usage of this drug. They invested heavily in its promotion, employing an influential spokeswomen like Lauren Hutton to promote its secrets to keeping women feeling and looking young. As a salesperson with a social consciousness, familiar with the scientific studies, you risk engaging in immoral and harmful practices that contradict your company's beliefs about the benefits of one of its products. The opportunity to reduce dissonance is very low. Exercising voice about the product's flaws is highly risky (Mokhiber and Weissman, 2002). One could lose one's livelihood, status and be pulled into a legal swamp. One could even disappear in the night.

In this situation (and they may be multiplying exponentially in our world where corporate malfeasance is common), the worker can vent her frustration with other colleagues. This may reduce stress and anxiety, but this does not remove the dissonance. As Morrison and Milliken observe, 'there will be a stark contrast between what one expresses behind closed doors and what one expresses (or fails to express) in public (Bies and Tripp 1999; Morris and Feldman 1996)' (p. 721). Those who differ significantly from the majority will be pressured to remain silent. This may be particularly difficult personally for women and black or Asian people (as we will see in the following section) who challenge managerial (or behaviour of other workers) actions as reflecting gender or racial bias.

Morrison and Milliken conclude with the sobering observation that 'behavioral cycles that maintain organizational silence will be extremely hard to break' (p. 722). They are not subject to direct observation and, once people stop trusting a system, it is almost impossible to restore the lost trust. Cynicism settles in for the long haul. They think a revolutionary change to the system may be required to move from a climate of silence to one that encourages voice. This demands a strong external force. Even in the face of the most dire evidence of managerial failure, strategic reorientation seldom happens. But even if top management has the energy and will to execute system-wide change, they face employees who either do not believe that speaking up is wise or do not trust top-down initiatives for participation. True pluralism remains elusive – even for liberal organisation thinkers.

116

Gender and race-related inhibitors to learning in organisations

Management researchers and theorists like Morrison and Milliken provide us with many insights. But they dance around speaking of the class dynamics of organisational life. The revolution they whisper of so gently to managerial readers would be rejected out of hand. It would require that the owning class's exercise of power through hierarchical structures would be overturned. If organisational learning theorists are reluctant to speak of class, they are also wary of serious analysis of the way gender and race relations play themselves out in organisational life.

In the last three decades, however, the contemporary scholarly scene has witnessed an explosion of studies of gender and race. All disciplinary studies have been touched, including organisation theory (Mills, 1988; Nkomo, 1992). In this section, then, my intention is to highlight some of the ways gender and race relations inhibit organisational learning dynamics.

One only has to spend a few days in any reasonable hotel in North America or Europe to realise that gender and race are markers of status and power in organisations. In Toronto, for instance, the chambermaids are usually black women from the Caribbean. Walking to one's room, one is met by that open smile and lilting Jamaican accent. Few, if any, white faces are evident anywhere. Who are the cleaning ladies who enter the houses of upper-middle-class men and women? They're usually from the Third World – places like Guatemala or Peru and Trinidad. One can, of course, press this obvious sort of analysis into other sectors of the low end service economy; in fact, most of the dirty jobs of the post-industrial economy. These workers are members of organisations. What lessons do they carry within their psyches and bodies? How often do they get to have a say in how the hotels or fast food outlets run? Travel into upscale corporate offices. How many women are in top management? Do you notice any aboriginal people anywhere? Is everybody white? If not, what jobs have they been assigned?

The ideal of the just learning organisation assumes that all employees (regardless of race or gender) have access to the latest in training techniques, that all employees are engaged in communication towards enhancing productivity and performance. But the research evidence indicates that there really is no such thing as an abstract employee. They always come with bodies, skin colour, cultural formation, values, beliefs, passions. Swedish researcher Lena Abrahamsson (2001) states that 'the learning organisation, with its focus on integration and decentralisation, challenges the gender order, which is a strong system built on segregation and hierarchy. Knowledge of the factors and power structures that restore old patterns is necessary when working with organisational development' (p. 112). This latter point is made strongly by Stella Nkomo who argues that using race as a category of analysis suggests a 'view of organizations made up of race relations played out in power struggles . . .' (1992, p. 507).

By now, it is common knowledge that women are still grouped in the gender-specific lower paid occupations and do not receive equal pay for equal work. Most striking, perhaps, is the way skills definitions are 'saturated with sexual bias' (Phillips and Taylor, 1980. p. 79). Many feminists have argued that the classification of women's jobs as unskilled frequently is not synchronised with the actual amount of knowledge and skill required for their jobs – that is, they have pointed to the socially constructed nature of skill. In Phillips and Taylor's words, 'skill is often an ideological category imposed on certain types of work by virtue of the sex and power of the workers who perform it' (1980, p. 79). Feminists also worry that the social and political processes of job redesign will not only lead to specific job losses for women, but will also lead to women's exclusion from 'technical knowledge and know-how' (Knights and Willmott, 1986). They fear that the new technologies will be masculinised. Women will be locked into low-skill jobs with no opportunity for either job enrichment or vertical career mobility. These concerns have led to impassioned calls for the transformation of pre-adult female socialisation to counter trends to steer girls away from science and technology and for training initiatives for women (Gaskel and MacLaren, 1987).

Male managers often bristle at the thought that the organisations they preside over are, in fact, patriarchally constituted. Labelling an organisation as patriarchal (or racist), while provocative, focuses attention on the mechanisms that reproduce the gender and race systems within the organisation. In her important article, 'Hierarchies, jobs and bodies: a theory of gendered organisations' (1991), Jane Acker states, that,

> Abstract jobs and hierarchies, common concepts in organizational thinking, assume a disembodied worker and universal worker. This worker is actually a man; men's bodies, sexuality, and relationships to

> procreation and paid work are subsumed in the image of the worker. Images of men's bodies and masculinity pervade organizational processes, marginalizing women and contributing to the maintenance of gender segregation in organizations. (p. 53)

Filtering organisational life through their perceptions, men easily think that their experience is the norm. All sorts of unquestioned assumptions creep into the male managerial outlook. By nature, they ought to lead. By nature of their roles as men, they ought to be paid more highly. By nature, their jobs are inherently more knowledge- and skill-demanding. The organisational maps and memories so prized by organisational learning theorists are often, in fact, male versions of organisational history and struggles. The organisation takes its shape over time around the needs of men's bodies, centred on a 'full-time, life-long job, while his wife or another woman takes care of his personal needs and his children' (p. 63). Women's needs and life trajectories are not inscribed in the organisation's way of operating. Discussing obstacles to transforming companies into learning organisations, Abrahamsson (2001) observes that gender-related organisation patterns must be rendered visible. She identifies four patterns: (1) segregation of the sexes within companies; (2) myths of women's and men's work; (3) gender labelling; and (4) stereo-typical ideas of gender specific attributes. One can easily see a similar pattern for race-related patterns (racial segregation, and so on).

Each of these patterns reproduces the unequal distribution of learning opportunities within the organisation. Women and black or Asian people are rendered inferior by isolating them spatially, within society and within organisations. Baldry et al., in their article, 'Bright satanic offices' (1998), argue that,

> When women first entered offices . . . [they] were located in separate rooms, often entering by a different door from the men and working different hours (Crompton and Jones 1984). The reason for this gender apartheid, while justified [at the time] in terms of decorum and the maintenance of seemly behaviour, was actually so that women would not be able to see and envy the more interesting work of the men (Dohrn, 1988) and, in this, the use of space must be seen as an instrument of managerial control. (p. 165)

Thus, as Acker reminds us, 'Gender enters the picture through organizational roles that carry characteristic images of the kinds of people that should occupy them.' Gendered and racialised perceptions

119

prompt our expectations that the person occupying the CEO's position ought be of a certain race or gender. In some societies – Jamaica is a good example – the social structures are so racialised, that one has to be the right shade of brown to 'get the job.' Black at the bottom, white at the top. This is the way it was centuries ago, this is the way it is today in the tourist industries, in the cane fields, in the gouged-out bauxite hills.

The myth that women (or black or Asian people) are suited uniquely for certain kinds of work is deeply anchored in the Western mentality. The bitter experience of aboriginal people in Canada attests to this fact. Their schooling in the gruelling nineteenth century was designed to fit them for menial agricultural and industrial labour. African-Canadians and African-Americans have not forgotten how they were perceived and treated and mis-educated through the centuries. They were segregated into certain spaces and work locations. All of this was made possible because of the white colonisers' beliefs that this was what they were only capable of. The sexual segregation of labour is also a powerful mechanism for ensuring that the potential of women to learn, grow, and gain mastery over their life situations – in work and elsewhere – is either thwarted or slowed down. Women are still segregated into certain occupations (they are channelled into the so-called 'caring' occupations). However, because these occupations end up being extensions of women's domestic work (childcare and lifeworld management), which our society does not value highly, women end up doing invaluable work for little pay (Hart, 1995). Graham Lowe argues that '[w]orkplace structures and policies tend to favour those already in good jobs. Training patterns are consistent with this tendency: workers who receive employer-sponsored training have higher incomes and formal education than those who do not' (2000, p. 88). Women's location in lesser status spaces in the organisation cuts them out from learning opportunities. The gender hierarchy is maintained by men because it suits them nicely! They will not give up this power easily.

N.T., a navigator with the Canadian Armed Forces, relates the story of working in a non-traditional role (95 per cent of her co-workers were men). During her training and socialisation into the organisational culture, she had been unconsciously socialised to think that women's interpretations were wrong because it deviated from the accepted norms of the 'malestream.' She recalls one event in particular on a course occurring in the early 1990s. She was watching a video with male colleagues about the effects of cold water and temperature on an exposed person.

The demonstration was conducted using an actual woman in a bikini. Two women objected, but she was embarrassed to admit that she thought they were overreacting; it was just a video, after all. Later, she concluded that this everyday act reinforced society's unjust belief that women are objects and should not be shown the same respect as men (N.T., 2002).

Albert Mills (1988), a critical management theorist, argues that women had considerable difficulty being accepted in organisations. Drawing on available research, he notes that researchers like Dubeck (1979) have identified men's dominance of formal networks as an 'important causal factor. Such networks, she argues, function on a basis of trust rooted in assumptions of shared characteristics between key actors. The more unlike those actors an outsider appears to be, the more likely they will remain an outsider. Thus, in a male circle of management, a female has an immediate handicap' (p. 365). Analogously, if the male circle is white European, the African-Canadian, East Indian Sikh or James Bay Cree is outside their circle of comfort (the reverse situation could also be true, but it is much rarer). As many feminists have insisted upon – right across the theoretical spectrum – women are pressed to become 'social males' (the corridor talk in male circles is rough on these women) to make it in the company. Women and black or Asian people may also be excluded because they do not fit into the informal organisational culture. If management approves, even tacitly, of all male work and playgroups (with its attendant talk and horseplay), women are excluded from the '"body talk" of sex and sports' (Acker, 1991, p. 67). Analogously, if the organisational culture takes its flavour from Anglo-Canadian cultural mores and practices, even the styles of dress, of laughter and joke-telling, of celebration, of interacting, of speech, of eating, or singing may be in serious conflict with non-Anglo cultures. Aboriginals speak of becoming 'apples' (white on the inside and red on the outside).

Feminist scholarship reveals the subtlety of mechanisms for reproducing patriarchal institutions. Following Martha Nussbaum, Joyce Stalker (1998) argues that, 'Satire is a particularly effective tool of repression, since it allows its authors to separate from an emotional bond with women and yet express anger, violence or patronage.' Seemingly harmless jokes 'express sentiments of disrespect, dismissal and distrust. They are a canny way to limit, demean and stifle women's power' (pp. 247–8). Those with power assume the privilege of telling jokes that delimit those with lesser power's place beneath them. Men tell jokes that demean women. Whites tell jokes that demean aboriginal people. When women or black or Asian people object, they are accused of lacking a sense of humour. If the joke is masking some serious issue, as they can, then critical reflection is deflected or swept into the dirty corridors.

Abrahamsson's study of the effects of organisational changes in pulp and paper, electronic, food, and laundry industries posed the question of whether the attempt to introduce flat integrated organisational models in these organisations meant better possibilities for women workers. She wanted to know whether there would be learning for everybody and what the obstacles to learning might actually be. She observes that promoters of organisational change had high ambitions and held optimistic perspectives. They wanted '[l]ess bureaucracy, faster decision processes, and a group-based flow organisation thought to enable companies to react more quickly to the demands of the surrounding world.' They imagined that these organisational changes would offer 'working assignments with possibilities to learn and develop – both for women and men' (2001, p. 106). They also thought that these flat, open, boundaryless organisations would be better for women (providing them greater possibilities for gender equality). In its purest form, an integrated working model meant that the sexes would be mixed.

However, as we have already learned, there is often a gap between practices in the organisation and management discourse (Milkman, 1998; Thompson and Warhurst, 1998). Abrahamsson discovered that each of the companies studied ran into difficulties implementing the new organisational models. Her key concept is that of the 'restoring mechanism or action.' By this she means actions, either strategic or unconscious, that bring the organisation back into its previous form after an organisational change has been attempted. Sometimes the restorative action is obvious: appealing the position of 'foremen' to flatten the organisation, then, after a short period, reintroducing the position. Restorative actions can also, ironically, renew or even strengthen the segregation of work tasks. She doesn't think that every change is met by restorative actions. New patterns do appear. But some of the resistance is more inertial, actions that moderate the effects of organisational change.

Abrahamsson thinks that if the gender order is ignored, these very conditions will fuel restoration. In all of her companies, she found that work tasks were apportioned according to their 'female' or 'male' quality.

Most of the women performed typically female work tasks – often including repetitive, lower paid manual sub-operations. The intention of the new organisational changes was that men and women should share work tasks equally in some form of job rotation as well as working on the same teams. Some improvements in women's working conditions did occur. But she found that it was 'very difficult to mix women and men in the same groups and it was particularly difficult to bring them to perform each other's work tasks' (p. 108). Moreover, Abrahamsson discovered that if women worked in gender-mixed environments, they fared better than those with patterns of gender segregation.

Management also perceived women through gendered lenses. When conflicts arose or when employing new workers, management gave preference to men: 'it was easier with men' (i.e. male machine operators). Women were not viewed as familiar with the technical and mechanical aspects of the job. Even women, having internalised this perception, believed it was easier to get male operators to do repair work. Women refused to carry out adjustments or repairs. 'This', argues Abrahamsson, 'in spite of the fact that, in my opinion, they possessed good knowledge of different causal connections for different interruptions in production, and worked every day with technically advanced machines' (p. 109). This paradoxical situation had allies. One work manager of a laundry praised women for their adaptability, flexibility, mental strength and well-prepared suggestions. Despite this, he would pick only men for certain special tasks. All the salary increases went to certain men, and all his confidants were men. Managers left female machine operators to their fate, even though there was no intrinsic value in women doing 'technical' work. Here, Abrahamsson notes, there is a risk of women forming a 'B' team outside the new organisation.

She thinks that 'gender marking, gender segregation and gender hierarchical processing made it easy for people to re-create the old gender patterns in the new organisation' (p. 109). But one pattern became particularly evident. If the gender marking and gender segregation were strong and extensive at the outset, the more were the 'instances of restoration and the difficulties in introducing organisational change' (p. 109). These companies had trouble making sense of and managing gender-related problems. The trouble was enacted through the choice of methods of change. The more women at the workplace, the less democratic the methods. Managers used drastic methods and various forms of compulsion to establish work teams and job rotation. In male-dominated companies, instances of restoration decreased. Old models and hierarchies sneaked into the new projects little by little. Male workers held the most 'prestigious positions together with foremen, middle management and white-collar workers/specialists who took part in the project groups' (p. 110). In one electronic company, where the production force was used to change and gender mixed, with an organisational culture that treated men and women equally, the substance of the organisational change was greater than in other companies.

From the vantage point of the just learning society paradigm, Abrahamsson's conclusion that restorations also provide 'concrete obstacles to learning, both individual learning and organisational learning' (p. 110) is very important. She focuses on two aspects of this inhibiting process. Provocatively, she argues that if horizontal integration (job rotation) and vertical integration (de-hierarchisation and job enrichment) cannot be realised, then it will be very difficult to achieve a learning organisation. Unless the design of the work itself carries potential for knowledge and skill growth, an authentic learning organisation cannot be realised. In five of the eight companies Abrahamsson studied, companies tried to integrate different types of functions – technical functions, quality control and stores. In those companies where men were in the majority, after a time, the organisation 'often returned to the original structure with special divisions precisely for the technical function, quality control and stores' (p. 110). Why did this problem occur when managers wanted women and men to participate in the same job rotation? At one of the pulp and paper companies, women and men were to work at the same machines. But men refused to do 'women's work.' Conflicts arose and integrated maintenance, job rotation and learning crashed to the floor.

The attempt to create a flatter and more decentralised organisation is a salient part of designing a just learning organisation. One positive feature, Abrahamsson's research reveals, is that the new organisational structures vertically integrated work tasks. In all of the companies she studied, some of the foremen's former duties were re-assigned to workers. 'Five of the eight companies introduced a "co-ordinator", a blue-collar worker and member of the working team, who acted at the same time as a working foreman. At the same time the traditional position of foreman was removed. Many of the women, as well as the men, who were working in production obtained the opportunity to serve as co-ordinators' (p.

111). Workers appear to have had mixed feelings. One the one hand, they liked the idea of vertical integration. On the other hand, these new organisations did not mean that 'women acquired any better work or more power. Most of the women did not feel any work-enrichment, nor were they given any new work tasks. In one of the pulp and paper companies the coordinators said that they felt like "messenger-girls" or "mother-figures" that had to tidy up and put things in order' (p. 111). Oddly, these were the work tasks previously shared by all members of the work team. When women took over tasks associated with the foreman, but now without the support enjoyed from the position, men often found it very hard to take orders from a woman. So they chose to run around the foreman to the work manager (a man). In all the studied companies, former male foremen received qualified tasks and higher salaries, retaining their position in the hierarchy. Female foremen, in contrast, often reverted to production work. Sometimes, women working in production showed initiative in organisational projects. They seized opportunities within the new coordinator systems. But even in the laundry, the coordinator system was dropped after two years. The foreman – with only men doing this work – was reintroduced.

The hard-headed sociological research of Catherine Hakim (*Work-Lifestyle Choices in the 21st Century: Preference Theory* (2000)) contradicts Sweden's carefully cultivated image as a leading gender equity nation. Hakim's review of the empirical evidence indicates that OECD countries have significantly lower levels of occupational segregation than Sweden. Despite social engineering initiatives aimed at encouraging women to combine family work with paid work outside the home, half of Nordic women are in female-oriented occupations compared to one-quarter of women workers in other industrialised countries. Men continue to dominate at the upper levels of professional and managerial positions. Nor have the Swedes achieved sexual equality within the family. Despite generous provision for paternal leave, 50 per cent of all fathers refused to take any leave whatsoever. Like many other men, Swedish men were not prepared to care for small babies. One possible explanation for the subversion of attempts to introduce horizontal changes in organisations lies with the cultural attitudes of Swedish men and women. Seventy-seven per cent of Swedish men, and 57 per cent of women, believe that the father is the primary income earner. Both sexes may endorse egalitarian values, but these values are not enacted in either the family or workplaces.

Abrahamsson's work is sobering. At the 'studied companies gender segregating and stereotype gender coding of work places and work tasks were strong restoring mechanisms and obstacles for strategic organisational changes and also obstacles for organisational learning. My study shows that restoration responses in the work organisations brought the organisation back to its original form and function' (p. 112). It is as if these gender-restoring mechanisms operate powerfully underneath the surface rhetoric of democratic organisational change. Ironically, the attempts at job rotation and integration brought to the surface from the deep more clarity as to the patriarchal structuring of the relationship between gender and work task and function. The organisational change enabled men to learn how to maintain their privileged positions. In the end, Abrahamsson concludes that, 'The learning organisation, with its focus on integration and decentralisation, challenges the gender order, which is a strong system built on segregation and hierarchy. Knowledge of the factors and power structures that restore the old patterns is necessary when working with organisational development' (p. 112).

Thus, Hakim's urgent call for sociologists of the workplace to go 'beyond sex and gender' seems too hasty. Her preference theory suggests that we move away from the old structural analyses to look at the social roles that men and women 'prefer and adopt for their own lives' (p. 280). Indeed, her typology of women workers – work-centred, adaptive and home-centred – appropriately tries to understand the complexity of women and men's lives as they make their choices about who should work and how children fit into the overall picture. But preference theory can easily fall prey to imagining that patriarchal and class-based power belong to an earlier, now superseded, post-traditional world. Abrahamsson's case studies indicate that gender coding is still operative within these Swedish workplaces.

CHAPTER SIX

Ethics and empowerment in business organisations

Formulating the question

The notion of empowerment is dear to adult educators. In fact, along with civil society, it seems to have been the award-winning, celebrity word of the 1980s and 1990s. Years ago, I recall even seeing the wonder word on the back of a box of Kellogg's corn flakes. This was rather shocking for one with sympathies for marginalised and oppressed peoples of the world who were struggling to gain some control over their lives. Those of us nurtured on a diet of Paulo Freire and popular education were surprised to discover that the concept was used extensively by 'theorists to explain organizational effectiveness' (Conger and Kanungo, 1988, p. 471). The sacred grove had been invaded and ransacked. Wasn't it outcast socialists who advocated workers' right to democratically control their companies well over 100 years ago?

Yet we are aware of the 'perverse ways in which signs, representations, and language confuse rather than clarify an always elusive reality' (Harvey, 2000, p. 10). The sign – empowerment – does not appear to signify a stable, coherent reality. It can mean many different things to many different thinkers and actors in the world. What does it mean when management claims that it is going to empower its employees? What does it mean when a community organisation claims that its goal is to empower African-Canadians in their fight against city hall? How would empowerment advocates know that their projects have empowered others? How do those who are allegedly empowered know they are? Does the idea of empowerment hold different possibilities in business and civil society organisations? It is important that we clear up conceptual muddiness and confusion. It is crucial that we try to calibrate the forms and degrees of empowerment in business organisations. The conceptual arsenal necessary for the task must be capable of slicing through the murk of the lovely rhetoric of empowerment – which promises much that is good – as well as identifying the potential for increasing the efficacy of men and women who live out their lives in organisations producing goods and services.

At issue, then, is the ethical question of how much say and influence ought the members of a business organisation actually have in the running of its overall affairs? In this chapter, while the principles and matters discussed are pertinent to the idea of the empowered citizen, the focus is mainly on empowerment within business organisations. This chapter reviews literature that helps us think about power and empowerment, the divergence between empowerment rhetoric and reality in most organisations. I also consider whether the language and practices of empowerment in business organisations contain emancipatory potential.

Empowerment: Basic conceptual challenges

The *Concise Oxford Dictionary* (1990) defines empowerment as a transitive verb meaning to 'give power to.' To understand fully what this process signifies, we must first explicate the word power, itself a contested and confusing concept. How power is produced determines how powerlessness is understood, and empowerment advocacy strategies will tend to focus on the identified dimension of power. The just learning society paradigm (informed by various streams of critical social science) requires a sophisticated way of understanding how, in the face of determined opposition from those in power, those who are enlightened can stop power from wreaking havoc and mayhem in human and natural affairs. This certainly is not an easy question to grapple with. We know that the self-understanding, or consent, of people provides power with legitimacy. In the long run, power cannot do its work without the agreement of the governed. In the short term, power (whether in the form of dictatorships or liberal plutocracies) can proceed against the will of the majority of its people.

At its most elemental, power over others can be exercised through force (including coercion and manipulation) or, with others, through the voluntary consent of the governed. In the latter case, the assumption is that 'consensus has been arrived at without compulsion' (Habermas, 1990, p. 174). The power with/power over distinction was first articulated by Mary Follett in 1925. 'Power is capacity', she wrote, and 'power-with is a jointly developed power' (p. 115). Her core idea was picked up by Dorothy Emmett in 1953, who confronted the thinkers of her day who reduced power to coercion. This distinction between power with and power over would subsequently influence feminist discourse in the 1970s to the present.

For Habermas, the 'consensus-building force of communication arrived at agreement is an end in itself and cannot be instrumentalized for other purposes' (1990, p. 174). But we must understand that power can be enacted instrumentally, and must be separated conceptually from communicative power. In both types, power arises out of interaction. 'Power', as Brian Fay observes, 'must be dyadic' (1987, p. 120). By dyadic, Fay means that human activities are rule-governed. The exercise of power presupposes a normative and institutional context. A schoolteacher's exercise of power over a child (the teacher can get the children to do this or that activity) presupposes historical and institutional processes and procedures that create the context for school activities. Thus, Fay's definitions must be set within the interpretive school of social science that assumes that all human activity is mediated through language. Both the children and the teacher exercise power as capacity to act within particular social settings.

In his award-winning book, *Power and Powerlessness: Quiescence and Rebellion in an Appalachian Valley* (1980), and subsequent important texts on the politics of participation (Gaventa and Jones, c.2002), John Gaventa (following Lukes (1974)) argues that power has three dimensions. In the first, the liberal pluralist face, power is understood as a product of which interest group wins and which loses on salient, clearly recognisable issues. The political system is assumed to be relatively open to all participants. Powerlessness comes primarily from individual choice. Inaction reflects the relative contentment of the citizenry (or workers if we shift to the business site) with the status quo. Their lack of participation comes from their lack of resources to compete effectively. Within this model, empowerment (and related advocacy strategies) depends on professional policy leadership and expert advocacy on behalf of less powerful citizens. Focusing on narrow and winnable issues, they attempt to set, formulate and enact agendas (or repeal policies) that serve the interests of their clients. They play the game by the rules of the current system and do not question how the elites came to be the leaders of the game.

The second dimension of power focuses on which groups sit at the table and which issues or grievances are recognised. Unlike the liberal pluralist model, attention is shifted to systematic or structural barriers that keep certain groups and issues from the table. The empowerment strategy of the 'citizen action approach' attempts to enlighten people in community. Professional organisers build local leadership through educational strategies that galvanise grassroots and challenge structures. Powerful grassroots organisations struggle to gain clout and access. They want to get issues/policies to the table for action and enforcement. They play the game knowing that it has been rigged in favour of elites.

The third face of power, perhaps the most interesting, focuses on the insidious way power holders shape consciousness and awareness of issues through processes of socialisation, secrecy, information control, and so on. Powerlessness comes mainly from the governed's lack of awareness, critical consciousness and information. Oppression is internalised, the coloniser resides within the colonised, people blame themselves. The enlightenment process is particularly pertinent to the critical model of empowerment. Education must develop political awareness, confidence and a sense of rights. It must identify urgent issues that challenge structures. The collective agent attempting to transform structures must develop considerable group clout and accountability. Indigenous knowledge and leadership must be mobilised. In the third dimension, the means by which A affects B moves significantly beyond those permitted in the first two approaches. A affects B's 'conceptions of the issues altogether.' Thus, there may not be any observable conflict. But real contradiction exists between the interests of those exercising power and the real interests of those they exclude. Those playing the game may not even know that the game is rigged and the gambling table cunningly designed to the opponent's advantage.

In sum, the one-dimensional mode of power emphasises observable conflicts, and addresses who prevails in bargaining over the resolution of key issues. The second dimension focuses on the mobilisation of bias: how the powerless are kept that way through mechanisms ensuring non-decisions. The third dimension of power examines the 'means through which power influences, shapes or determines conceptions of the necessities, possibilities and strategies of challenging in situations of latent conflict' (Gaventa, 1980, pp. 12–15; 2003). Third-dimension scholars turn their attention to the way social myths, language, and symbols are shaped or manipulated in power processes.

The concept of empowerment in organisational theory

By the 1980s empowerment was a very popular concept influencing the actions of all sorts of powerful companies. Everywhere corporations – from Kodak to Wal-Mart to Kentucky Fried Chicken – were implementing employee empowerment programmes. Books extolling empowerment were selling millions of copies in a general atmosphere of corporate doubt and fear. Many fine ideas – freedom, dignity, and self-governance – swept into corporate boardrooms and on to factory floors. Yet the concept has remained enigmatic, with definitions and understandings pounded out on different forges (participatory management supporters, Total Quality Management (TQM), corporate culture theorists, organisational learning advocates, organisational development proponents and a stray socialist or two).

Corporate management's appropriation of the language of empowerment is intriguing. As a critical social learning theorist and historian of industrial societies, I have been continually amazed at how difficult it has been over the last 150 years for working people to gain control over or have security in their workplaces. In particularly heightened moments of history such as the end of World War I, the socialist left struggled for 'workers' control' of the means of production (Hunnius, Garson and Case, 1973). In Turin in 1919, for example, the Italian revolutionary Antonio Gramsci helped the workers form themselves into workers' councils. Gramsci believed that the workers could become aware of their own potentialities and abilities through the collective organisation of the productive and administrative apparatus. Mental and manual work would be united in the councils. Within the factories, labour schools would help the workers acquire new technical skills. Schools of culture in the evenings would help the workers make sense of their self-activity towards building a new social order. In the end, the army did not support the workers. Corrupt union men undermined the initiative of the workers' council (Welton, 1982). Industry's captains and ruling political and cultural elites could not tolerate workers controlling production. Contemporary managerial initiatives to empower workers seem tame to those who know that whenever self-directed workers try to gain more governing power in their workplaces, there has been bloodshed, beatings, baseball bats cracking skulls, even tanks in the streets.

In *The Business of Employee Empowerment* (1999), Thomas Potterfield argues that a critical examination of employee empowerment rhetoric and practices is necessary because of its widespread use by powerful companies, the enigmatic nature of the concept and its controversial ideological nature. Potterfield discovers the antecedents of empowerment in business management and organisational studies in the 1950s and 1960s in the works of Argyris (1957), McGregor (1960) and Likert (1961). But their call for expanded responsibility for workers and more democratic work environments went unheeded. If these ideas were so scintillating, why didn't corporate managers embrace them when first raised? Why are they resurfacing today? During the golden age of capitalism from 1945–1973, Potterfield contends, capitalist organisations were preoccupied with instrumental means to accomplish present goals. The pursuit of profit meant that there were no clear-cut, instrumental reasons for making the kinds of changes advocated by Argyris, Likert and McGregor. With the oil crisis of the early 1970s, US economic dominance began to be undermined. Global competition heated up considerably. So did the desperation of corporate managers to find ways of mobilising their employees' potential. Empowerment was the saviour of the hour.

Before the word empowerment became management's pet, the concept was widely discussed in civil society organisations. Potterfield surmises that Barbara Solomon was the first to introduce the term empowerment into social reform discourse in her 1976 text, *Black Empowerment.* Gaventa does not use the term in *Power and Powerlessness* (1980). Rappaport, Swift and Hess's *Studies in Empowerment: Steps Toward Understanding and Action* appeared only in 1987. Certainly the civil rights and feminist movements were articulating ideas, individually and together, that men and women could improve their personal, social, economic, and political fortunes, before they used this particular word. Indeed, empowerment ideas and beliefs can be located within a broad range of social and intellectual movements over the last three centuries. The key idea that breaks into Western history is the notion that men and women do not have to accept their situations fatalistically. They can use their rational and imaginative powers to understand why they are kept down. They can release their own personal and collective energies to change their circumstances.

One of Canada's leading philosophers of adult education, Moses Coady, never used the word in his voluminous writings or speeches from the 1930s to the 1950s. But the idea burns brightly in his works. He argued that the Antigonish Movement would 'enable the forgotten common people to educate themselves to the point where they can so manipulate the forces of society that they are their own masters – free men not serfs' (Welton, 2001, p. 140). This statement pulses with power imagery. Another of Canada's eminent philosophers of adult education, Watson Thomson, proclaimed the message of 'Power to the people' in his writings and lectures in Saskatchewan in the early 1940s (Welton, 1986a). In fact, one can readily argue that the Canadian adult education movement throughout the twentieth century has been animated by an empowerment model. It was only in the 1970s, though, that this ambiguous concept appeared as a sign.

The notion of empowerment appears to have jumped its tracks. Its deepest meanings lie with the agonies and struggles of the stigmatised, the small folks, the marginalised and oppressed. Transposed to the business management domain, the term signifies practices whereby 'corporate leaders choose to give more decision-making power to lower-level employees' (p. 45). Potterfield observes that, 'Interestingly, advocates of empowerment within business and organizational settings do not acknowledge being influenced in any way by the use of empowerment-related themes and ideas by the social activists and reformers of the 1960s and 1970s' (pp. 38–9). This historical development is fascinating. Now, it seems, reform impulses are being carried into the organisational domain by the very agents the workers have fought against for many centuries. Clearly, we need to settle down and clarify what recent scholarship thinks of this concept.

Conger and Kanungo wrote a seminal article ('The empowerment process: integrating theory and practice') based on the presupposition that our 'understanding of the construct is limited and often confusing' (1988, p. 471). The authors inform us that 'control and power' are used in two different ways in the literature. In the first, empowerment is a relational construct: power here is a 'function of the dependence and/or interdependence of actors' (p. 472). The bases of power have been identified as (a) legal; (b) coercive; (c) remunerative; (d) normative; and (e) knowledge/expertise. This focus on sources of power has led to the development of strategies and tactics of resource allocation for increasing the power of less powerful parties and reducing the power of the more powerful one. Thus, in terms of a relational dynamic, empowerment becomes the 'process by which a leader or manager shares his or her power with subordinates' (p. 473). A chooses to empower B: to delegate specified decisions and responsibilities. In the management literature, most of the emphasis is on 'participative management techniques such as management by objectives, quality circles, and goal setting by subordinates as the means of sharing power or delegating authority' (p. 473; see Schied *et al.*, 1998). However, this relational understanding may not address how empowerment is actually experienced by subordinates.

The second way of understanding empowerment is as a motivational construct. In the psychological literature, power and control are used as motivational and/or expectancy belief-states that are internal to individuals. Some psychologists (and adult education theorists) assume that individuals have an innate need for control over life situations. People have power when they believe they can cope adequately with events, situations, and/or the people they confront. Power needs are frustrated when they feel powerless or when they believe that they are unable to cope with the physical and social demands of the environment. Do we have an intrinsic need for self-determination? The well-known adult learning theory of Malcolm Knowles (1980) assumes that we do; the andragogical model builds upon this psychological assumption. Within this construct, power is less delegation of authority and resource sharing, but more enabling – motivating through enhancing personal efficacy. Conger and Kanungo suggest that management theorists prefer the first meaning, delegation, because the ones doing the delegating hold real power. In contrast, 'enabling implies creating conditions for heightening motivation for task accomplishment through the development of a strong sense of personal efficacy' (1988, p. 474). Thus, empowerment is 'defined here as a process of enhancing feelings of self-efficacy among organizational members through the identification of conditions that foster powerlessness and through their removal by both formal organizational practices and informal techniques of providing efficacy information' (p. 474).

Critical learning theory must not lose sight of the notion of personal efficacy. But, simultaneously, management will always prefer, I believe, a psychological perspective on empowerment. They desire that their employees feel efficacious regarding their role performance and find personal meaning in their work tasks without tampering too much with the organisation's goals and procedures. But examining personal feelings of efficacy in the abstract provides little insight into the existing patterns of participation in the state or in economic life. It is not feelings that determine participation. People must not only feel competent to participate. They need the requisite structures to make it worthwhile. Optimistic managerial proclamations about creating the powerful self – the 'power to get up and go, to pull ourselves up by the bootstraps, or to persevere in difficult circumstances' (Townley, 1994, p. 9) – are mostly delusionary.

Conger and Kanungo believe that the structural conditions that foster subordinates' sense of powerlessness must be identified. Once identified, empowerment strategies and tactics can be designed to remove them. They conceive of the empowerment process in five stages that include the 'psychological state of empowering experience, its antecedent conditions, and its behavioral consequences' (1998, p. 474). In the first stage, structural conditions (organisational factors, supervision, reward system, nature of job) are scrutinised to ascertain which conditions lead to a psychological state of powerlessness. The second stage points to the managerial strategies and techniques that create the pedagogical forms for the realisation of empowerment (participative management, goal setting, feedback system, modelling, contingent/ competence-based reward, job enrichment). Stage three assumes that subordinates need to receive 'self-efficacy information.' This can be facilitated through enactive attainment, vicarious experience, verbal persuasion, and emotional arousal. Stage three is the crucial moment: reception of self-efficacy information is tied to the removal of the conditions listed under stage one. Stage four focuses on the results, that is, the strengthening of effort–performance expectancy or belief in personal efficacy. The final stage examines the initiation/persistence of new behaviour task objectives. Social psychologists like Bandura (1977) argue that the 'strength of peoples' convictions in their own effectiveness is likely to affect whether they would even try to cope with given situations . . .' (p. 193).

Conger and Kanungo have constructed a dialectical model that assumes that internal psychological states (and the action consequences) are shaped by external conditions. They do not think that self-efficacy is independent of the organisational context. Without the transformation of the self (the state of 'learned helplessness' is not compatible with the just learning organisation), changing various dimensions of the organisation will not result in an empowered organisation. In fact, they argue that 'specific contextual factors contribute to the lowering of self-efficacy or personal power among organizational members' (1998, p. 476). Conger and Kanungo claim that the principal contextual factors contributing to lowered self-efficacy beliefs are (a) organisational; (b) supervisory style; (c) reward systems; and (d) job design. They think that events inducing 'significant alterations in organizational structures, communication links, power and authority relations, and the organization's goals, strategies, and tactics' unsettle and disorient workers' sense of control and competence (p. 477). In the end, Conger and Kanungo present us a critical humanist vision of the self-efficacious individual who is enabled to be such by leadership or supervisory practices that design the procedures that foster this deep sense of personal and collective mastery. What is missing from their normative model is a serious confrontation with power, interest and greed in organisational life.

Conger and Kanungo open the way for a more subtle analysis of the types, degrees and agents of power. Frederick Bird, author of *The Muted Conscience* (1996), is part of a network of international scholars probing the meanings of ethics in business life. In his contribution to the important text, *Ethics and Empowerment* (1999), Bird searches for a just form of empowerment fitting for workers and their organisations. To probe this question, he constructs a typology that enables us to calibrate the types and degrees of power in the workplace. Most discussions of empowerment leave one with the impression that empowerment is a kind of zero-sum game: either you are or you aren't empowered. Bird's analysis of the different forms of power provides proponents of the just learning organisation with a way of breaking with an all-or-nothing approach to organisational transformation.

His first form of power assumes that all persons have acquired a repertoire of know-how and skills. When they enter the workplace, they want opportunities to use their unique know-how and personality characteristics such as wit, charm, strength. Task powers are different from personal powers. This second type is linked to persons' abilities and opportunities to influence and shape the character, scope, conditions and pace of work. This is the much talked about realm of job enlargement and job enrichment. The third type, contractual powers, refers to the 'capacity of workers to determine the basic conditions that affect the status of their employment' (p. 47). The historic struggle of the trade union movement has sought to establish contractual relations free from coercive or manipulative forces. That this struggle is far from over is attested to by the virulent opposition to trade unions manifested by mega-corporations like Wal-Mart (Olsson, 2003; Cusac, 2003).

Through this optic, empowerment advocates can determine precisely whether workers have some say in the 'terms of contract', whether they are able to freely choose or reject these terms, whether they can bargain for changes and have complaints heard. The fourth type of power, adjudicatory power, focuses on a worker's 'capacity to raise complaints and to defend oneself against complaints made by others' (Bird, 1999, p. 47). The final type of power has most at stake – governance power. Who has the power to 'establish policies, to develop organizational strategies, to set budgets, to apportion resources among units and functions within organizations and to appoint administrators to direct organizations' (p. 48)? Bird's typology of power challenges one to consider the interrelation amongst the different forms of power. What is the relationship between having task power without governance power? Does the absence of contractual power undermine personal senses of efficacy and well-being? Is it really possible to have authentic empowerment if employees have no governance power? What are the appropriate ethical considerations regarding who ought to have a say in the governing of the corporation? Boards of directors and shareholders only? Can we talk of governance without raising pointed questions about ownership of the means of production?

Bird thinks that writers are 'notoriously vague about the degrees or extent of power they have in mind.' To this end he proposes a scheme to calibrate different degrees of power in order to provide benchmarks for determining if particular objectives have been realised. A vague statement like, 'our employees have been empowered by our new managerial schemes', Bird would proffer, requires a differentiated understanding of both the form of power they have newly acquired as well as their actual capacity to 'realise valued objectives even in the face of possible resistance' (p. 50). Within his scheme, employees can have six degrees of power. First, employees may have a scant degree of power. They are unable to exert any appreciable influence in realising their objectives. One need only think of an illegal worker who crosses the border of his or her own country to take up dirty, low-paying work in a chicken processing factory. They have low wages, no benefits, and live in dilapidated housing. They dare not say a word about their working conditions. Secondly, workers may have a marginal degree of power, able to exercise only a modest, but not decisive, influence in realising their objectives. With the third, consultative power, employees are able to partially realise their objectives. When workers attain co-determinative power, they have the capacity to significantly shape outcomes. In many liberal-progressive sectors of the European trade union movement, trade unions have succeeded in gaining positions on policy making councils. Bird thinks that his fifth degree of power, effective power, differs from the fourth in that, with effective power, workers have the capacity to determine outcomes. The final degree of power is total. Here, a collectivity realises its objectives without having to consider any effective opposition or resistance (1999, pp. 50–3).

Bird studied several different empowerment programmes (including a plywood co-op and a programme management initiative at a university hospital) to test his typology of power. His observations are incisive and illuminating. For example, one of his propositions is that increases in one form of power do not necessarily occasion or produce increases in other forms of power. Workers in the plywood producer co-op had effective governance, but not much task power. This observation pinpoints one of the fundamental contradictions within co-operative forms of organisation. They claim that they are radically democratic through collective ownership, yet may not allow any redesign of the jobs themselves. In fact, Bird observes that in 'no case were workers able to radically redesign the jobs . . .' (p. 72). However, they did increase task powers, in 'varying degrees' gaining a 'sense of ownership over the jobs they performed' (p. 73). They also increased personal powers (courses on interpersonal skills helped). But in none of the cases did workers increase any adjudicatory powers. Little attention was paid to 'issues related to the rights and prerogatives of workers with respect to the handling of disputes, complaints and grievances' (p. 74). Further, only in modest ways did any of these empowerment programmes 'extend or strengthen the contractual powers of workers' (p. 74). Bird notes that workers at several sites increased their governance powers. At the Plywood co-op, which was worker-owned, the employees governed their own plants through annual meetings and elected boards. But their governance powers did not 'translate into any significantly greater task, personal or contractual powers' (p. 76).

Empowerment in action

Potterfield studied Farbrook Technology (FT), a pseudonym for a Fortune 100 corporation, to ascertain Farbrook employees' understanding of the goals of the empowered work environment. He discovered that, while senior executives spoke of the 'need for responsible freedom', they actually meant that 'employees should be free to make decisions within limits that are clearly defined by senior management' (1999, p. 80). Management set the overall goals and objectives and determined how money would be expended. FT's empowered workplace only permitted employees to have more say in how (the means) they might achieve predetermined goals. They could not decide what those goals would be. Directives cascaded downward with management setting boundaries at the top. Those further down the ladder, like the manager of engineering, complained that 'cost management measures are taken out of our hands' (p. 83). Most of the employees thought that 'being empowered' was 'largely a function of the individual employee's personal attributes and characteristics' (p. 85). They had bought into the psychological perspective on empowerment. Yet their suggestions did press beyond the ideology of individual efficacy. Employees wanted to have a broader perspective on business. They were critical of their company's feedback mechanisms and didn't think that FT had a systematic procedure for rewarding employees. They wanted senior management to allow more decisions pertaining to spending and hiring at the local levels.

In his reflections on the FT interviews, Potterfield believes that some attempts were made to 'flatten the organization and to extend some additional decision-making authority to lower-level employees.' But FT was hesitant to 'share information and rewards with lower-level employees.' FT made no effort to nurture the participation of lower-level employees in the 'formation of an overall corporate vision' (p. 97). Rather, they preferred that senior management develop the vision and cascade it down to the broad base of their employees. Also, the company failed to initiate pedagogical processes to 'help employees cope with the turbulent, fast changing business environment' (p. 98). But Potterfield does think that FT's empowerment initiative awakened many employees to think about the current conditions of the business world and the limitations imposed upon their work lives by their company.

Christopher Moon and Celia Stanworth (1999) studied the case of teleworking. Although they know that empowerment has different meanings, they argue that it is 'generally related to the ideas of "excellence" held by managers, rather than to unequivocal rights to liberation for the workforce, so that the promise of self-actualization for workers is at best a secondary consideration compared to "bottom-line" outcomes' (p. 326). Like Potterfield, they think the contemporary usage of empowerment originated in the women's movement of the 1960s and 1970s. But they assert that 'worker empowerment' was first referred to by Juran, a TQM guru who linked empowerment with 'quality systems' (that is, the responsibility for quality was delegated closer to the point of production). They are suspicious of managerial usages of empowerment, claiming that managers try 'to make us think that things are different from what they really are . . .' (p. 327). Their core question is provocative: What are the ambitions or consequences for empowerment in work organisations?

They think that management gurus like Tom Peters (1982) and Charles Handy (1996) articulate a 'discourse of chaos' for senior managers. Indeed, the chaos thematic threads through the organisational learning and empowerment literature. Once the global business environment is perceived as chaotic and turbulent, the 'function of the term empowerment is to form part of the rhetoric concerning how employees should be managed in order to achieve competitive advantage, and this is just as important as its practice' (p. 328). In the 1990s, Moon and Stanworth observe astutely, the 'cult of the customer' – constructed as a discerning and fussy aesthete – 'provoked much organizational change' (1999, p. 329). Companies now required a staff committed to serve the ever more demanding and discriminating needs of their customers (which leapt over business boundaries and entered every domain of our lives as patients, clients, students).

The need for 'responsiveness to customers and to "delight" the customer has led organizations to empower workers, by increasing employee involvement through devolving authority to self-managing teams' (p. 330). They think that, in fact, the exemplary cases of devolvement in the literature (Cadbury's, OCS Smart's Group (laundry), Harvester Restaurants, Ciba UK and Frizzell's) reveal that the results were actually rather modest. The material changes, they say, were 'more in the direction of work-intensification than multi-skilling through training. It is the feeling of being empowered, rather than any objective increase in power amongst employees, that is the required outcome' (p. 331). TQM's revered rhetoric of 'empowerment, trust and mutual dependency' can be compared with the reality some researchers have discovered: 'pervasive regimes of constant electronic and peer group scrutiny' (Sewell and Wilkinson, 1993, p. 98; see Townley, 1994). The vaunted self-managing teams set up under TQM and just-in-time (JIT) systems are miles away from the European worker co-determination movements in the 1960s and 1970s to give workers greater control. In the brutal, no-holds-barred 1990s, team working has been described by Parker and Slaughter as 'management-by-stress' (cited, Legge, 1995, p. 230). Garrahan and Stewart (1992) found 'peer surveillance operating at Nissan which encouraged workers to identify defects caused by other workers. This had the effect of creating pressure on individuals not to let down other team members, and encouraging competition between teams to increase output' (cited, Moon and Stanworth, 1999, p. 331).

In their particular case study of teleworkers, Moon and Stanworth define telework as a 'form of "flexible" work which involves distance work, remote work or telecommuting which is dependent upon the use of information and communications technologies (ICTs)' (p. 336). Workers work at home or in satellite centres away from central organisations. The teleworker is often celebrated as the epitome of the information age. These postmodern workers no longer work in organisations fixed in space and time. They are supposedly free from the dreaded hierarchical office. According to Toffler (1980), who never catches the shadow in the sunlight, the 'teleworker has increased autonomy, independence and ability to organise his/her own time, to combine work with domestic and community activities' (p. 336). Teleworker independence and empowerment appear to reduce the need for control. But Stanworth and Moon observe that the management and control of teleworkers remains troublesome for companies.

Management worries that new workers will not be sufficiently enculturated for physical absence from the workplace. They worry that they will have to spend more time controlling off-site workers than the convention work site. Management theorists ponder this latter problem, wondering if managers having troubles with off-site workers are insufficiently accommodated to their new roles as developer-consultants. But some managers have had positive experience, developing high-trust relationships with their often high-status employees (whose jobs are intrinsically interesting and may well have internalised the corporate culture). Despite this, managing telework is 'still often seen as a severe test of management competence' (Moon and Stanworth, 1999, p. 337). Thus, there is lots of talk about 'managing by output, or by milestones, and a rejection of over-formal checking systems and Tayloristic methods . . .' (p. 337). Before the IT bubble burst in the opening years of the new millennium, the teleworker was identified as the avant-garde worker of the new age. They were self-employed believers in an enterprise culture. They were pioneers and risk-takers in contrast with the old bureaucratic, dinosaur firms. Their self-employment (and perhaps their bohemian lifestyles) seemed to release them 'from the shackles of the conventional workplace', enabling them 'to take control of his/her own destiny' (p. 338). The latest technology enabled them to engage in high-level knowledge work far from organisational centres.

In fact, Moon and Stanworth inform us that 'teleworkers who were managerial or professional staff were more likely to be fully integrated into the company enjoying high-trust relationships involving a high degree of discretion' (pp. 338–9). The literature on telework and virtuality assumes a radical reduction in the 'numbers of routine, lower-status teleworkers, employed or self-employed, such as data-entry clerks, or word-processor operators who may work at home or in telecentres' (p. 339). But the numbers of less cerebral or highly qualified workers may well increase. Less likely to be empowered, these workers may have their work closely monitored (technologies measuring the number of strokes, error rates or time taken on telephone calls have all been introduced). Many home-based workers are just as tied to their workstations at home as they were in traditional situations. The segmentation of the labour force leaves us with 'drone' workers of the information age, many of whom will be women. And there is scarcely any more security working at home than there is working down town in an office.

Moon and Stanworth believe that the 'promise of empowerment' has been oversold and ignores the political reality of most workplaces. Often moves to empower employees follow layoffs and delayering, which are then followed by work intensification. JIT and TQM systems obliged workers to become empowered. It was 'thus an obligation rather than a right, and has been imposed where resistance is low' (p. 340). They think that the employer right to be as 'competitive as possible appear to be at odds with the rights of employees to be empowered' (p. 340). Nor can one assume that either 'personal growth' or 'high morale' – the pre-condition for 'bottom-line success' in the excellence literature – lead causally to more profits. The

> empirical evidence tends to support the conclusion that at best
> worker empowerment is tolerated insofar as it contributes to profits,
> and at worst is a mechanism to persuade workers into the false belief
> that they have been given more discretion, so that they feel more
> committed and will work harder. In postmodern organizations all

should become empowered, whereas in reality empowerment may be experienced only by a privileged minority, whether a certain group of managers or an elite group of teleworkers. Other workers may be excluded from empowerment, and may in fact feel more oppressed under empowering regimes. (pp. 340–1)

Empowerment as an ethical endeavour

The critical and empirical literature casts considerable doubt on managerial claims to empower their workers through various kinds of programmes and projects. The gap between the rhetoric of empowerment and the reality for most workers is immense. Certainly management's pushing of decision making lower down the corporate order may enable some workers to acquire new skills and competencies. Some may even increase their feelings of self-worth and efficacy. But the evidence is overwhelming that companies are not introducing empowerment strategies because it is the 'right thing' to do (Quinn, 1999, p. 31). In fact, management-induced empowerment is essentially an adaptive strategy for organisational survival. It is a deliberate strategy to extend management's control over workers (Burawoy, 1985, p. 150).

Potterfield argues that the language of empowerment performs several key ideological functions. First, it masks corporate practices that are actually not in the workers' interests. Empowerment advocates (Hammonds, Kelly and Thurston, 1994; Jaffe, Scott and Tobe, 1994; Keichel, 1989; Waterman, Waterman and Collard, 1994) promote 'beliefs and values that support the major interests of corporate owners and leaders and a corresponding denigration of beliefs and values that challenge those interests' (1999, p. 118). Some companies are interested in more satisfying conditions for their workers. But their primary interest in cost cutting, increasing productivity and other bottom-line concerns – the business of business is business – take priority over the values of mutual loyalty, job security and organisational stability. Corporations routinely subordinate these employee interests to their profit commitments. Second, empowerment language, by denouncing the old organisational models as paternalistic and calling for a new covenant with workers, normalises insecurity and instability. Empowerment advocates like Waterman (1994) argue that the new workplace requires innovative and resourceful individuals who don't need unions or bosses to protect them. Perhaps he could be so audacious before we

143

learned that Enron's bosses stole their pension funds and left them with nothing. Potterfield says that the 'belief that values like mutual loyalty, job security, and employment stability are no longer possible to attain is also reflected in the FT interviews' (1999, p. 121). It seems that if advanced capitalism is going to survive intact, it must convince workers to accept insecurity and instability. Potterfield claims that 'while there is a lot of rhetoric about employees being mature adults who are responsible for making the decisions that affect their lives, the structures and policies at Fairbrook conspire against sort of genuine participation . . .' (p. 125).

Third, empowerment language assumes that the turbulent and insecure environment is a 'permanent, unchanging, naturalized state of affairs' (p. 126). The current status quo is accepted without question. Empowerment writers and advocates rush in to help their workers cope with the 'unpredictable, ever changing business environment' (p. 126). Potterfield says that he has not found one example of 'writers exhorting workers to change or transform these insecure and unstable conditions' (p. 126). External conditions cannot be altered. 'This distortion', Potterfield argues, 'tends to support the existing relations of power and dominance within corporate organizations' (p. 127). This rules out any reflection on alternative imaginings and ordering of just economic organisations. Empowerment texts emanating from management intellectual circles do not acknowledge the 'freedom to challenge and change external reality . . .'(p. 127). Thus, the learning challenge for management is to devise pedagogical strategies and procedures to redesign 'expectations of company loyalty . . . making workers more responsible for certain limited types of decision-making, their own employability, retirement fund, etc.' (p. 129). To meet these challenges, managers must charge workers up, get them committed to corporate goals, and fired up about the new requirements of their jobs. Moreover, these challenges are supposedly to be met within the corporation as a self-contained unit. But the big troubles plaguing contemporary businesses are linked to the larger socio-economic system of advanced corporate capitalism. Empowerment texts never make connections between the problems facing workers and the larger global system itself.

Can we make a convincing argument for empowerment as an ethical endeavour? Can we argue for empowerment as a human right? Can we make the case for non-instrumentally oriented empowerment projects? Harry van der Linden provides us with the argumentative structure in 'A Kantian defense of enterprise democracy' (1998). Kant's famous categorical imperative affirmed that moral law had to be universal and that humanity had to be treated as an end in itself. Van der Linden builds his case for democratic firms on these two normative assumptions. The Kantian moral imperative requires universal respect for persons. There must be universal respect for individual autonomy and universal mutual promotion of individual ends. But to enact these moral imperatives, 'dialogical and institutional action is needed to arrive at universal laws' (van der Linden, 1998, p. 220). Like Habermas (1984, 1987), van der Linden pulls Kant into the social realm.

For van der Linden, this means that in the political realm, the Kantian individual is a co-legislator and the political system must 'guarantee for all the conditions that enable one to be a co-legislator' (1998, p. 220). This requires constitutional democracy, the protection of basic civil and political rights. But the pedagogical procedures enabling participation must also be in place (the latter is the missing dimension of liberal democratic regimes). In the economic context, van der Linden argues that the categorical imperative requires that all 'workers become co-legislators in their companies and have various economic rights that protect their conditions of participatory autonomy or co-legislatorship . . .' (p. 221). He thinks that employees are usually treated as 'means only' because they are 'systematically denied the opportunity to co-determine the rules governing their company and work' (p. 221). The absence of the right of co-determination undermines the well-being of the workers. And the interest of the employers – the corporate managers – may also violate the public interest.

It is the 'realm of ends as the ultimate end of the moral law [that] makes the ideal of enterprise democracy imperative' (p. 221). But objections to enterprise democracy are often raised. Workers are said to lack the competence to manage firms, and they have insufficient motivation to participate in decision making. Van der Linden's retort is that, in fact, workers do manifest sufficient motivation to engage in decisions pertaining to the day-to-day conduct of their jobs (work pace/schedule, distribution of specific tasks, and so on). They also participate in many of the particular decisions concerning grievances and other personnel matters. They have the incentive at these levels. The main problem pertains to their competence and motivation to engage in decisions that affect the entire enterprise (introduction of new technology, distribution of profits, investment and product diversification). Here, matters are more complex and challenging. Indeed, mainstream empowerment advocates will not even pose the haunting question of ownership. And those proposing the transition from private to social forms of ownership offer a bewildering array of scenarios and practical experiments. But the just learning society framework would, minimally, goad companies and workers into 'creating relations between workers and experts in technology and business [so] that the idea of enterprise democracy can still be upheld' (p. 223).

Why bother? Van der Linden argues that self-respect, self-realisation and improved material conditions are the intrinsic rewards of democratic decision making itself. He recognises that persons can achieve self-realisation and self-respect outside the work domain. As well, some workers may just travel along for a 'free ride' on the efforts of others. But the question of 'active participation' at all levels of work organisation, he argues, ought to be understood as a responsibility. Each of us, then, has the moral duty to be committed to the well-being of others. It is our 'duty to help to shape both the internal and external decisions of one's firm so that autonomy and happiness are promoted in general' (p. 224). Within the Kantian moral framework, non-participation signifies that 'one's fellow workers are not positively respected as co-legislators' (p.224). In earlier chapters, I have alluded to the way life in the consumer paradise turns us inward and away from social and public commitments. We do not usually consider that when we opt out, remain silent, mute or deaf to the other (Bird, 1996), that we are not being morally responsible. Van der Linden counsels us to perceive the 'autonomous self . . . as a co-legislative self' (1998, p. 224).

Van der Linden states forthrightly that enterprise democracy 'requires that private productive property ownership be socialized' (p. 227). One can only imagine how that message would play in the Harvard School of Business luncheon seminars with Fortune 500 executives. He thinks that democratic firms would 'provide all workers with the opportunity for decision-making and thus enable the development of participatory autonomous individuals' (p. 229). A radical shift away from the idea that the 'business of business is business' is thus required. The problem with leaving the big picture decisions to highly paid executives (the ratio between their salaries and benefits and that of the average worker has increased exponentially in the last decade) is that the corporate interest cannot pursue policies that are universal in import. He thinks that the 'interests of workers are more representative of the interests of most consumers and citizens' (p. 230). If workers had 'more control in democratic firms', van der Linden avers, they would be enabled to take 'increased moral responsibility for, and awareness of, possible economic harm' (p. 230).

The firm must be transformed into a 'social good' (Davies and Mills, 1999). Davies and Mills argue persuasively that the 'term "empowerment" shall also be considered in terms of justice (as well as control) particularly from the point of view of a human being's inalienable right to be treated with dignity, as well as the individual's perception of justice arising out of their experience of the organisation' (p. 180). They resist, then, the notion that empowerment is something to be easily cast aside at first sight of a new management fad or twist in the economic climate and ethos. They add their voice to the growing chorus of international voices that challenges the transnational corporation's right to dispose of people and goods and services any way their managers see fit. Thus, current company law unjustly divorces ownership from responsibility: the 'requirements of justice and participation in industry are seriously lacking' (p. 183). The results of this great divorce are devastatingly evident everywhere in the world. Davies and Mills believe that 'as long as the law effectively sanctions the huge gap in reward and decision-making power between those who contribute their capital, and those who contribute their work, then empowerment can only remain denuded of any real meaning' (p. 184). Distributive justice calls for the 'just distribution of decision-making' (p. 184).

Davies and Mills raise the difficult question of 'how such ethical imperatives [can] be translated into the practical production of goods and services?' (p. 185). Are there seeds of empowerment within managerial rhetoric and practices? What can we hope for at work within the just learning society paradigm? Matts Alvesson and High Willmott ('On the idea of emancipation in management and organization studies' (1992)) are well-known critical management theorists. They think that some forms of critical theory promote an all or nothing mind set. Its worst manifestation might be the sentiment that men and women have to wait for some mysterious big bang end to the dastardly capitalist economic system. Alvesson and Willmott eschew this sort of left melancholia in favour of a commitment to micro-emancipation. By micro-emancipation, they mean an 'emphasis on partial, temporary movements that break away from diverse forms of oppression, rather than successive moves toward a predetermined state of liberation' (p. 447). This attractive idea assumes that control does not mean only 'discipline and restriction of the space for action.' It can also be perceived as a 'potential source of critical thought and emancipation' (p. 446). This is consistent with the relational conception of power and empowerment.

They realise that an over-reliance on local projects of emancipation in specific companies can leave the 'vital sources of oppression associated with the laws and principles of capitalism' (p. 449) undisturbed. However, they identify three types of emancipatory projects: questioning, incremental, and utopian, and three foci of emancipatory intent: means, social relations, and ends. On the first dimension, the authors distinguish a 'questioning from a utopian type of emancipatory project' (p. 450). I would argue that the introduction of empowerment rhetoric into companies opens up possibilities for employees (and management) to 'combat the self-evident and the taken-for-granted' (p. 450). Bird's forms and scale of empowerment provides the critical tools needed to investigate and problematise actually existing practices within workplaces. Alvesson and Willmott argue that the 'utopian element emerges when the current conditions are confronted with a new form of ideal, which aims at opening up consciousness for engagement with a broader repertoire of alternatives' (p. 450). For me, the ideal of enterprise democracy (with its grounding in the Kantian moral imperative) provides us with the utopian dimension needed to impel us along the bumpy road. One might even consider Bird's forms of empowerment as signposts pointing to just organisational life. Better to achieve level two than no level at all.

To consider the 'primary object of emancipatory efforts', the authors make an 'analytical distinction among means, social relations, and ends' (p. 450). They say that the 'emancipation of ends is concerned with the unfreezing institutionalized priorities and, thereby, opening up debate about the practical value of economic growth, consumption, the quality of life and so on' (p. 450). Emancipatory projects addressing means 'challenge the necessity and value of established methods of organization . . .'. Finally, the 'inclusion of social relations as a focus draws attention to distributions of equalities/inequalities in terms of privileges and power' (p. 450). Alvesson and Willmott's matrix is helpful for adult educators who work within the just learning society paradigm. For example, they observe that means such as 'participatory styles of coordinating work for the attainment of goals' (such as ecologically sound production in a lumber mill) does not 'necessarily touch upon issues like segmented labour markets, or other forms of class, gender, or race inequalities' (p. 451). They think it is possible to imagine emancipatory projects aimed at transforming social relations (reducing power asymmetries) that leave the ends and means unaffected. They argue that their matrix can also help us to determine empirically if management schemes (like QWL or TQM) are emancipatory on the ground floor.

In the end, Alvesson and Willmott counsel us to 'resist the equation of micro-emancipation with (pseudo)humanistic versions of management and organizational studies, which promise full integration of human needs and dominating bureaucratic ideals, thereby devaluing if not denying the emancipatory impulse as it contributes to manipulative forms of practice and obscures contradictions' (p. 452). They insist that emancipation (or empowerment) is incompatible with any effort at improvement that directs attention to a very narrow target and away from the social context in which it is produced. The emancipatory ideal cannot be 'adequately developed without consideration of macro-level ideas, ideologies, class, race and gender structures, economic principles and laws, and so forth, that organize the world of organization and management' (p. 453).

CHAPTER SEVEN

Citizenship in the age of information

The foreclosure of the political?

In his classic text, *Class, Citizenship and Social Development* (1965), T.H. Marshall identified three elements of citizenship: civil, social and political. Civil rights protected the citizen from the state; social rights ensured the citizen of a material safety net; political rights allowed for the participation in the governing of society. Civil and social rights, however, help secure the 'individual's position as a private actor.' They secure the 'legal and material basis necessary for the realization of political rights and are thus justified.' Adult educators have focused their attention particularly on the political rights of participation because the act of taking part in deciding how society is to be governed requires citizens predisposed to learn, and structures that enable wide-ranging communicative interaction. This ideal assumes that citizenship is not simply a passive state of entitlements. Rather, citizenship is one of the fundamental roles to be learned and enacted by men and women as they deliberate with one another about matters pertaining to the public good. Many adult educators posit that the 'skills of civility' (McKinnon and Hampsher-Mon, 2000) are acquired by participating in the voluntary associations ('schools of citizenship') within civil society. Men and women took responsibility for the local commons by participating in a wide variety of organisations. There they learned how to respect, if not love, others, how to listen, how to make arguments and how to act strategically. They also forged connections between and amongst people, creating a social infrastructure with enough resilience to catch those who fell into various kinds of trouble or sickness. Adult educators assumed, moreover, that citizen performance of their role in the local surroundings served as a bridge to the larger world of representative political

150

engagement. Those men and women who were active in a multiplicity of associations or movements within civil society (here denoted as the social space comprising family, voluntary associations, movements and various public spheres) would have acquired the self-confidence, know-how and connections to participate in party politics. They would be informed and competent citizens. Active citizens would gain a return on their investment of time and energy: they would take pleasure in policies, laws and institutions that were the outcome of complex conversations among an engaged and alert citizenry. Whether a rapid transit system, a community health centre or an urban wilderness space, all the citizens could say that they had considered a wide range of viewpoints, and that the resulting decisions were anchored in the best arguments and ethical commitment to promote the well-being of most and not one's self primarily. In other words, the deliberative learning process would not be governed by the instrumental logic of efficiency, but rather a communicative logic governed by the norm of universal justice.

Anyone who observes the contemporary political scene knows that this idealised depiction of the active citizen is under serious challenge. There is enormous dissatisfaction with the workings of parliamentary democracy in Western liberal democracies. Far-right, xenophobic groups are on the rise in liberal democracies. Growing numbers of citizens have disengaged from voting processes. Many young activists are rebelling against corporate globalisation, protesting from Seattle (1999) to Mumbai (2004) without giving a thought to parliaments. For their part, many intellectuals (working different seams of the knowledge mine) raise questions about the meaning of the political in an age when capitalism is the only game in town. Stephen Talbot, in *The Future Does Not Compute: Transcending the Machines in Our Midst* (1995), announces dramatically that, 'It is not easy to see where you and I might step into the picture and make a discernible difference' (p. 77). Talbot thinks that the problems – be they famines regularly scything millions of people, or massive assaults upon mother earth, have become 'so systemic, the cases become so tortured and inaccessible, the interrelationships grown so intricate, that we cannot imagine how to fix one thing without fixing everything' (pp. 77–8).

To clarify our understandings of adult learning and citizenship – what do we mean by active citizenship in the information age? Qhat ought we to be able to know and do to perform our citizen roles in the global, networked era? – we will survey some of the writings of political thinkers who are meditating upon the meaning of the political in a very turbulent, confusing and contradictory world. In the first part, I examine thinkers who suggest that we inhabit a post-political world; in the second, I analyse several thinkers who maintain that the political has, in fact, been reconstituted in accordance with postmodern realities. Special attention is given to Habermas's elaboration of deliberative democracy, mainly because he consciously thinks about the learning dynamics in civil society. I then conclude with some axioms drawn from complex and contradictory analyses of our global situation.

Zygmunt Bauman: In search of politics

The prolific Bauman is a weathervane for understanding the economic and social storms and intellectual winds sweeping around us. In *In Search of Politics* (1999), Bauman worries mightily about the state of politics in the contemporary world. Bauman begins one of his first reflections on politics with a brief discussion of the meaning of freedom in the postmodern world, namely the freedom to choose. After clearly expounding the notion that all 'individual freedoms' are 'confined by two sets of constraints. One set is determined by the agenda of choice: the range of alternatives which are actually on offer. All choice means "choosing among" and seldom is the set of items to be chosen from a matter for the chooser to decide. Another set of constraints is determined by the code of choosing: the rules that tell the individual on what ground the preference should be given to some items rather than others and when to consider the choice as proper and when as inappropriate' (pp. 72–3). In the modern era, Bauman tells us, legislation set the agenda of choice, and education was the primary institutionalized effort to supply choosers with orientation points' (p. 73). Now, however, agenda and code-setting agenda of 'extant political institutions' have been either abandoned or trimmed down. But this does not mean that individual choice is actually expanding because the agenda has been ceded to 'forces other than the political' (p. 74).

For Bauman, then, the 'retreat or self-limitation of the state has as its most salient effect a greater exposure of choosers to both the coercive (agenda-setting) and the indoctrinating (code-setting) impact of essentially non-political forces – primarily those associated with financial and commodity markets' (p. 74). Like many other scholars (such as Benjamin Barber – *Jihad vs. McWorld* (1995)), Bauman identifies a 'marked tendency of our times' as the 'ongoing separation of power from politics: true power, able to determine the extent of practical choices, flows; thanks to its ever less constrained mobility it is virtually global – or rather, extraterritorial.' Thus, the 'hub of the present-day crisis of political process is not so much the absence of values or confusion caused by their plurality, as the absence of an agency effective enough to legitimate, promote, install and service any set of values or any consistent and cohesive agenda of choices' (p. 74). Market pressures have replaced political legislation as principal agenda-setters. Although we are not focusing attention here on the way the code of choice has been commodified, it is worth noting that the current code educates desire such that the world is treated 'primarily as a container of potential objects of consumption', inducing individuals to 'view the arousal of desires clamouring to be satisfied as the guiding rule of the chooser's life and a criterion of a worthy and successful life' (p. 76). One of several available roles for persons, that of consumer, has elbowed out that of citizen.

Bauman is alarmed at the epochal 'departure in the history of the modern state: the separation and increasing gap between power and politics' (p. 97). He thinks that political agents have 'lost the certainty of their roles' because the 'political economy of post-industrial and global capitalism no longer provides the clear-cut categorization of "places within the system of production" in which forms of collective action (political parties, associations, trade unions) were once anchored' (p. 98). The traditional question – What is to be done? – Bauman concedes, is

> asked less frequently, and if when asked it tends to be quickly dismissed on the ground of TINA (There is no Alterative) creed, this is not so much for the lack of ideas as for the absence of agencies which could conceivably carry them out. The assessment of the feasibility of actions and practicality of projects is a function of the relative strength of the agent and its adversary; and under present circumstances the main question, the question to be asked more urgently but a question to which no clear answer is in sight, is the query 'Is anybody capable of doing whatever needs to be done? (p. 98)

We return again to our central question – Can citizens make a discernible difference in this seemingly post-political era?

Bauman is also troubled that the

truly powerful and resourceful agents have escaped into hiding and operate beyond the reach of all established means of political action – let along the democratic process of negotiation and control centred on the agora. These new agents celebrate their independence and detachment from the agora . . . They see no profit in normative regulation and so do not need the agora; but they sense profit in having their hands untied and so do their best to keep their distance from the agora and to stay out of sight of the crowds that fill it. (p. 98).

This hiddenness and secretness of power is, in my view, the fundamental factor animating the anti-corporate protesters in Seattle and other sites. It is part of a growing rage against the disengagement (and apparent heartlessness) of global elites (and intellectuals for that matter) from the concerns of citizens everywhere. As proponents of deliberative, strong or participatory democracy insist, the republic idea 'puts critical inquiry in the heart of community membership; citizens belong to the republic through the active concern with the values promoted or neglected by their polity' (p. 168).

However, in Bauman's estimation, the republic is emigrating from the nation–state. This startling observation assumes that democracy is

> becoming increasingly toothless and impotent to guard or adjust the conditions vital for the life of the citizens . . . . [C]ontemporary states fail to meet the other necessary condition of a viable republic: the ability of the citizens to negotiate and jointly decide "the public good," and so to shape a society which they would be prepared to call their own and to which they would gladly give their oath of unswerving allegiance. (p. 169).

Bauman thinks that the concept of '"global powers" captures the emerging, indomitable reality, while the concept of "global citizenship" thus far stays empty, representing a postulate at best, but in most contexts not much more than wishful thinking' (p. 170). The debates at the World Social Forum, where sectarian leftists (associated with the Mumbai Resistance 2004) advocated a total break with capitalism, suggest that the left imagination cannot yet dream beyond its failed historical projects. Bauman believes that the lives of global peoples are shaped decisively in areas beyond the nation-state's reach, while those instruments controlled by citizens remain locally confined. This bitter reality is the primary cause of the very uneasy tension in the World

Social Forum gatherings between those who want to keep it an 'open space' for learning and deliberation, and those who want to create a 'movement of movements' to confront global capital.

Darin Barney: The hope for democracy in the age of network technology

Few may have noticed that, precisely at the moment when many exhausted left intellectuals were putting away their critical tools for the long winter ahead, cyber-romantics were busy crafting new grand narratives about the hope for democracy in the age of network technology. These dreamers imagined network technology (NT) as the 'medium through which a democratic revolution is being, or will be, enacted' (Barney, 2000, p. 264). While admitting that computer networks are 'not completely without democratic benefits', Barney is sceptical about NT as harbinger of strong democracy. He argues that NT 'fails to live up to its democratic image precisely because of its many non-dialogical applications are un- or anti-democratic, and these eclipse, and even undermine, the democratic potential of applications such as network-mediated civic discussions' (p. 264). Indeed, Barney wonders why so many of us have become 'seduced by a democratic potential that is at best marginal in relation to the predominantly anti-democratic attributes of this technology. Is it simply that, as the children of Prometheus, we have been blinded by hope?' (p. 264).

For Barney, a viable definition of democracy must have three elements: 'equality, participation, and a public sphere from which sovereignty emanates' (p. 22). Equality refers to an 'equality of ability to participate, rather than simply to an equal opportunity to do so' (p. 22). His definition also 'stipulates that citizen participation must be meaningful in order for it to qualify as democratic' (p. 23). In other words, participation cannot be frivolous or merely symbolic.

> Democratic participation must be clearly and decisively connected to the political decisions that direct the activity of the participants' community. By this definition, polities in which citizens' participation is limited to legitimizing deliberations and decisions made without their participation is not a democracy. Thus, democracy requires that citizen participation be specifically linked to policy outcomes, rather than relegated to the general role of system legitimation. (p. 23)

155

Barney wants to differentiate strong democracy from liberalism, namely that 'democracy is not constituted wholly by freedom of consumer choice in a market or the freedom to do privately whatever one likes. Instead, democracy is about the taking of collective decisions that are to govern the common and public practices of the members of a community' (p. 23).

Barney's version of the post-political thesis hinges on his belief that our global, networked world has closed off political options. 'Taken together, capitalism, liberalism, and technology form a trinity of sorts, outside of or beyond which there exist no political options capable of being persuasive in the modern (and, even more so the postmodern) world. The modern capitalist, liberal, technological state is thus "a universal and homogeneous state [that] is the pinnacle of political striving"' (p. 252). This trinity is the master signifier of our symbolic universe, now so utterly taken for granted that their distinctive ideological character saturates our psyches, the human lifeworld, colonising our sense of what is good and worthwhile. Thus, liberalism

> cannot tolerate a good that flatly prohibits certain activities or ends by deeming them unambiguously harmful. Technology cannot realize its essence if its setting upon the earth and human beings is constrained by the limitations imposed by a transcendent good. Beings committed to the belief that their essential humanity is expressed in their ability to make themselves and their world cannot be obligated to a good emanating from some other conception of their essence. (p. 252)

Like Bauman's 'migration of power' thesis, Barney's 'closure of the political universe' is shocking. Barney illustrates his provocative thesis by arguing that North American, European and some Asian governments have not been able to resist embracing making massive financial commitments to building network infrastructures. The ethos guiding them all is 'animated by liberal notions of progress, capitalist visions of prosperity, and an abiding faith that technological progress is central to both' (p. 260). There is only one symbolic universe. No alterative goods have been able to penetrate into the majority consciousness.

Barney thinks that there can be no vital political meaning and life unless we can make choices about the direction of our public life.

In a democracy it must be possible for people to allow certain virtues to constrain the untrammelled expression of human freedom, material accumulation or technological advance. In genuine democracies, in other words, citizens must at least have recourse to a good that might impose significant limits on the pursuit of these ends. No such recourse is available in a liberal, capitalist, and technological society, in which a human being's essence is believed to be his or freedom, and the fulfilment of that essence is achieved through unlimited acquisition and endless progress.

As long as the universal homogenous state is a liberal, capitalist and technological one, it must, by virtue of its ends and what it truly is,

deny outright the imperatives of the good – in which 'the people' as a collectivity cannot effectively choose virtue over liberty, wealth, and progress – it cannot be a democracy ... The homogenous state of modern capitalist, technological liberalism denies people this opportunity, and so cannot accommodate genuine democracy. In so far as it contributes substantially to the entrenchment of this state, network technology is an instrument of democracy's continued impossibility in the modern world. (pp. 263–4)

Barney asserts that many people believe that NT is a revolutionary democratic medium. He thinks that our strong appetite for good self-government and community with our fellows and sisters bewitches us into accepting NT as the 'ultimate stand-in, capable not only of satisfying the baser human appetites for material wealth and mastery, but also of gratifying certain nobler human appetites without actually satisfying them' (p. 265). He maintains that digital networks cannot stand in for the genuine arts of government and democracy. Networks are able to distribute information and facilitate communication. But these attributes

do not encompass the resources necessary for the practice of the genuine arts of self-government, politics, and democracy . . .. In a time of weakened spirit, wherein wisdom and courage are conspicuous by their absence from public life, these surrogates are able to flatter our collective appetite for a more genuine politics. They are, however, ultimately unable to satisfy that appetite, a fact that may account for the residual cynicism, alienation, and dissatisfaction afflicting many of the so-called advanced democracies. This malaise provides fertile soil for claims that network technology can satisfy more substantially our yearning for an authentic democratic politics . . .. Under the sway of these stand-ins, we have become habituated to practising a diminished politics that bears a name it does not deserve. The regime of network technology offers scant hope for the shattered of this ignoble delusion. (p. 268)

We may be learning all over the place, but it is mainly contained within the technological frame.

Manuel Castells: Informational politics and the crisis of democracy

In volume two, *The Power of Identity* (1997), of his massive three-part study of the information society, Castells presents us with another version of the post-political thesis. Like Bauman, Castells believes that the blurring of the boundaries of the nation-state has confused the definition of citizenship. Citizens are no longer certain, he claims, of where power resides (everywhere? nowhere?). The rise of tribalised identity politics weakens the solidarity bases of political sharing. The state's inability to control capital flows and ensure social security diminishes its relevance for the average citizen (who may even watch his job disappear into cyberspace). Even the evident turn to the local to exercise some control over one's life situation helps to increase the 'distance between mechanisms of political control and management of global problems.' And the erosion of the welfare-inspired social contract between capital, labour, and the state, weakens social capital and sends everyone scurrying to 'fight for their individual interests.' Castells appears to agree with the French iconoclast Jean-Marie Guehanno who argues that the liberal democratic state has disintegrated into a society 'endlessly fragmented, without memory and without solidarity, a society without citizens . . .' (pp. 309–10). Guehenno's opening two chapters (1995) are aptly entitled, 'The end of the nation' and 'The end of politics.'

Developmental humanists who still ascribe to the ideal of the active citizens find these perceptions distressing. If that weren't enough, Castells informs us that the 'transformation of politics, and of democratic processes' is 'even deeper . . .' (p. 310). One now has to add, Castells purports, the direct consequences of new NT on political debate and power-seeking strategies. He believes that in the information society the electronic media have become the 'privileged space of politics' (p. 311). This is the heart of his argument. Although Castells does not think that all politics can be simply reduced to 'images, sounds, or symbolic manipulation', he underscores the 'critical role of electronic media in contemporary politics' (p. 311). Castells claims that the 'logic, and organization, of electronic media frame and structure politics' (p. 312). This framing of politics by their capture in the learning space of the media impacts not only elections, but political organisation, decision making and governance, ultimately modifying the nature of the relationship between state and civil society.

If Castells is correct in this contentious claim, deliberative democrats need be alerted to the dangers inherent in this trend of the information age. Castells believes that electronic media has become the critical public space for communicative interaction. Without an 'active presence in the media, political proposals or candidates do not stand a chance of gathering broad support. Media politics is not all politics, but all politics must go through the media to affect decision-making. So doing, politics is fundamentally framed, in its substance, organization, process, and leadership, by the inherent logic of the media system, particularly by the new electronic media' (p. 317). Castells engages in an extensive analysis of the way the media actually gets framed, the way information is managed. This topic has particular salience in the post-11 September 2001 world. Once the electronic media becomes the premier public space, power moves quickly to colonise this space. Indeed, other theorists of the media in the information age have written perceptively on the explosive growth of the information management industries (spin doctors, media consultants, pollsters, and so on). Governments, corporations and civic groups increasingly rely on communication and information in their attempts to manipulate public opinion and maintain social control. In the famous phrase of Edward Bernays (1955), 'consent is engineered.' In the information age we are assaulted by 'endless propaganda' (Rutherford, 2000) attempting to control and guide our actions in every dimension of our lives. Advertising and propaganda fuse into 'public relations' which dedicates itself to 'producing information to persuade audiences of a course of action which promotes the interests they are paid to serve – i.e. to control people's information environments the better to exercise some control over their actions' (Webster, 1995, p. 126). The information (or learning) society we actually inhabit is really a 'promotional culture' (Wernick, 1991) that uses powerful methods of persuasion to train us for our main role as consumers and customers. Emptying civil society of dialogical interactions, promotional culture scarcely frets for a moment about the degradation of everything public, from broadcasting, libraries, parks, information to education.

The director of the influential *Le Monde Diplomatique*, Ignacio Ramonet, believes that with the acceleration of globalisation the 'fourth estate' has been stripped of its potential to criticise power. Massive transnational media corporations have evolved into formidable profit-making machines themselves as well as acting as the ideological arm of globalisation. Thus, they contain demands from the grassroots and, where possible, seize political power (like Berlusconi of Italy). They have proved capable of trying to undermine governments like Hugo Chavez's Venezuela, and of serving as an instrument of the US Empire in the Middle East. Ramonet thinks that like our food, our news is contaminated – 'poisoned by lies, polluted by rumours, misrepresentations, distortions and manipulation' (2003, p. 7). *Le Monde Diplomatique* has called for the creation of Media Global Watch, arguing that 'freedom of enterprise cannot be permitted to override people's right to rigorously researched and verified news . . .' (p. 7). *Adbusters* has joined them in this mission, boldly calling for a 'Media Carta' to seek a 'new human right for our information age, one that empowers freedom of speech with the right to access the media' (2004).

Vaclav Havel: The power of the powerless

The Czech dissident, playwright and politician, Vaclav Havel, rejected the view that power is a lost cause, that we are condemned to play in our little private sandboxes while the larger world outside our playground goes to hell. In the late 1970s, Havel wrote his famous essay, 'The power of the powerless', the immediate aim of which was to explain the significance of Charter 77 to potential supporters within Czechoslovakia and encourage opponents of late-socialism in the Soviet bloc. Havel works with a fairly standard conception of power (the ability of certain humans to exercise their will over and against others). Yet the striking aspect of Havel's essay is its lack of deference to power. He questions the cynicism of those who 'curse the bastards' and then drift with the tide or drink themselves into oblivion. 'The power of the powerless' is definitely not attracted to institutional politics. Nor does Havel subscribe to a kind of anti-politics stance. His essay is more subversive. He proposes that under any circumstances the downtrodden and oppressed always contain within themselves the power to remedy their own powerlessness. Consequently, they are the cause of their own continuing subordination.

Havel arrived at this startling idea (oppression never displaces political (or agentic) subjectivity entirely) through his own eastern European experience, namely that late socialism could not be reformed from within. The centre of potential resistance was, in fact, the lifeworld. Here one could 'live in truth' (what he would later call 'anti-political politics'), shaking off the muck of the system. 'This system serves people only to the extent necessary to ensure that people will serve it', he wrote. 'Anything beyond this, that is to say, anything which leads people to overstep their predetermined roles is regarded by the system as an attack upon itself. And in this respect it is correct: every instance of such transgression is a genuine denial of the system.' Thus, as long as individuals act as if they accept the system, the system will continue to be confirmed. As Havel counsels us, citizens can say enough is enough. The green grocer can simply refuse to keep the party's sign in his window.

Havel's daring thesis upended the presumption that the Gullivers who command states and have the weapons of coercive power at their disposal (guns, armies, propagandists, and so on) will have things their way, forever. Those who speak of sovereign power should not have the last word in politics. In effect, Havel argues that under certain circumstances the powerful are powerless. Their powerlessness is traceable to five related factors. To start with, the powerful can never control the micro-movements of all of their subjects. They can never find quite enough spies to sit in every coffee shop; they cannot watch every living room. The powerful may wish to reduce the citizen to a cog in the machine, but usually they are too stupid or conservative to do that all the time. Second, the power structure depends upon ideological rituals that become less and less credible (as well as bypassing public debate) as the people become less and less happy. Here a third consideration arises: some may call the ideology a lie, declaring the emperor's thoughts naked. This possibility, Havel says, is nurtured by the ontological fact that the 'everyday, thankless, and never-ending struggle of human beings to live more freely, truthfully, and in quiet dignity' is ultimately not completely repressible. Fourth, misery appears to nip at the heels of imagination, forcing the mind to reflect on the human condition. How has life come to this? Does it have to remain this way? Who is responsible for our suffering? Finally, individuals who live in truth reject the innocent fiction that power is a thing to be grasped or abolished. For Havel, power is not something one has; it is relational, so power relations are not reducible to the instruments of power. Each individual is caught within a labyrinth of influence, repression, fear and self-censorship which swallows everyone within it, at the very least rendering them silent. Every person is both the victim and supporter of the system – and potential opponent.

Since the lines of organised power within the system pass like low-current electricity through all its subjects, the latter can defend themselves only by preventing the system from ruining their personal lives. Those who choose to live in truth effect something of an existential revolution. They must agree that there are some things worth suffering for, and be prepared to say out loud what others think only in solitude. We have arrived at the heart of Havel's affirmation of political agency: the person can always act (write an open letter, hold a rock concert, a demonstration, go on a hunger strike). The effective power of these acts cannot be judged in conventional political terms. Yet living in truth is a risky business. The consequences for the individual are unclear, but these acts can be surprisingly effective. To be sure, totalitarian regimes can hound citizens, drag them from their beds, lock them up in psychiatric wards, beat them silly, even murder them. But such tactics prove the point: the powerless have within themselves the power to obstruct normality, to embarrass the authorities, to point to the possibility of living life differently – according to values like trust, openness, responsibility, solidarity, love.

Living in truth begins, then, at the existential level. Although it can manifest in collective actions, it is essentially local, invisible, anti-political. The strategy of living in truth is not interested in becoming an institutional party. Living in truth is for this reason most ethically effective when it keeps its distance from formal politics. They must grasp that a better system will not ensure a better life. In fact, the opposite is true: 'Only by creating a better life can a better system be developed.' Living in truth requires the cultivation of mechanisms of individuation, self-protection and co-operation in areas underneath and beyond the reach of the state – within the household, among friends, at the office, within the parallel economy and sphere of unofficial culture. In a phrase, the empowerment of the powerless first and foremost requires individuals to build open, flexible structures of resistance that run parallel to and underneath the late-socialist state.

This is best accomplished from below through small-scale initiatives.

There are some limitations to Havel's arguments. Havel avoids the different interpretations of what it means to live in truth. He may also downplay the truth that we generally do not love truthful living very much (it is very hard), and the hypnotic effects of the system bind us tightly. The pessimistic proponents of the post-political thesis would query Havel's abandonment of politics – the messy and complicated activity of collectively encouraging individuals to live in truth and thereby decide who gets what, when and how. Perhaps Havel and other eastern European intellectuals so fear the actually existing world of corrupt party politics that they think it is non-redeemable. Deliberative democrats would find troubling Havel's failure to mention politics as a form of collectively-based speech and interaction oriented to the attainment of the good life (the orientation of Darin Barney). Havel also eschews talk of parliaments, armies, police forces, civil service or local government. Always, for Havel, the primacy of the individual's existence over the institutional frameworks within which they live. For me, Havel's separation of the person from institutional framework reflects an important historical moment, a way of conceiving resistance and hope; it ought not be generalised into a normative politics for everyone. Developmental humanists and proponents of the just learning society must always attend to the institutional preconditions for communicative processes in civil society. On the other hand, Havel's recovery of the person as moral agent is a necessary conceptual retrieval for contemporary learning theory.

Havel believes that Heidegger's diagnosis of the crisis of modern technological society (there appears to be no way out of the powerlessness produced by modern regimes of power) can be countered from below against the odds. Only when the 'independent life of society' is cultivated can the powerless be prevented from becoming new masters. Havel called this new and desperate possibility 'social self-organisation.' Soon thereafter, with greater confidence and precision, it would be called civil society (Keane, 2000, pp. 268–86).

Anthony Giddens: The emergence of life politics

In *Modernity and Self-Identity* (1991), Giddens (like Ulrich Beck of 'risk society' fame) launches his attack on Gulliver by arguing that transformations within modernity itself have precipitated a new form of

163

politics he names 'life politics.' Giddens assumes that the modernist project (increasing knowledge about the social and natural worlds would enable us to control and direct it to our own purposes) has been surpassed. Today we live in a world of 'manufactured uncertainty.' We are less certain that our know-why can translate crisply into know-how (or, inversely, that we even have the know-how to deal with the threats of new, virulent diseases such as H5N1, the avian disease). Giddens thinks that the 'ethos of self-growth signals major social transitions in late modernity as a whole.' He labels these transitions 'burgeoning institutional reflexivity, the disembedding of social relations by abstract systems, and the consequent interpenetration of the local and the global' (p. 209).

These transitions, Giddens insists, issue in a new life politics (Beck, for his part, speaks of 'sub-politics' (1994)). To help us grasp this new politics, he distinguishes emancipatory from life politics. For Giddens 'emancipatory politics as generic outlook concerned above all with liberating individuals and groups from constraints which adversely affect their life chances. Emancipatory politics involves two main elements: the effort to shed shackles of the past, thereby permitting a transformative attitude towards the future; and the aim of overcoming the illegitimately domination of some individuals or groups by others' (pp. 210–11). Emancipatory politics, perhaps integral to modernity, achieves substantive content when it focuses on divisions between human beings (like class, for example). Whether the division is class, ethnicity or gender, rich or poor nations, the 'objective of emancipatory politics is either to release underprivileged groups from their unhappy condition, or to eliminate the relative differences between them' (p. 211). Emancipatory politics wants to reduce or eliminate exploitation, inequality and oppression.

Emancipatory politics is guided by the imperatives of 'justice, equality and participation.' The norms of justice determine what passes for exploitation. Above all, emancipatory politics is preoccupied with overcoming exploitative, unequal or oppressive social relations. Its orientation, says Giddens, is 'away from' rather than 'towards.' The actual content of emancipation is not fleshed out. Behind most versions of emancipatory politics lies the principle of autonomy. 'Emancipation means that collective life is organized in such a way that the individual is capable – in some sense or another – of free and independent action in the environments of her social life . . . . The individual is liberated from constraints placed on our behaviour as a result of exploitative, unequal or oppressive conditions; but she is not thereby rendered free in any absolute sense' (p. 213). Habermas's framework for emancipatory politics offers the ideal-speech situation, immanent in all language use, as an animating vision of emancipation. 'The more social circumstances approximate to an ideal-speech situation, the more a social order based on the autonomous action of free and equal individuals will emerge' (p. 213). The substance of the choices is left open.

Giddens believes that life politics is more expressive of the conditions of late modernity. If, as Beck argues, unmoored individuals have been forced to be the 'stage director of their own biography, identity, social networks, commitment and convictions' (1994, p. 14), then we might imagine that we would see a decline in emancipatory politics (the position of Castells and Bauman). In its stead, a 'politics of self-actualization' appears as agency retreats from grand theatrics. Life politics 'concerns political issues which flow from processes of self-actualization in post-traditional contexts, where globalizing influences intrude deeply into the reflexive project of the self, and conversely where processes of self-realization influence global strategies' (p. 214). Life politics, then, is a politics of life decisions. They are decisions affecting self-identity itself. Unhinged from traditional scripts, individuals must reflexively craft their own biographies in a world of great risk, insecurity and anxiety. With power evidently diffused through the different domains of society (work, state, civil society, private), the individual must negotiate power as she moves from setting to setting to realise her potential and desires. 'Only if the person is able', Giddens argues, 'to develop an inner authenticity – a framework of basic trust by means of which the lifespan can be understood as a unity against the backdrop of shifting social events – can this be attained' (p. 215). A tall order, given the volatility erupting in power-infused domains like work and state systems.

Life politics plays itself out on the terrain of body and self-image. Feminist analyses and politics have made us aware over the last three decades how significant life politics (identity and constructing new life-plans) has been to their liberatory project (likewise, with the various strands of gay struggles for recognition). Giddens thinks that the 'body' used to be simply given, but today it has 'become emancipated – the condition for reflexive restructuring' (p. 218). The increase in the 'reflexive practices of everyday life' (Philippe, 2000) – weight watchers, appearance, exercise, lovemaking manuals – indicates that the body is no longer simply the object of industrial discipline. Rather, it is immediately pertinent to the person's identity. Now individuals, stage directors of their shifting identities, must 'make choices concerning strategies of bodily development in life-planning, as well as to determine the "disposal" of bodily products and bodily parts' (p. 219). These choices force a reflexive engagement with power, coded into various products pushed (or branded) by the promotional culture. This, I think, is the essential argument of Naomi Klein's popular text, *No Logo: Taking Aim at the Brand Bullies* (2000).

The discussion thus far draws in the world of social relations external to the self mainly in terms of their reflexive impact on self-identity and lifestyle. But personal decisions, Giddens argues, also link person to planet. Ecological concerns, largely responsible for the 'unexpected renaissance of a political subjectivity' (Beck, 1994, p. 18), acknowledge that 'reversing the degradation of the environment depends upon adopting new lifestyle patterns' (Giddens, 1991, p. 221). As Giddens observes: 'Widespread changes in lifestyle, coupled with a de-emphasis on continual economic accumulation, will almost certainly be necessary if the ecological risks we now face are to be minimized' (p. 222). A poignant example of the linkage between the person's body and the planet is EarthSave Canada's stark message on their brochure. 'What you place on the end of your fork', they observe, 'has profound implications for the environment . . .'. Like other eco-activists, EarthSave connect our Western eating habits (a diet with excessive amounts of protein, saturated fat, cholesterol, pesticides) with many of the main environment issues – desertification, fresh water availability, ocean pollution, biological diversity, and rainforest destruction. They argue that, once the veil on the ecological perils of the meat-centred diet is lifted, a plant-based diet can transform one's fork into a 'powerful tool for environmental protection and restoration.'

In sum, Giddens believes that the life-political agenda has been produced by the emancipatory impact of modern institutions. It emerges from the centrality of the reflexive project of the self in late modernity. What is the sense of politics in 'life politics'? All issues of life politics, says Giddens, involve questions of rights and obligations, and the state thus far continues to be the main administrative locus within which these are settled in law. Life-political issues are likely to assume greater and greater importance in the public and juridical arenas of states. Today life-political issues permeate many areas of social life in late modernity. In my part of the world, the Comox Valley on Vancouver Island, a significant minority of citizens have chosen lifestyles that continuously confront the economic and political elites with demands to protect wildlife, watershed areas, urban wilderness parks, river walkways and estuaries, wild salmon, fresh water, and toxic free goods. Giddens reminds us that emancipatory politics will not simply come to an end. 'In late modernity, access to means of self-actualization becomes itself one of the dominant focuses of class division and the distribution of inequalities more generally' (p. 228). The ecology movement is a potent illustration of the fusion of life politics and the old emancipatory orientation to overcoming fundamental splits in the human community and natural world.

Jurgen Habermas: The learning dynamics of civil society

In his recent text, *Between Facts and Norms* (1996), Habermas continues to evolve a view of democracy that challenges both the cynicism of contemporary political theorising and the idealism of the comunitarians. Habermas remains committed to a deliberative form of democracy, the foundational importance of the lifeworld for healthy human existence and civil society as the pre-eminent learning domain. Habermas's famous transformation of critical social theory into a critical communicative learning theory was a revolutionary conceptual move for the just learning society paradigm. Unlike other contemporary political thinkers, Habermas consciously constructs civil society as a learning infrastructure. As new problems are fed into (or arise out of) civil society, this infrastructure is mobilised to process these problems pedagogically and translate learning into action agendas. Or, conversely, the learning infrastructure is so damaged and dysfunctional that citizen voices are defeated, muffled or muzzled.

Habermas's text is very complex and problematic. In fact, *Between Facts and Norms* offers us two versions of deliberative democracy, one radically democratic, the other more accommodative to the realities of actually existing democracies. In the strong version, Habermas emphasises that all manifestations of political power must ultimately derive from communicative power; even if indirectly, administrative power tends to legitimise itself by reference to discursive (or learning) processes based in civil society (1996, p. 169). The medium of law merely transfers or translates communicative power into administrative power. The primacy of deliberatively derived law assures that communicative power effectively 'determines the direction' (p. 187) of the political system; in another formulation, Habermas claims that communicative power 'maintains' or 'asserts' itself against administrative and market mechanisms (p. 299). Habermas does not intend to deny that complex markets and bureaucracies are relatively autonomous from the integrative power of communicative action. But some formulations in *Between Facts and Norms* indicate that their autonomy can be contained by a relatively far-reaching set of democratic checks and controls on their operations. The strong model suggests that communicative power gains a pre-eminent position against money and administrative power. Habermas builds on the argument of Nancy Fraser, who has openly criticised Habermas (as has Thomas McCarthy (1991)) for giving away too much to systems theorists (like Niklas Luhmann). Fraser offers us an important distinction between 'strong' and 'weak' publics.

For Fraser, weak publics are unburdened by the immediate task of formal decision making, whereas strong publics (an elected legislature) are those 'whose discourse encompasses both opinion formation and decision making' (1992, pp. 109–42). Habermas reproduces this formulation in chapters four and seven. For him, parliament at times is conceived as an extension of the deliberative networks constitutive of civil society, as an 'organized middle point or focus of a society-wide network of communication' (1996, p. 182). Parliament is merely a technical device necessary in large, complex societies to 'focus' the process of political debate and exchange, but this technical feature need not extinguish parliament's own deliberative attributes. The task of making certain that parliamentary bodies are 'porous' to civil society, to use Habermas's expression, is thus eminently realistic in light of the fact that there is nothing structurally distinct between weak and strong publics. In both, communicative power is predominant (Scheuermann, 1999, p. 159). The ideal of the strong public is most compatible with the just learning society paradigm.

But Habermas admits that in parliament, time constraints necessitate that actors are less concerned with the 'discovery and identification than the treatment' of problems, 'less with developing a sensibility for new problem positions than with justifying the choice of problems and deciding between competing solutions' (p. 307). Parliament still serves as a site for impressive debate and exchange, even if the imperatives of the formal decision-making process reduce the 'wild' and 'anarchic' features in civil society. Habermas also suggests that 'deciding between competing solutions' is likely to heighten the importance of compromise within the 'strong' parliamentary public. If compromise is to be fair it must be in accordance with three conditions: (1) it provides advantages to each party; (2) it tolerates no 'free riders'; (3) no one is exploited in such a way as to force them to give up more than they gain by compromise (pp. 165–7). As Stephen White has noted (1988, pp. 76–7), this theory of compromise means that 'it is the privileged agent who is confronted with the choice of . . . demonstrating to what degree his inequality can be discursively justified', of showing that it is in accordance with standards of procedural equality, participation, non-deception and non-manipulation. In this model, the process of reaching and then defending any particular compromise seems unlikely to suppress dialogical learning processes. On the contrary, it seems destined to encourage debate in so far as citizens are required by it to consider whether compromise procedures actually compensate for 'asymmetrical power structures' (Habermas, 1996, p. 177; Scheuermann, 1999, p. 160).

The model of the parliament–civil society interaction in the just learning society requires the encouragement of debate. Citizens cannot always be waving every issue or problem in the face of a distracted parliament. But Habermas's mention of 'asymmetrical power structures' is very telling because Fraser's distinction between strong and weak publics relies on the insight that 'where societal inequality persists, deliberative processes in public spheres will tend to operate to the advantage of dominant groups and to the disadvantage of subordinates' (1992, pp. 122–3). Thus, the achievement of a truly freewheeling, vibrant, effusive civil society, as well as a parliament responsive to its dictates, demands that we radically challenge asymmetries of power. Habermas reproduces Fraser's explicitly socialist argument: 'All members of the political community have to be able to take part in discourse, though not necessarily in the same way' (p. 182). In order for this requirement to gain substance, an egalitarian social environment needs to have been achieved: 'Only on a social basis that has transcended class barriers and thrown off thousands of years of social stratification and exploitation can we achieve a fully thriving civil society' (p. 308). At another point Habermas describes the merits of a civil society 'adequately decoupled' from class structures. Then he adds that 'social power should only manifest itself [in civil society] to the extent that it enables and does not hinder the exercise of citizenship' (p. 175).

Habermas rightly follows Fraser in focusing on the social barriers to deliberative democracy: the idea of a freewheeling deliberative democracy (or just political learning society) remains utopian as long as avoidable social inequalities undermine the deliberative capacities of the vast majority of humankind. To the extent that civil society is especially vulnerable to the pressure of class domination, then, it would see incumbent on a democratic theory which places special emphasis on the importance of unhindered debate within civil society – the just learning society's aspiration – to salvage something of the socialist critique of the crippling inequalities of capitalist society, even if we now surely need to acknowledge the undeniable virtues of complex markets and bureaucracies in modern society. But *Between Facts and Norms* does not say anything systematic about 'social asymmetries of power', let alone how to counteract them (Scheuermann, 1999, pp. 160–1).

Placing Habermas in critical dialogue with the likes of Barney and Bauman leads William Scheuermann (and myself) to wonder if *Between Facts and Norms* fails to 'give adequate expression to legitimate unease and anxiety about the fate of representative democracy at the end of the twentieth century' (Scheuermann, 1999, p. 155). In a provocative essay, 'The talking cure in Habermas's republic', Deborah Cook observes that many citizens are not

> even sufficiently motivated to put a mark on a ballot every five years, let along to engage in sustained, reasoned discussion of public affairs. The privately owned media pander primarily to the profit-making interests of their owners and advertisers. Even when information is not withheld altogether, coverage and analysis is often biassed, sometimes actually impeding responsible opinion-making. Despite recent experiments in electronic town halls and citizens' forums, there are far too few institutionalized channels of communication between the public and the political realm. Even when politicians are made aware of the opinions of their constituents, they will often ignore them in favour of their own interests, or those of their financial backers or other allies. (2001, pp. 135–6)

Despite the flooding of millions of protestors into the world's streets on 15 February 2003 to protest against the US invasion of Iraq, the present moment in global history has intensified the concern that communicative power (critique, argument, persuasion, warnings) – so valued by deliberative democrats – is far removed from the centres of decision-making powers. Despite this wonderful display of public morality, the war went ahead. In our unipolar world, proponents of dialogue face a US Empire that negates opposition, shunts intellect and culture to the sidelines. The Empire is a monologic space. President Bush gives declarations. He appears to be unopen to learning anything. Bernhard Peters, a German political theorist, thinks that the ideal of radical, or deliberative democracy is mainly a myth, seldom (if ever) realised in practice (see Scheuermann, 1999, pp. 163–4). I would not go that far, but it does seem that the enemies of deliberation, of the just learning society (fundamentalist mind-sets, a war ethos with its incessant propaganda, willingness to lie and deceive on part of political leaders, the dumbing-down effect of the media and television) abound in our day.

Between Facts and Norms articulates another, less radical, more defensive vision of democracy. At best, Habermas's model of parliament is an ideal of how parliament should operate. But most parliaments today continue to rubber-stamp decisions made elsewhere, doing the bidding of economic power. In British Columbia, Canada's polarised west coast, one searches in vain for evidence of fair compromises. Two lines of Habermas's argument are troublesome. First, Habermas uses the metaphor of centre and periphery to illustrate how themes emerge 'at the periphery and pass through the sluices of democratic and constitutional procedures situated at the entrance to the parliamentary complex or the court' (1996, p. 356). This metaphor helps us to understand how the learning process works in the civil learning infrastructure. But Habermas informs us that the 'deliberative periphery inevitably plays a minor role in determining the policy-making process' (Scheuermann, 1999, p. 165; Habermas, 1996, pp. 356–9, 379–91). Thus, in normal times communicative power is dormant. Only when crisis moments erupt in the society do 'communicative processes within civil society and parliament . . . take on a renewed significance for decision making' (Scheuermann, 1999, p. 165).

Within Habermas's scenario, the new social movements can play a 'surprisingly active and momentous role' (1996, p. 371) in crisis situations. In these times, citizens get the opportunity to 'reverse normal circuits of communication' (p. 381). Habermas argues that the controversial topics of our day – genetic engineering, ecological threats, spiralling nuclear arms race – were not 'brought up by exponents of the state apparatus, large organizations, or functional systems. Instead, they

171

were broached by intellectuals, concerned citizens, radical professionals, self-proclaimed "advocates"...' (p. 381). The new social movements raise their issues, dramatising and presenting them so that the media will take up them up. Movements have to get the attention of the public and 'gain a place on the "public agenda"' (p. 381), and then follow an often tortuous route to parliamentary gates without any guarantees that the issue will even be addressed. Andrew Parkin contends that the new social movements may fulfil four functions. First, they strengthen civil society by forming independent associations and organisations within civil society. These associations produce social solidarity and renew the spiritual and organisational resources needed for efficacious collective action. Second, by cracking open blocked public space, the new social movements ensure that reflective learning processes occur outside the control of government and private corporate interest. More public participation is demanded and new channels of communication are opened up beyond the grasp of the state and direct control of private capital. Third, the new social movements signal the importance of creating a global civil society to counterpoint the globalisation of capital. Finally, the new social movements practice a politics of inclusion by incorporating marginalised perspectives into their public deliberations. 'Each of these four dimensions', Parkins says, 'of new social movement practice – the strengthening, defending, and the expanding of the scope and inclusiveness of civil society – help to tilt the balance of power away from government, bureaucracies and privately owned corporations, in favour of individuals and independent public associations active within civil society' (Parkin, 1996, pp. 16–18).

This second line of Habermas's argument – giving pre-eminent role to social movements as radical democratic learning sites – is not without its conceptual and practical problems. Scheuermann believes that 'passing reference to a panoply of left-liberal social movements hardly constitutes adequate evidence for an empirical claim as ambitious as this one.' In fact, Scheuermann thinks that one can present social movements in a rather less favourable light.

> Whatever their undeniable merits, these movements may also provide evidence for worrisome tendencies within contemporary representative democracy: precisely because the 'centre' has gained exorbitant power in relation to the 'periphery,' extra-parliamentary social movements, engaging illegal action (i.e. civil disobedience),

have emerged to fill the gap left by a formal political system increasingly dominated by ossified parties and organised vested interests. Similarly, civil disobedience often represents what Habermas himself calls "the final instrument" (BFN 382) whereby political groups hope to ward off state action which they consider altogether unbearable; emphasizing this rather defensive form of political action hardly seems the best way to demonstrate the continued vitality of civil society in contemporary democracy. (Scheuermann, 1999, pp. 166–7)

Proponents of the just learning society paradigm are also faced with several disconcerting matters. For one thing, how might we be so sure that civil society will reactivate itself during crisis moments? Habermas thinks that as long as the periphery is 'able and effective to identify outbreaks of illegitimate social power' (1996, p. 167), the power of political elites can be counteracted. But a dormant public, subjected to privatising tendencies and entrenched old-style politics, can be easily manipulated by public relations tricks and tactics. The reactivation of civil society presupposes two things: the citizenry must have the requisite virtues and the motivation to be active. Simone Chambers says that

> [i]mplementing practical discourse, then, is not so much a matter of setting up a constitutionally empowered 'body' of some sort as it is of engendering a practice. It involves fostering a political culture in which citizens actively participate in public debate and consciously adopt the discursive attitudes of responsibility, self-discipline, respect, cooperation, and productive struggle necessary to produce consensual agreements . . .. The road from public debate in which strategic actors compete in a marketplace of ideas to public debate in which discursive actors democratically work through their differences is a long one. Its length, however, is a poor argument for not setting out on the journey. (1995, p. 177)

Civil societarian adult educators would be committed to realising the following learning objectives: learning how to compromise; to take reflective distance from our own perspectives so as to entertain others; learn to value difference; recognise or create anew what we have in common; come to see which dimensions of our traditions are worth preserving, which ought to be abandoned. But these communicative virtues can easily remain lovely ideals when those with money and political power control the means of communication (the mass media).

When these virtues are absent from civil society, civil society can go bad. Without deep and persistent traditions of tolerance and respect for the other, a crisis moment for any society may be turned against particular ethnic groups who become the cause of the crisis itself. During World War II in Canada, for instance, the 20,000 Japanese living on Vancouver Island and the mainland of British Columbia (B.C.) were evacuated from the coastal region. They lost their houses, boats, possessions. They were displaced to internment camps or sugar-beet farms in Alberta. At the height of the hostility to the 'enemy alien' after the bombing of Pearl Harbour on 7 December 1941, the stereotypical image of the Japanese – as unassimilable and innately aggressive – was used as a pretext for anti-Japanese B.C. politicians to 'cleanse' B.C. of its enemy within. Both Adachi (1976) and Sunahara (1981) document the relative ease these politicians had in mobilising civil society against the Japanese. The sparks of racist attitudes lay smouldering in B.C. civil society; B.C. advocates of a 'white Canada forever' (Ward, 1978) were able to fan these sparks into a bonfire that swept through the churches, voluntary associations, political parties and the media. Without traditions of rational public debate and governmental willingness to forgo self-interested decision making in the interest of just treatment of all members of the society, the communicative potential of civil society is blocked, and civil society itself is actually degraded.

Feminist scholars (Benhabib, 1992, 1995; Fraser, 1989, 1992; Fleming, 1997; Ryan, 1992) have explored the way social inequalities between men and women (enacted in patriarchal beliefs and practices) can infect civil society. Fraser (1989; reprinted in Meehan, 1995a) argued that Habermas failed to consider that 'gender', in fact, might be a code similar to 'money' or 'power' that mediated the relationships between men and women. Male interest, prestige and power are at play in the internal constitution of both the family and work. Fleming (1997) is particularly troubled by Habermas's failure to denote child-rearer or nurturer as one the fundamental roles played by men and women in late modern societies. Feminists have also questioned Habermas's stylised account of the emergence of the liberal bourgeois public sphere. Eley (1992) argues convincingly that the network of clubs and associations – philanthropic, civic, professional and cultural – were not accessible to everyone. He thinks that these associations were 'the arena, the training ground, and eventually the power base of a stratum of bourgeois men who were coming to see themselves as a "universal class". . .' (1992, p. 114). These men had an interest in restricting women to the domestic (or private) sphere. The irony here is that men touted rationality, accessibility and suspension of status hierarchies while simultaneously using them as markers of gendered distinction. This commentary does not, I think, undermine Habermas's basic argument that the liberal public sphere introduced a universal norm that carried the potential to undermine its particularistic historical practice. Ryan (1992) introduces an important insight from her historical investigation of nineteenth-century American women who created a women-centred alternative public sphere. Habermas (1992, 1996) now recognises that societies have a plurality of publics. These feminist critiques recall Gramsci's powerful analysis of the way ruling elites rule by gaining hegemony over civil society.

Politically responsible adult education

We have travelled through the landscape of contemporary political theory, searching for the main ingredients to craft a conceptual framework for citizenship in the age of information. Of all the theorists discussed, Habermas is the one who consciously thinks about the learning dynamics of civil society in its multiple interactions with state administrative systems and the economy. But one of the main problems we have identified with the Habermasian framework is how, in the actually existing world of democracy, communicative power can be transformed into administrative power. The works of Bauman and Barney provide the necessary substantive analysis of what the just learning society paradigm is up against. Bauman's 'migration of power' thesis stretches the idea of communicative power out beyond its nation-state borders. Castells confronts us with the incredible power of the electronic media. In our historical moment, economic globalisation appears to be driven by gargantuan transnational corporations who are wealthier than most of the world's nation-states, and command the ability to subject national state administrative systems to their wishes (privatisation, de-regulation, and so on). To be sure, Habermas has insisted in *Between Facts and Norms* (and elsewhere) that the system and the individual biography are never completely uncoupled. Although this may be true (it seems so: there is a thread connecting the slums of Port-au-Prince in Haiti to the World Bank and IMF), there can be no denying the pervasive sense of powerlessness to influence the system amongst the world's peoples.

Barney's version of the foreclosure of the political challenges the just learning society paradigm from another angle. He thinks that the world's leading liberal democracies are, in fact, bound to a monofocal way of imagining the world. Capitalism, liberalism and technology comprise a holy trinity that brooks no opposition. Barney's thesis gains considerable power in the aftermath of the collapse of the socialist project throughout the world. The international left is in utter disarray, unable to penetrate the illusion that there is no alternative to the holy trinity. Habermas, for his part, would not be so despairing. Barney has closed off the political universe prematurely. Constitutional democracies have evolved legal systems that contain hard-fought human rights for its citizens. Legal systems in liberal democracies filtrate universal norms (or tolerance and respect for the other) into the everyday workings of civil society and the system. Though degraded, multiple public spheres do, in fact, function in the liberal democracies. The new social movements, as flawed as they may well be, contain utopian potential to confront liberal democracies that ascribe to a philosophy of no limits (or restrictions) on growth. The ecology movement (with its many tendencies) erects roadblocks to untrammelled economic development, everywhere in the world. Still, one cannot deny the power of Scheureman's critical observations that the presence of the new social movements also signals deep flaws in actually existing democratic societies. It is not clear how proponents of the just learning society paradigm will grapple concretely with the yawning chasm between civil society and administrative systems.

I think it is important for communicative action procedures to be an integral part of the daily functioning of administrative systems. But even communicative mechanisms such as hearings and commissions never seem to break the stranglehold that money has on decision making. Thus, at the normative level it is relatively easy to say that administrative systems must be open to deliberative processes, or that communicative processes must be enabled by dynamic public spheres within civil society itself. It is not so easy to know, given existent social inequalities within liberal democracies and other non-democratic states, how the sluices or gateways between a mobilised civil society and administrative systems could be designed, such that parliamentarians would have to implement policies that the people have deliberated upon at length and concluded that a particular policy is in the best interests of the commonwealth. Citizen's assemblies, consensus conferences and juries are among several successful deliberative procedures promoted by adult educators throughout the world. Though tension always exists between administrative and communicative power, parliamentarians would have to provide good reasons for the decisions they have made. They would not be able to get elected through image manipulation and money-mediated interests alone. They would be more accountable for their decisions. Their decisions would have to enhance the life chances of the worst off and not simply perpetuate the opportunities for the better off to accumulate more wealth and goods. We seem rather far removed from these ideals at the moment.

Havel, Giddens and Habermas – each in his own way – affirm the existential power of the person to act. Havel insists that 'even a purely moral act that has no hope of any immediate and visible political effect can gradually and indirectly, over time, gain in political significance' (1990, p. 115). This deep existential commitment to the spiritual-moral power of the person is 'insistently rebellious' (Isaac, 1992, p. 249). Havel maintains that the powerless have more power than they ever imagine and moral acts of the person may reach beyond the isolated self-resonating deeply with those who are oppressed. Our oppressive conditions, be they South African apartheid, brutal communist regimes or the soft terrorism of consumer democracies, never totally exhaust us. We always possess the capacity to 'resist indignity and reconstitute community that can never be written off nor saddled by a political ideology' (p. 115). Like Habermas's communicative reason, human freedom is history's stubborn presence. Although Giddens does not embrace existential language, his thinking about life politics detects agency propelling the choices that citizens are making regarding their bodily presence in a socially fragmented and individualised world. We do not have to stretch too far to link Giddens' life politics and the dynamics at play in the new social movements. Citizens acquire knowledge in social movement activities because they have the learning space to do so. Anchored in their bodily sensibilities, new social movement participants seek to block certain forms of development (such as mining incursions into provincial parklands). In doing so, they make arguments that propose that blocking mining in a parkland, for instance, enhances the commonweal and does not simply advance middle class cultural interests. If intra-public deliberative learning procedures and processes are in place, it becomes possible to filter particular interests out from those claims that a said policy will benefit everybody.

Adult educators committed to the ideal of active citizenship have laboured innovatively to provide the learning contexts that would enable adults to become 'masters of their own destiny' (Coady, 1939; Welton, 2001). This often meant starting at square one: courses in public speaking and discussion facilitation. This sort of ordinary work, with its nose close to the grassroots, is usually invisible to political theorists. It may be invisible; it is not non-essential. Proponents of the just learning society should try to help youth and adults to acquire the know-how and skills of active citizenship as they participate in various groups. Associations can be schools of citizenship: places where people learn to respect and trust others, fulfil obligations and press their claims communicatively. The cluster of socialising agencies have to create internal pedagogical environments characterised by a firm commitment to foster an inquiring, sceptical attitude to authority's beliefs and actions (indoctrination is not permitted). There ought not to be a contradiction between the values of open and dialogic primary educational formation and the young adult's participation in associations, organisations and movements.

Oskar Negt (2000), a former student of Adorno and Habermas, argues that the learning potential within a society's civil infrastructure may, in fact, be dormant. Negt thinks that, 'We live in a world of epochal changes; traditional values and orientations are questioned, new binding values and orientations have not yet been established' (p. 9). New problems are constantly being fed into civil society. These 'trouble spots' (such as the requirements of globalisation or threats to the family unit), as Negt labels them, demand that the civil society infrastructure be mobilised so that, say, government decisions, measures and bills, can be translated into the 'curriculum of civil society' (my phrase) and processed for action. This mobilisation process requires that the learning potential residing within civil society (particularly the voluntary movement and public sectors) be released through intentional consciousness-raising in these sectors. It may also require the creation of new organisation forms to enable a society to provide its harried citizens with new qualifications and orientations for a world in transformation. Negt worries that European societies lack the 'manageable institutions in which people can recognize themselves in their thoughts and actions, so that they are approved and acknowledged in their personal environment.' He also thinks that the 'real problem with learning and education is not the amount of information but the ability to process the information.' He thinks that this pedagogical processing is the 'core function and task of further education in Europe' (p. 12). Another suggestive idea is Negt's identification of the new key qualifications and orientations that Euro-citizens require to attain full citizenship in an emergent cosmopolitan global order (identity, ecological and economic competencies for example). Civil society's functional tasks – transmitting meaningful life programmes, teaching social obligations and nurturing personally competent men and women – require continual responses from the civil learning infrastructure. In our fast-paced world, one can easily imagine that the problems feeding into the lifeworld of citizens could outpace the infrastructure's responses. The civil learning infrastructure could ossify around the formation of the industrial worker and citizen, and, as such, be completely inadequate for post-industrial (or other) societal formations. Even more serious, economic globalisation processes could so utterly damage the lifeworld foundations of society that the arduous task becomes that of painfully putting in place a minimally functional civil society.

CHAPTER EIGHT

The lifeworld curriculum:
Pathologies and possibilities

The concept of the lifeworld

The grand corpus of Jurgen Habermas offers a cornucopia of concepts and approaches for proponents of a just learning society. The lifeworld is an especially important notion because our attention is drawn to the ground of our learning capacity as human beings. If this general assertion is correct, then any damage to the lifeworld – it has elemental tasks to accomplish in time and space – has dire consequences for human well-being. Although there are different theoretical frameworks that are available to us, Habermas's recasting of historical materialism as an evolutionary social learning theory immediately entices me to see historical unfolding and contemporary societal dynamics, be they pathologies, problems, accomplishments, through his optic. In an earlier work, *In Defense of the Lifeworld: Critical Perspectives on Adult Learning* (Welton, 1995), I thought that defending the lifeworld was both a necessary collective action project for adult educators (and others of course) and an appropriate analytical tool for illuminating the learning processes of our species. Although I haven't changed my view, the account of the lifeworld offered in *In Defense of the Lifeworld* was too schematic. I am also aware that the pathologies of the lifeworld in both Western liberal democracies and many other non-democratic places on earth have become more pervasive. The glaring deficits of modernity – loss of meaning, feelings of powerlessness, unhappiness in the midst of a glut of material possessions, despair over deepening discrepancies between rich and poor, social fragmentation, moral confusion, personality disorders and addictions – are wreaking havoc in Western liberal democracies and elsewhere in the suffering world. This disconcerting reality beckons counter-proposals and action to enable the lifeworld to carry out its life-sustaining functions.

Habermas's way of understanding historical evolution provides the just learning paradigm with a useful way of thinking about social learning dynamics. He uses the social science concepts of 'social' and 'system' integration to describe the defining moment of capitalist modernity, arguing that system integration does not require communicative coordination. While drawing life sustenance from its tendrils in the rich soil of the lifeworld, the system is impelled along its learning trajectory geared to instrumental-rational efficiency. Social integration, in contrast, is symbolically structured. Social evolution manifests itself along two axes of human learning: one, an instrumental logic of learning how to find efficient (or successful) ways of producing and administering one's existence; the other, increased potential for reflexive action in a rationalised lifeworld bound together through communicative processes. Increased reflexivity means that with the advent of modernity traditions are constantly questioned and revised. In all of his work, Habermas argues that the lifeworld is the source of human activity, connectedness and meaningfulness.

Habermas posits that communicative actors always move within the horizon of their lifeworld (1987, pp. 179, 187–9, 192). By this, Habermas refers to the culturally transmitted and linguistically organised reservoir of meaning patterns – background knowledge or cognitive maps – available to members of society. No single actor, Habermas is at pains to inform us, is ever fully aware of the background assumptions informing one's horizon. As a phenomenological sociologist like Alfred Schutz might say, the person is thrown into a world already sedimented with layers of interpretative patterns, normative orientations and myriads of recipes for relating to people and things. Lifeworlds are patterned ways space is organised to help us order our lives. We devise category systems to order our kitchens and our cooking activities. We are adept at making our personal lives functionally meaningful. Towels here, sporting equipment there, bikes kept outside.

Yet the use of 'we' in the preceding sentences may blind us to the bedrock reality that women are the managers of the lifeworld. Women dwell in the connected worlds of the homeplace (Gilligan, 1982; Hart, 1992, 1995; Gouthro, 1999, 2002). They tend to be more attuned morally to the needs of those close at hand than men, whose energies are consumed in workspaces. Women do the lion's share of the work of transmitting meaning-systems to dependent children. They provide the children with necessary stories to knit the various strands of living into a coherent pattern for negotiating life's pathways, fraught with the unexpected and the surprising. They perform the daunting, awesome work of ensuring that the vulnerable infant is nurtured in a respectful manner. They are the child's first moral educators as they teach them how to relate to other 'I's present in their lifeworlds. Feminist social and moral theorists (Benhabib, 1987, 1995; Cooke, 1999) alert us to the way the gender-sex system is both historically constituted and embodied in taken-for-granted cultural norms. All human societies have been patriarchal and have not valued women's lifeworld work as of equal value. Thus, oppressive and exploitative gender-sex arrangements bind women to the homeplace (the private sphere) and constrain women from being full and equal participants in public spaces. To be sure, women make choices and do, in fact, often accept the normative status quo. Pulled between the system and the lifeworld, many modern women struggle to balance paid work and family work (Hakim, 2000). But patriarchal values and systems may place brakes on the full human development and possibility for some women. These values present themselves in the intricacies of everyday lifeworld processes whereby boys and girls learn their status-differentiated places in the world (Dinnerstein, 1976; Balbus, 1982; Chodorow, 1978). Girls are tugged towards the lifeworld more strongly than boys.

Habermas's idea that the lifeworld is communicatively structured is, as feminist theorist Marie Fleming reminds us, central to his 'understanding of the problem of meaning and to his reconstruction of historical materialism' (Fleming, 1997, p. 192). Habermas's ambitious (and often controversial) theory of communicative action assumes that post-traditional persons learn to adopt different attitudes toward corresponding worlds. 'It is raining' refers to an objective world, 'I have a headache' to the subjective and 'Abortion is morally wrong' to the normative. In some traditional cultures, for example, a statement such as 'It is raining' is inextricably tied to the 'gods are blessing us.' For the experiencing subject, then, the lifeworld is 'constituted by interpretative patterns organized in language and handed down in cultural traditions' (1987, p. 135). Sociologists Peter and Brigitte Berger and Hansfield Kellner remind us in *The Homeless Mind: Modernization and Consciousness* (1974) that modernity creates a plurality of lifeworlds. We all have lifeworlds. We do not all share common understandings of what constitutes the life well lived. Intractable debates on what life is and when it begins is but one telling illustration of this reality.

Modernity not only uncouples the system from the lifeworld. It also produces separate institutional spheres (like formal schools for children and youth that originate only in the early nineteenth century) to perform the work of making meaning (cultural reproduction), stabilising personal identities and solidarity (social reproduction) and fostering individual skilfulness (socialisation). The lifeworld provides actors with narratives and vocabularies to orient their actions in and with the world and others. Actors make sense of their everyday world by drawing upon taken-for-granted funds of myths, sagas, sacred scripts, sentiments, common sense and science. Traditionally, religion has been the storehouse for orienting stories, filtered and adapted through time in response to changing circumstances. This stock of knowledge supplies interpretations as we come to an understanding about the objective world of natural things and processes, other people close to us and far away, and our inner selves. It also provides participants with norms to regulate their membership in social groups. The lifeworld pedagogical processes produce the competences that enable actors to speak and act with confidence, resilience, verve and imagination, placing them in a position to take part in processes of reaching understanding and thereby asserting their own identities. Thus, if the socialisation processes are functioning adequately, actors make sense together and are motivated to act normatively. The way we live our lives is interwoven with the language we are immersed in.

For actors to speak and act with confidence, verve and intelligence, their lifeworlds must provide them with the right nutrients for the growth (and unfolding) of sense-making in the midst of the hurly-burly of life. The bedrock of the lifeworld is the provision of safety, security and sustenance for all of us, but particularly the children, youth, the frail elderly, the mentally retarded, the homeless. Harmful, anxiety-producing and unstable conditions distort the socialisation process, giving rise to numerous pathologies amongst children. One need think only of the devastating consequences of wars on the lives of children, unspeakable damage, in fact. Wars of all sorts leave children orphaned, often homeless, left to fend for themselves amongst the rubble. In the former Soviet Union, to provide but one tragic illustration, World War II left 600,000 parentless children. Today, a social crisis has now left 700,000 'social orphans' in Russia. These children, abandoned by the state and dejected parents, are left to scrabble out a terrible existence without affection and care in metro underpasses (Walsh, 2004). They find their counterparts in most of the teeming cities of our world, from Mumbai to São Paulo. Once safety and security is gained (no easy matter in most of the world), it becomes possible to speak of needs for competence, efficacy and self-esteem. The attainment of competence and feelings of efficacy are intimately related to our need for connectedness and relatedness to other people. Masterfulness requires arenas for its expression. Isolation from others and feelings of unworthiness drive us away from situations where we could express our know-why and know-how. We also have needs for autonomy and authenticity. We must be able to engage in activity that is challenging, interesting and enjoyable.

The idea of the self as relational (or situated) is fully compatible with the paradigm of the just learning society. Until recently, Western philosophy and psychology has been saddled with a debilitating vision of the solitary self. One thinks immediately of Descartes' 'I think therefore I am' or Hobbes' metaphor of the 'self as mushroom.' These ideas imagined that the human self was unitary, containing some essential substance that did not change over time, conceivable apart from others. Although the idea of a unitary, substantial self had been challenged convincingly by the Buddha in the axial period of history (Jaspers, 1962; Armstrong, 2001; Mishra, 2004), contemporary critical, feminist and post-structural thought challenged the prevalent, masculinist view on two fronts. Habermas and his colleagues replaced the solitary self with a self formed inter-subjectively. Like Habermas, cultural feminists (such as Gilligan (1982)) insisted that the self was embedded and embodied in a web of relationships. But they were reluctant to admit that men and women moved along a single trajectory of ego, moral and ethical development. Post-structural feminists (Flax, 1993; Butler, 1992) offered a third view of the self as fractured, fluid, multiple. Perhaps each of these views captures a dimension of the ever-elusive self. The unitary view names the constancy of the 'I' even as time and circumstances change. The relational self is sociologically credible. 'I' am utterly dependent on the air surrounding me and the intricate web of relationships extending to the far reaches of the globe for my nurture, shelter, food and spiritual sustenance. The post-structural sense of the self captures the often distressing daily experience of conflicting passions, changing moods, uncalled for thoughts whistling through the mind, constantly shifting contexts and relationships. One moment one is elated, the next moment, for no apparent reason, down in the dumps. I am confident and assertive in one situation, a confused, bewildered person in another. No wonder that some social theorists would doubt the idea that there is, in fact, a substantial, unchanging self.

But post-structural conceptions of the self drift inexorably towards erasing the possibility of human agency. Habermas insists that we ought not discard the ideal of autonomy. We have the capacity to be self-determining moral agents. Following Kant, he argues that agents are 'autonomous to the extent that they judge and act in accordance with morally valid norms and principles that they themselves accept as such' (Cooke, 1999, p. 195). What is fair for one, is fair for all. Perhaps the greatest learning challenge for children and youth is to break free from thinking of themselves as self-encased egos towards a deep openness to the vulnerable face of the other (Levinas, 1969; Hendley, 2000). Habermas distinguishes self-determining moral action from self-expression. To be self-expressing, I must shape my life project in a personally meaningful way while recognising the equally valid existence of other projects. My view of the 'good life' cannot be imposed on anyone else. In a post-metaphysical world, there are no universally valid views of the good life. But I would argue that the positing of a regulative ideal, like the just learning paradigm, can act as a 'filter that will enable us to reject certain kinds of conceptions of the good while allowing for a broad spectrum of possible ones' (Cooke, 1999, p. 200). One cannot, then, split absolutely concerns about the good life from moral ones. Indeed, the ideal of the just learning society identifies the good life with the conscious design of structures, in the system and lifeworld, that foster the unfolding of developmental potential of all human beings and earthly creatures (from inherent capacity in its givenness to acquired knowledge and action competencies to the structural preconditions for its realisation). This regulative ideal 'forbids us to turn away from the vulnerable other' (Cooke, 1999, p. 202). The good society is a just one.

With the wheels of modernity grinding away at received ideas and practices since the sixteenth century, Habermas notices that the authority of the sacred gradually weakens, unable to block developmental learning processes from unfolding, pressing cultural traditions to become more reflexive and subject to incessant testing. For their part, societal institutions can no longer find their legitimacy in transcendental locations. Personality systems extract their 'egos' from both 'culture' and societal embeddedness, giving rise to self-planning. But with the gains of modernity – increased reflexivity, more options in life-planning, openings for self-expression – come possible deficits and losses. With the secularisation of society (God, as German theologian Dietrich Bonhoeffer (1962) once said, explains less and less of life's situations and predicaments, and has been banished to the outer edges of the cosmos), a prolonged crisis of meaning is precipitated in Western societies. Since human beings have immense trouble living in a meaningless world, devoid of the succour of the gods and the promise of happiness beyond the grave, people are driven to create replacement narratives. Adherents of traditional religions are forced into defensive postures in the face of God's removal to the outskirts of society. Perhaps the central question for the just learning society paradigm is whether the host of new spiritual narratives (or re-fabricated old ones) foster resilient, tolerant engagement with the world.

The lifeworld can be pathologised when the world becomes too complex and events too random and unpredictable to make sense. The loss of meaning is not replaced adequately. People thrash around rather desperately to make sense of their everyday troubles, suffering, problems, let alone figuring out why the world beyond the vulnerable self seems so dangerous and risky. The lifeworld can also be destabilised when the individual is unmoored from community embeddedness. Our intertwinement in informal networks of family and friends – they funnel lifeworld resources to persons in need – gradually unravels. Divorce rates increase dramatically; families disintegrate. We become less dependent on our informal networks for insights, recipes for life's problems, care when we are buffeted by the vagaries of life. We lose our anchor points in the lifeworld. Our sense of social solidarity thins, society fragments into little lifeboats floating around, sometimes touching, mostly not. We don't participate in trade unions the way we used to. We attend fewer PTA meetings. We bowl by ourselves. We no longer imagine that we can master our life situations. We learn to be helpless by constantly per-mitting others to act while we feign passivity. The loss of meaning, the erosion of solidarity and moral uncertainty produce various psycho-pathologies in personality formation. In such a situation, the lifeworld is flooded with therapeutic imagery: we are all damaged, addicted, victims of an ever-multiplying host of illnesses.

Habermas's metaphor – the 'colonisation of the lifeworld' – provides us with a powerful analytical tool to grasp how the lifeworld loses its capacity to provide meaningful life scripts and orientation to life's pathways. Like his Frankfurt School forebears, Adorno and Horkheimer, Habermas believes that the fundamental disordering principle at work within capitalist modernity is the illegitimate intrusion of instrumental rationality into the lifeworld domain. The pathologisation occurs when '[m]oney and power – more concretely, markets and administrations – take over the integrative functions which were formerly fulfilled by consensual values and norms.' Habermas's thesis is that 'those domains of action which are specialized for the transmission of culture, social integration or the socialization of the young rely on the medium of communicative action and cannot be integrated through money or power. When these domains are commercialized or bureaucratized, disturbances or pathological side effects appear' (Habermas, in Dews, 1992, pp. 171–2). Habermas's successor, Axel Honneth, considers his mentor's approach to pathologisation overly cognitive. Honneth believes we must understand that 'with regard to an individual's relation to self, there exists under certain circumstances the threat of a disintegration of identity, because a person's particular motivational complexes have not been sufficiently integrated' (1995, p. xxi). This threat of disintegration must be grasped on its own terms, and not simply as a by-product of instrumental action. The new thematic of post-Habermasian critical social theory – the 'struggle for recognition' – will be taken up in the final section of this chapter.

Before this happens, I will examine some of the pathologies afflicting the contemporary Western lifeworld in the following two sub-sections. Taking my cues from Habermas and Honneth, I will argue that (1) the market system has achieved a god-like status in contemporary globalised capitalism. It measures 'value' and 'worth' only in terms of the production of commodities which can be exchanged on the market. It wants only to enhance profits; and, to do so, jumps its boundary and presses lifeworld institutions into its service, foreclosing deliberative learning processes about alternative ways of being in the world. We can, I think, consider high intensity consumer capitalism as a surrogate religious system: it offers to fill the deep lack in Western being (Loy, 2002). If consumerism pretends to resolve the crisis of meaning for the collectivity, I will argue that (2) 'therapeutic culture' (Furedi, 2004) of Western liberal democratic countries offers itself as a compelling way of interpreting everyday suffering, pain, problems, and disappointments. Although the therapeutic culture may well be a variant of high intensity consumerism, it can be analysed separately. Both consumerism and the

187

therapeutic culture, at their deepest level, undermine the central pedagogical aim of the just learning society paradigm: to create authentically empowered persons inhabiting lifeworlds that compel the system domains to respond to their needs and aspirations. Consumerism orients us away from contesting the system realms (of work and politics), offering us pleasurable fare and dessert to assuage our nagging sense of emptiness and powerlessness. Therapeutic culture, for its part, gently fosters the idea that it is just fine to accept one's self as a survivor and to not become co-dependent on others. It presents itself as the antidote to social fragmentation.

The religion of the market

David R. Loy, a professor of international studies at Bunkyo University in Japan and a Zen Buddhist teacher, offers us a compelling viewpoint on why we ought to understand our present economic system as the West's dominant religion. In *A Buddhist History of the West: Studies in Lack* (2002), Loy argues that, although religion is 'notoriously difficult to define', if we 'adopt a functionalist view and understand religion as what grounds us by teaching us what this world is, and what our role in the world is, then it becomes evident that traditional religions are fulfilling this role less and less, because that function is being supplanted by other belief systems and value systems' (p. 197). This is a shocking statement for those of conventional religious sensibility. Certainly the monotheistic religious traditions have not just disappeared into the thin air of modernity. One could make a solid case that Islamic cultures contain strong currents of resistance to Western consumerism (perceived as decadent and nihilistic). But in the West, Christianity in particular has lost much of its power to resist the new god that has (and is) conquering the old ones (just like Christianity did in its displacement of Roman deities). Although the monotheistic religions contain many different streams and tendencies (including ascetic and contemplative traditions), these minority traditions have not been able to prevent the market from becoming our 'first truly world religion, binding all corners of the globe into a worldview and set of values whose religious role we overlook only because we insist on seeing them as secular' (p. 197). Economics is the new theology of this global religion of the market; consumerism its highest good; all religions must come bearing gifts to Moloch, an ancient tyrannical object of sacrifice to whom children were offered, and those who do not are under fierce assault.

Loy wonders why we acquiesce in the appalling realities of global inequities and are able to sleep so peacefully at night. He finds his answer in Rodney Dobell's (1995) explanation that 'lies largely in our embrace of a peculiarly European or Western [but now global] religion, an individualistic religion of economics and markets, which explains all of these outcomes as the inevitable results of an objective system in which . . . intervention is counterproductive' (p. 232). Any intervention in the 'world of business' is perceived as a threat to the 'natural order of things', a direct challenge to the 'wisdom of the market.'

> The hegemony achieved by this particular intellectual construct – a 'European religion' or economic religion – is remarkable; it has become a dogma of almost universal application, the dominant religion of our time, shoring up and justifying what would appear to be a patently inequitable status quo. It has achieved an immense influence which dominates human activity. (p. 232)

Thus, the new theology teaches us that business activity is right and just because the market made us do it and that value can only be adequately signalled by prices. We sacrifice our time, our families, our children, our forests, our seas and our land on the altar of the market, the god to whom we owe our deepest allegiance. Forsaking the consumer paradise for a life of poverty, wandering with an empty begging bowl or a life devoted to alleviating the plight of others is scarcely an option for most religious persons.

Today we can scarcely find a moral perspective resident in the world religions to challenge the hegemony of the religion of the market. Indeed, globalising capitalism seems natural, the perfect fit with our human nature as essentially greedy and self-interested beings continually at war with one another over scarce resources. But economic historians (Weber, 1946; Tawney, 1926; Polyani, 1944) inform us that in pre-modern societies the 'material necessities of life were embedded within a total cultural milieu which regulated the circulation of goods according to social norms' (Leiss, 1976, p. 3). Pre-capitalist man (can we imagine such a creature?) values material goods only as long as they serve moral ends (enhancing social status and reinforcing social obligations). The famous potlatch ceremonies of the Kwawaka'wakw ('Kwakiutl' in the older orthography) native people of British

Columbia's majestic north-west coast, so abhorrent to nineteenth-century missionaries, was both a dramatic display of chiefly status and a mechanism for redistributing goods to less fortunate coastal communities. Ironically, the missionaries interpreted the potlatch through the eyes of materialistic Europe. They sought to ban its practice all the while bringing various European material goods and conceptions of private property into the traditional culture.

Beginning in the late middle ages and reaching its first plateau in the late eighteenth century, the capitalist market began to assume an autonomous, god-like existence. As Max Weber understood so well (*The Protestant Ethic and the Spirit of Capitalism* (1946)), gradually the inner worldly ascetic impulse to know and serve God, who would reveal himself in the silence of the prayer chamber, evaporated. Protestant believers began to measure God's favour by their economic success. Economic success was the means to achieve the end of God's favour and eternal salvation. But this fragile link could not abide centuries of unrelenting capitalist achievement and success. Eventually, the means, economic blessings, displaced God himself. God was now the Market, dwelling in the transcendental mist and the source of all hopes. Who today questions the need for growth, for a higher standard of living or disputes the gospel of sustained economic development? Even Jesus would drive an SUV, if we can believe the Rev Jerry Fallwell, the formidable American leader of the Christian Right.

Eighteenth-century Scottish Enlightenment thinker Adam Smith (1976) warned us over two centuries ago (in his *Theory of Moral Sentiments*) that the market was a 'dangerous system because it corrodes the very shared common values it needs to restrain its excesses' (Loy, 2002, p. 204). Two hundred years later, Polyani inveighed against a system that annihilated 'the human and natural substance of society' (1944, p. 163). These are prescient words that reverberate through Habermas's fears about the system's desiccations. Doesn't everyone know that the god we serve requires clear cut forests, depleted oceans, empty oil wells, toxics dumped into the biosphere? 'A direct line', Loy observes sadly, 'runs from the commodification of land, life, and patrimony during the eighteenth century to the ozone holes and global warming of today' (Loy, 2002, p. 204). Everyone also knows, deep down, in their heart of hearts, that the god we serve actually has no life of its own. It feeds on the life force of the natural and human worlds. It needs men and women who have energy and the motivation to work with others to produce the goods. Yet its production modes generate endless sickness amongst the workers and eternal problems for families. It needs the biosphere, but depletes it shamelessly. It needs the lifeworld, but leeches it of its nutrients. The money-code is at war with the life-code. Ironically, if the money-code wins out in the end, that, indeed, is the end.

William Leiss *(The Limits to Satisfaction: An Essay on the Problem of Needs and Commodities* (1976)) provides us with a lucid account of how the religion of the market seeks to meet the needs of its adherents. He argues that the high intensity market setting manipulates people into believing that they can meet their needs and fulfil their desires through purchasing particular commodities. Leiss sees some serious problems with this mode of needs–meeting. For one thing, individuals must have competent craft knowledge of the product that is supposed to meet the specific need. With goods proliferating endlessly and quickly, most people have neither time nor inclination to research the product. We rely on common-sense judgments. But these judgments are usually questioned by some recent scientific report. Ever attuned to what will sell while appearing to be good (or healthy) for you, corporations marketing wares that only yesterday were bad for you, now tell us, so assuredly, that the product is free of bad fat and is now good for your family's nutrition. We make our decisions about the food we eat in a whirl of uncertainty and conflicting messages from the media and the halls of science. The controversy around the Atkins Diet – which advocates eating no carbohydrates – illustrates well some of the problems we face in our lifeworld decision making. Even a cursory investigation of the scientific criticisms of this diet leads us to seriously doubt Atkins' claims. But the appeal of this counter-intuitive diet (What? I shouldn't eat potatoes? Red meat is ok?) is basically media-manipulated. North Americans are obsessed with being thin and so are easily influenced to try anything to shed the pounds. The Atkins' Diet is adopted by many people without any adequate craft knowledge of what effect the lack of carbohydrates will actually have on their health in the long run. Thus, guileful advertising, sloppy and irresponsible reporting of scientific research and blinkered scientific work itself linked with inadequate craft knowledge generates behavioural dissonance and inner confusion in those who are purchasing goods.

In the high intensity market setting, individuals are taught to 'identify states of feeling systematically with the appropriate type of commodities' (Leiss, 1976, p. 19). This is an insidious and dangerous learning process because individuals are being carefully led away from finding satisfaction in active citizenship, good work and aesthetic self-expression (making a living, living a life and expressing ourselves was the way Violet McNaughton, a brilliant early-twentieth-century Canadian adult educator, put it) to imagining that particular products actually do what their messages iterate. The job of advertising within the religion of the market is, as journals like *Adbusters* proclaim, to educate us incessantly to imagine that there is a real link between an impulse and the sacralised commodity. To illustrate: advertisers prey upon our authentic needs for self-respect and respect from others by decomposing the body into various parts. Then the authentic need for self-respect is channelled towards the consumption of various chemical mixtures that promise a pleasing appearance and recognition from others. Self-respect and respect from others, however, does not reside in any commodity. It is generated, if you will, through mutual, communicative activity. My self-respect is strengthened as I demonstrate mastery and skilfulness at work, at play, in various community activities while hearing the words 'nice effort' or 'job well done.' Simply consuming a commodity has nothing to do with what I, as a unique person, have thought, accomplished, struggled with others to fashion or build. In well-functioning healthy communities, it seems to me, most persons would not be seduced into really believing that self-respect (or self-esteem) could be gained through consuming the right product cluster. Once cut loose from traditional bonds and obligations, individuals easily become the playthings of marketing trends.

The religion of the market can maintain its grip on its devotees by constantly destabilising the categories of human need. Corporations spend billions of dollars annually on advertising (these agencies are our 'captains of consciousness' (Ewen, 1976)) designed only to make us feel dissatisfied, unsettled, ill at ease, without any deep harmony between our inner and outer worlds. We must be willing to believe there is something fundamentally defective with our bodies, minds and souls. We must also believe that the act of consuming – both simple and exquisitely executed products – will meet our needs, fulfil our heart's desires and make us happy. But fulfilment channelled through consumption is mainly a delusion. Leiss observes, tellingly, that, 'The constant re-division and recombination of need – fragments renders it increasingly difficult, if not impossible, for individuals to develop a coherent set of objectives for their needs and thus to make judgments about the suitability of particular goods for them' (1976, p. 88). Thus, having displaces being as the core value of the upstart religion.

The iconoclastic Buddhist scholar, Stephen Batchelor, offers penetrating commentary on 'having and being' in *Alone with Others: An Existential Approach to Buddhism* (1983). 'Having', he observes, 'is characterized by acquisitiveness. Our worldview is dominated by the notion that the aim of personal existence is fulfilled in proportion to what we are able to amass and possess' (p. 25). Craving, the source of endless suffering for Buddhist teachers, impels men and women to possess material objects that appear to 'offer protection, security, and social status through their tangible and starkly present solidity' (p. 26). We are also impelled to possess people – husbands, wives, children, friends, acquaintances – 'all arranged in a circle around us connected to the center by threads of attachment and possessiveness' (p. 26). We can also crave immaterial things, like thought, acquiring 'new possibilities' for further knowledge acquisition. Batchelor argues that 'even our bodies and minds are regarded as "things" we "have". Life is said to be the most valuable thing we possess' (p. 26). For Batchelor, 'having always pre-supposes a sharply defined dualism between subject and object. The subject thus seeks his or her well-being, as well as his or her sense of meaning and purpose, in the preservation and acquisition of objects for which he or she is necessarily isolated' (p. 27). 'I am what I have' is the way Fromm (1976) puts it in *To Have Or To Be?* But any 'sense of fulfilment will necessarily be illusory, because there is nothing one can have that one cannot fear to lose. Absorption in the horizontal dimension of having is the origin of all states of ontological insecurity' (Batchelor, 1983, p. 26). Buddhist social philosophers like Loy and Batchelor believe that compulsive motivation to have things attempts to fill the lack in people's lives. In fact, this motivation to fill the lack through possession has penetrated our consciousness so deeply that the traditional sphere of religion – the 'receptacle for the traditional symbols of being' – are approached as 'another region of having' (Batchelor, 1983, p. 28). One can possess eternal life, immortality, enlightenment, and the kingdom of heaven.

But the delusions fostered by the religion of the market are not limited to individual consciousness and needs satisfaction alone. The production and consumption cycle of high intensity consumer capitalism plunges onward, blind to the consequences on both non-human and human nature (Leiss coins the term 'discommodities' to refer to the 'residuals or waste products' (1976, p. 33) generated by the market system). It is common knowledge that capitalism is indifferent to the 'ecological context of human activity' (Leiss, 1976, p. 36). The production of discommodities, like various kinds of toxic poisons, is seldom ever fully revealed, even if known, to those who produce the goods. I recall driving through New Waterford, Nova Scotia, a working-class town full of telltale modest wooden bungalows, and being greeted by the cardboard sign, 'Welcome to the gates of hell.' This community was situated on the boundary of the Sydney Steel Company's eerie tar ponds (the moon was glittering beautifully on the dark surface), the largest toxic site in Canada. All sorts of evidence had come to light of various kinds of cancers among the residents. But neither the company nor the government health authorities took any responsibility for the sickness of workers and community members, despite numerous inquests, investigations and citizen protests.

Consumers have great difficulty associating consumption with the risks and the social conditions of production. The religion of the market is a hard and unforgiving taskmaster. Leiss believes (and I am in full agreement) that we can hold the high-intensity market order accountable for 'having dissipated much of the planet's readily available resources, for making the survival of the existing population dependent upon energy-intensive agriculture, for creating the necessity of future reliance upon nuclear energy (with its attendant dangers), and for introducing massive quantities of toxic compounds into the biosphere' (p. 100). He also thinks that the 'hunt for resources with which to continue feeding our industrial technology is pointless and self-defeating. Indeed, it has all the makings of a massive social obsession whose destructive aspects can only worsen with every further achievement in extending the interplay of needs and commodities' (p. 130).

Tim Kasser, an American social psychologist, provides us with a fascinating (and personally provocative) empirical account in *The High Price of Materialism* (2002) of how this massive social obsession with materialism does not actually make people happy. He begins with the observation that '[s]ages from almost every religious and philosophical background have similarly insisted that focussing on attaining material possessions and social renown detracts from what is meaningful about life' (p. 1). Lao Tzu's words stand in for many – 'Chase after money and security/And your heart will never unclench.' Kasser informs us that prominent psychologists (Rogers, Maslow, Fromm) insist that the 'focus on materialistic values detracts from well-being and happiness' (p. 3). But this normative vision – one thinks of Fromm's *The Sane Society* (1955) or *To Have Or To Be?* (1976) – is corroborated by substantial empirical studies. Kasser and his associates discovered through careful survey work that 'people who strongly value the pursuit of wealth and possessions report lower psychological well-being than those who are less concerned with such aims' (p. 5). Indeed, strong materialistic values (these values take hold of the centre of the person's value system) are associated with a 'pervasive undermining of people's well-being, from low life satisfaction and happiness, to depression and anxiety, to physical problems such as headaches, and to personality disorders, narcissism, and antisocial behavior' (p. 22).

Kasser argues that when our basic needs for sustenance and survival are thwarted, people buy things to help them feel safe and secure. Thus, materialistic values are 'both a symptom of underlying insecurity and a coping strategy' (p. 29). Kasser and associates' research indicates that, if parents (for a variety of reasons, including divorce) are unable to provide a nurturing environment for their children, their children will be more likely to embrace materialistic values. By so doing, they are compensating for an inadequately functioning lifeworld. But setting out down the materialistic pathway holds many dangers. The consumer paradise promises that 'if we reach our goals, our self-esteem and satisfaction with life should consequently rise' (p. 43). Beyond simply having enough, research reveals, 'attaining wealth, possessions, and status' does not 'yield long-term increases in our happiness or well-being' (p. 43). At first glance, this hypothesis seems counter-intuitive, particularly when one drives through an upper-middle-class suburb with lovely freshly mown grass, two cars in the driveway, garden in full bloom, and then swings through shabby, run-down neighbourhoods, where nothing much seems to be blooming. But the glitch in the high intensity consumer lifestyle lies with the way 'people with strong materialistic value orientations experience persistent discrepancies between their current status and where they would most like to be' (p. 48). The businessman who has made a million thinks of how measly this fortune is when compared with the Wal-Mart clan. Desire for more always outruns what we have at the moment. It is true as well that persons who grow up, let us say, in a materially poor environment where they are neglected, belittled and unable to get they want, may well seek to boost their low self-esteem through longing for material goods. Both ends of the economic

195

spectrum, however, pay a severe price for harnessing their sense of self to contingent circumstances. There will always be 'new challenges and threats' to positive feelings that easily puncture their self-esteem. Money, fame, and image are extrinsic to the person's being. Materialistic people measure their self-worth against the imagined ideal. In North America, the celebrity popular culture feeds these ideals into our consciousness. If only we could be like so-and-so! This desire for fame and image has recently been taken to extremes with young men and women undergoing facial surgery so they can look like Brad Pitt or some other movie star. Kasser's elegant summation of the psychological research asserts that our psychological health 'depends in part on whether we feel close and connected with others, and whether we can give and receive love, care and support' (p. 61). But Kasser observes that 'something about materialism conflicts with valuing the characteristics of strong relationships (loyalty, helpfulness, love) and with caring about the broader community (peace, justice, equality)' (p. 65). Materialism, it seems to me, both breeds self-centredness and attracts those relentlessly pursuing wealth, status and fame. As Kasser puts it, others' 'qualities, subjective experiences, feelings, and desires are ignored, seen as unimportant, or viewed only in terms of their usefulness to oneself' (p. 67). Jewish philosopher Martin Buber names this the I–it relationship in his celebrated text, *I and Thou* (1923). Illustrations of I–it relationships abound in our contemporary society. Parents are pressured to mediate their love for their children through money. Romantic relationships get twisted and distorted as men and women prepare themselves as attractive exchangeable commodities on the dating market. Friendships get infiltrated by instrumental values as people, perhaps without even thinking about it, use their friends for their own business or other ends. 'Materialistic values of wealth, status, and image', Kasser concludes, 'work against close interpersonal relationships and connection to others' (p. 72).

Kasser contrasts the materialistic life project with a life characterised by 'intrinsic motivation, and flow' (p. 76). The idea of flow, popularised by Csikszentmihalyi (1997), 'occurs when an individual is doing something for no other purpose than the sheer joy, interest, and challenge involved' (Kasser, 2002, p. 76). Children's play (I like to watch kids, with their floppy hats and plastic shovels and pails, digging merrily away on the beach) is an obvious example of flow. So are activities like looking at alpine meadows, climbing mountains, playing sports, volunteering,

196

having picnics or busying away in one's garden. High-flow activities are pursued for 'what the activities themselves have to offer, not for rewards or praise' (p. 77). Drawing on empirical research, Kasser argues that materialism is associated with low-flow activities. TV watching 'causes people to feel zoned out or apathetic' (p. 81). In his magisterial comments on TV watching, Putnam (2000) blames too much TV watching for much of the erosion of social capital in American society. If we're sitting at home, we aren't doing anything. In fact, research even suggests that too much TV viewing decreases the well-being of elderly people. Shopping is another low-flow activity. The malls serve as the secular temples of the religion of the market. But hanging around them doesn't increase our sense of well-being or happiness or deepen our sense of the mystery of life. Overwork also diminishes intrinsic motivation. We're exhausted making money and all of those near to us feel the deleterious effects. Thus, intrinsic motivation, or flow, emerges from 'high levels of autonomy and self-causation' (p. 86). The challenge for the just learning society paradigm is to press these psychological ideas into the institutional structures that are often designed to perpetuate low-flow activity and put severe breaks on self-causation.

Therapeutic culture as antidote to social fragmentation

British sociologist Frank Furedi has captured the attention of the British mass media in the last few years with his probing analysis of the way contemporary Western consumer societies inflate the uncertainties and risks of life out of all realistic proportion. We now live in a 'culture of fear' (2002). We have lost confidence in our capacity to master our own life situations. We have become emotional basket cases, weak, vulnerable, at risk. Furedi (2004) believes that we inhabit a 'therapy culture.' Of relatively recent origin, this culture constructs the individual as an emotionally vulnerable and unstable entity who lacks the 'resilience to deal with feelings of isolation, disappointment and failure' (2004, p. 6). 'Today', Furedi writes, 'a low level of self-esteem is associated with a variety of emotional difficulties that are said to cause a range of social problems from crime to teenage pregnancy' (2004, p. 2). The pathway has been cleared for rise of a new priestly class (psychologists, psychiatrists, therapists) who promise to cure emotional distress.

Furedi's originality lies with his argument that therapy culture not only provides counselling, but also offers itself as a 'system of meaning in

197

our time' (2004, p. 17). All cultures offer systems of beliefs about the meaning of life and a vocabulary to help us make sense of the individual's relation to society. If the religion of the market provides the ontological framework for contemporary being, then therapy culture plays an important role in addressing the anxieties and difficulties arising from living in the hectic high intensity market setting. The new priestly class crafts a powerful script for making sense of everyday trials and tribulations. Like the shaman in traditional cultures, the new priests place their clients' problems in a larger context of human suffering and dilemmas. All events are seen through the 'prism of therapeutics' (2004, p. 14), be they rites of passage across the life cycle or the planes crashing into the World Trade Center in New York on 11 September 2001. The therapy culture wants us to find our 'sense of unity around the common experience of vulnerability' (2004, p. 14). 'We are all New Yorkers now' and 'we all weep for Princess Diana.'

The therapy culture works by recasting social problems as emotional ones. C. Wright Mills' (1959) counsel to always link personal troubles with public problems is set aside and the self defined through feelings alone. The structural conditions of our everyday lives (political economy, administrative systems, incessant advertising, non-democratic communicative practices) vanish in the therapy culture. Now the focus is on the emotional damage experienced by poor kids. We don't think about why they are poor or how lousy their schools are. We design programmes to cure racist attitudes and forget to confront the way racism is institutionalised. In the 1990s, during the miserable decade of downsizing and massive firings, fired workers were told to pick up their counselling chits on the way out the door. Today we are more apt to lament the mental health consequences of free market capitalism than the depredations of the market as an intentionally designed system. Daniel Goleman's *Emotional Intelligence* (1995) dares to offer us 'emotional education' (self-help books, conferences, workshops) in response to society's 'collective emotional crisis.'

Furedi thinks that the therapeutic imperative is 'not so much towards the realisation of self-fulfilment as the promotion of self-limitation' (2004, p. 21). The therapy culture undermines the critical humanist vision of our capacity to realise our human potential to a preoccupation with the self 'underpinned by anxiety and apprehension' (2004, p. 21). Therapy culture promotes a view of the individual as 'distinctly fragile and feeble' (p. 21). In fact, Furedi argues that this culture actually interprets the 'aspiration for control' as 'especially damaging to the emotional well-being of man' (p. 35). The individual's informal relations of dependence (my web of connections and obligations to family, friends and colleagues) are stigmatised and labelled co-dependence. The self is distanced from others. According to Furedi, therapy culture has a 'deep-seated aversion towards family and informal relations' (2004, p. 75). The family is constructed as the source of emotional and psychological problems. They are mostly toxic environments, the cause of the defilement of the emotions. Within the therapy culture, families become dangerous sites where children are abused and emotionally damaged. This stigmatisation of the family seeps into other socialisation spheres. Parents panic and pressure their children's schools to forbid any kind of touching. Educators introduce self-esteem classes for their stress-ridden students. But this often backfires when self-esteem deforms into self-centred forms of behaviour, like bullying and picking on children from other ethnic groups. Children who think too highly of themselves may not think very highly of anyone else.

Furedi thinks that the 'growth of emotional determinism, the rise of public emotional culture and the stigmatisation of private, informal relations are relatively recent developments' (p. 84). He attributes this trend to three interrelated developments: the decline of tradition, the decline of religion, and the decline of politics.

Cultural critics (Lasch, 1979, 1984; Sennett, 1976; Rieff, 1966) have attributed the rise of therapeutic culture to the erosion of social solidarity and of communal norms, and the weakening of the influence of traditional authority on the conduct of everyday life. There is little doubt that the fragmentation of social life opens the way for the 'construction of an intensely individualized private existence' (Furedi, 2004, p. 85). We know that the freeing of the individual from the repressive constraints of some forms of traditional life contains some emancipatory potential. The dangers lie with selves no longer situated within a wider sense of purpose and selves uncoupled from widely accepted ways of doing things. The decline in 'collective visions that could inspire significant sectors of society' (2004, p. 87) – one thinks here of socialism, communism and cooperativism – has left individuals in the lurch. Now they are easy prey for cultural scripts offering to re-enchant subjective experience. This is the shadow side of the uncoupling of person from community and widely shared moral codes. We expect children to make up their own life scripts. They cannot really do this, and usually buy in to whatever the popular culture prepares for them.

With the decline of traditional religions, shared moral norms and the erosion of communal solidarity, therapeutics orients itself to the 'experience of the atomised individuals . . .' (2004, p. 89). Therapeutics interweaves itself with the contemporary quest for an individual identity free from pre-determined, traditional definitions. 'Therapeutic identity' provides a special meaning to the individual's emotional life. 'I am what my feelings are telling me.' 'Get in touch with your feelings.' 'Feel good about yourself.' These new age shibboleths are taught in many of the new forms of spirituality that have migrated from the mysterious East into Western consumer cultures hungry for depth and being. But this pushing of emotionality to the forefront of individual self-expression, Furedi laments, displaces rational, enlightened dialogue with the 'language of therapeutics' (2004, p. 45). Therapeutics teaches us to control our emotions. A powerful emotion such as anger, for instance, often managed by specially trained counsellors, is a legitimate, passionate emotion that fuels resistance towards those who exploit, oppress and maim us. Furedi believes that passion has exited from politics. Our emotions have been de-politicised. This penetrating insight seems well-sustained. Simply consider how US president Bill Clinton emoted so convincingly in public about the suffering of the world. 'I feel your pain.' We hardly even noticed that 'I feel' was the end of it. He did not say – 'I feel that we must act to right the injustices meted out to you.' In the therapeutic culture, it is as if the symbolic expression of sympathy is all that is required. These rituals of grieving are participated in, and then we move on to our next world problem and ribbon-wearing. All the while, the heel of oppression keeps a tight grip on the necks of the suffering. We remain, as de Tocqueville once said, 'enclosed within our own hearts' (cited, Taylor, 1991, p. 9).

In the *Theory of Communicative Action* (1983, 1987), Habermas worried about the way bureaucratic modes of administering people could prevent the self-determination of individuals in the various activities in the lifeworld (like maintaining their health). He also acknowledged that with the rise of the 'expert culture' – specialists monopolise various competences – knowledge is blocked from flowing into the various channels of the lifeworld. In my opinion, this is a more serious problem than Habermas allows. Furedi wonders how individuals gain insight and guidance once they are isolated from a 'supportive institutional fabric' (2004, p. 98). The therapy culture, for its part, renders the 'routine forms of social interaction' as 'difficult and complicated' (p. 98). It conveniently provides experts to help us manage the difficulties. For example, the knowledge and skill needed to raise children is carried in culture's traditions, and transmitted down through maternal kinship lines (Hart, 1992). But with the rise of child-rearing experts, parental confidence is unsettled. Every day forms of knowing and self-determination, rather than being affirmed and deepened, are undermined as parents are pressured away from common-sense forms of knowing and time-tested ways of nurturing into the comforting arms of professionals. 'There, there . . . we will help you to administer "tough love" to your angry teenager . . .'.

Furedi worries about the medicalisation of the problems of everyday life. He informs us that there has been a huge growth in the late twentieth century of 'non-physical diseases' having to do with 'emotional problems' (2004, p. 99). Stress, rage, trauma, low self-esteem, environmental sensitivities, addictions, Attention Deficit Disorder – to name but a few. The demand for medicalisation is generated by 'cultural changes that inflate the sense of individuation and powerlessness' (2004, p. 99). People definitely have a heightened sense of 'personal vulnerability.' But Furedi thinks that this may be part of the reason why Bush and the neo-conservatives around him keep stoking our fears about a 'war on terror' that may strike at any time, any moment, in your backyard, in your school, perhaps on the plane, and will continue for a very long time. Imagining ourselves as vulnerable, gripped by mild or severe panic, we crave the comfort of the great leader. Critical questioning of anything goes out the window.

In the end, therapy culture promotes a 'diminished view of the self' (p. 106). The therapeutic culture casts serious doubt on the ability of contemporary men and women to 'deal with disappointment, misfortune, adversity or even the challenges of everyday life' (p. 106). We are offered a 'distinctly feeble version of human subjectivity' (p. 106). The just learning society paradigm must contest the therapy culture's enfeeblement of the lifeworld. First, we must assert the 'capacity of the individual to manage the challenges of everyday life that insights may be gained into the workings of the self' (p. 106). Second, we must acknowledge that 'powerlessness is central to the newly reconfigured self' (p. 122). Third, we must realise that the 'moralisation of addiction has as its premise a radically fatalistic view of the process of socialisation' (p. 124). Classic thinkers like Freud, Mead and Dewey eschewed any kind of 'fatalistic formula that denied the potential for individual choice or self-determination' (2004, p. 124). Rather, they emphasised that being with others constitutes our humanness. We make choices; the self is 'product and producer of social reality' (p. 124). Furedi claims that the 'sense of powerlessness' assigned to the 'contemporary self is unprecedented in the age of modernity' (p. 127). The potentialities of human subjectivity, imagination and creativity are deflated, the disempowering threats of external circumstances are inflated. At risk for the just learning society paradigm is the core teaching of Enlightenment humanism: that human beings are active creators of their own existence, able to take risks, to imagine alternative worlds beyond the limited ones we inhabit. But to take risks and not simply be at risk means that we must forsake our assigned role of passive consumers and vulnerable selves.

The struggle for recognition: The elemental learning dynamic of the lifeworld

The task now facing us is to rescue the contemporary self from the clutches of the therapy culture. I need to articulate a framework that enables us to sift through the rather promiscuous way terms such as self-esteem, self-confidence, self-realisation, self-respect and identity are tossed around. I also need to be able to specify the pre-conditions for life trajectories that are confident and open to engaging a world believed to be worth knowing and inhabiting with others. The socialising agencies within the lifeworld (in particular, parental care and the formal schooling systems) must interact with the dependent child to create the psychological-spiritual foundation for the unfolding of the person's potentialities. Damage at this elemental level can thwart (or block) the learning capacities of the individual as he or she moves through the lifespan. If I, as a black or Asian child, have to navigate my way through a playground full of hostile, jeering white children shouting dirty little ditties, I can easily be humiliated and develop a fearful and angry self-identity. A poignant moment for me occurred while watching a recent documentary on the CBC about Chinese immigrants' experience in early twentieth-century Canada. Recalling his own childhood experience of being mocked, beaten and urinated upon by white schoolboys, an elderly Chinese man broke down in tears. Wiping his eyes, he marvelled at how much it still hurt, 70 years later. The just learning society, then, must grapple with a profound threat to its realisation: the early impairment of the child's self-confidence. We can also argue, I believe, that the institutions of civil society and the system domains must be structured pedagogically so that the self-confidence of the individual can be fostered as he or she lives out daily life. This latter theme has been accentuated in many different ways throughout this text.

Critical theory now understands that contemporary (and historical) social movements and conflicts cannot be comprehended in terms of either material interests or self-preservation alone. Workers' movements in the nineteenth century and early twentieth century were infused with a moral concern for the dignity of human beings (Thompson, 1963; Moore, 1973). Workers certainly wanted better working conditions (I think immediately of a little coal town near where I live in the Comox Valley on Vancouver Island called Cumberland, where hundreds of men died in unsafe mines). But they also did not want to be humiliated. Injustice has two faces – the denial of material resources (redistributive issues) and the denial of recognition. Like Hegel, G. H. Mead, Habermas himself, and many other thinkers, Honneth stresses the importance of social relationships to the unfolding of a person's identity. As Canadian philosopher Charles Taylor puts it, 'Due recognition is not just a courtesy we owe people. It is a vital human need' (1992, p. 26). Taylor argues that a

> person or group of people can suffer real damage, real distortion, if the people or society around them mirror back to them a confusing and demeaning or contemptible picture of themselves. Non recognition or misrecognition can inflict harm, can be a form of oppression, imprisoning someone in a false, distorted, and reduced mode of being. (1992, p. 25)

Honneth (1995) identifies three distinct forms of mutual recognition: self-confidence, self-respect and self-esteem. Each form is grounded in a specific intersubjective relationship which he labels love, rights and solidarity. In the first, the parent or care-giver must facilitate skilfully the development of the basic relation-to-self that Honneth terms self-confidence (trust in oneself). The child is utterly helpless and dependent upon the care-giver for life and sustenance. Care-givers are symbiotically bound to the dependent infant, each needing the other's love. The bedrock learning challenge for the child is to learn how be alone without feeling abandoned. Child and care-giver must negotiate separateness from each delicately. 'Good enough' infant care (Don

Winnicott's (1965) phrase) requires a high degree of emotional and intuitive involvement if the individuation of the child is to proceed without damage. The child must 'trust the loved person to maintain his or her affection, even when one's own attention is withdrawn' (1995, p. 104). For their part, care-givers must permit the infant to work through the rage at withdrawn total attentiveness and trust that their own love is up to the task of negotiating the transition to ego-demarcation. They must also be able to return from symbiosis to their own sense of separateness from the infant.

Honneth argues that this 'fundamental level of emotional confidence – not only in the experience of needs and feelings, but also in their expression – which the intersubjective experience of love helps to bring about, constitutes the psychological precondition for the development of all further attitudes of self-respect' (p. 107). The child, friend or erotic partner must be assured that the loved one will continue to love them. This capacity to trust, operating at deep levels of the human psyche, means that one can express one's needs and desires without fear of being abandoned. 'For it is only this symbiotically nourished bond', Honneth continues, 'that produces the degree of basic individual self-confidence indispensable for autonomous participation in public life' (p. 107). We have discovered an important elemental foundation for the just learning society. The bond between child and care-giver may be harmed, ruptured or shattered. Utterly poverty stricken families, families with addicted care-givers, conditions of war and mayhem, rape and torture, are all conditions that shatter self-confidence and impair one's ability to access one's needs (as one's own) and to express them without anxiety. Without the capacity to trust, the individual will not be able to be present with voice and openness in the learning encounters continually present in daily life.

Honneth links rights and self-respect in an insightful way. 'Just as, in the case of love, children acquire via the continuous experience of "maternal" care, adult subjects acquire via the experience of legal recognition, the possibility of seeing their actions as the universally respected expression of their own autonomy' (p. 118). This new self-understanding has only been made possible with the emergence of modern legal systems based on rights. Pre-modern societies granted certain rights only to those of particular status groups. With the emergence of universal modern law, all individuals are perceived to possess the capacities of legal persons able to make decisions as morally responsible agents. As a person I have legal rights along with all other persons. None is discriminated against. I am respected, under law, as a fully autonomous person possessing 'the qualities that make participation in discursive will-formation possible' (p. 120). To have minimal self-respect I must see myself as a holder of rights. I must be able to stand face to face with other human beings and not feel belittled. Conversely, when the rights of persons and groups are violated (or not recognised), men and women have a 'crippling feeling of social shame, from which one can be liberated only through active protest and resistance' (p. 121). The contemporary political struggle in Canada and the US over granting gays and lesbians the legal right to marry aptly illustrates the bond between self-respect and legal recognition.

In his summation of Honneth's argument in *The Struggle for Recognition* (1995), Joel Anderson (1996) observes that while rights are a pre-condition for self-respect, individuals need real opportunities to exercise this universal capacity. To participate equally in practical discourse, individuals must respect themselves and be socially recognised as competent public actors. This analysis adds a vital psychological dimension to the analysis of civil society as pre-eminent social learning domain. The human capacity for recognising and being recognised must be nurtured, carefully and attentively within the family and community surround. But civil society must be organised so that what has been put in place in early childhood and youth is sustained, and persons can develop the precise competencies for lively engagement in both the power-infused domains of work and governance, and the more communicatively focused life of civil society. If the institutions of adulthood fail to live up to the moral demand of respecting the rights to voice of its members, then the self-confidence of individuals may be eroded. Capacity needs competencies and competencies require suitable contexts.

Self-respect, then, permits persons to declare that they are entitled to the same status and treatment as every other person. This is the great Kantian moral imperative, a triumph of our now somewhat tarnished Enlightenment heritage. Self-esteem, in contrast, is the sense of what makes one special, unique and particular. We have already presented some critical thoughts on inauthentic modes of self-esteem in the high intensity consumer society. Honneth insists that human subjects always need a 'form of self-esteem that allows them to relate positively to their concrete traits and abilities' (1995, p. 121). But self and other need to value each other's contributions for their own life fulfilment. If they do not share a common orientation, then they will tend to devalue the other's qualities. I am different from you, and my qualities contribute more to the realisation of societal or cultural goals than yours do. Pre-modern societies organised social esteem differently from modern societies. If I was born into the aristocracy, I would acquire the characteristics appropriate to my estate. I would view those outside my estate to be placed there by divine mandate. In my interactions with others, I would assume that the peasantry, let us say, would manifest certain traits that I could take for granted and predict. My sense of social solidarity would emerge from the belief that each estate had its function to maintain the hierarchical chain leading from God to the lowest orders. With the birth of capitalist modernity, this divinely sanctioned honour-based hierarchy lost its objectivity because one could not 'provide unambiguous information about the relative measure of social honour' (p. 124).

The bourgeoisie's toppling of the aristocratic and noble classes in early capitalist England introduced the principle of self-esteem based on achievement and personal self-realisation. In this new post-traditional world, persons 'feel themselves to be "valuable" only when they know themselves to be recognised for accomplishments that they precisely do not share in an undifferentiated manner with others' (p. 125). Now, how-ever, tension and conflict are introduced into the field of social esteem. Modern liberal democracies provide a legal framework for the development of self-respect. They also provide rather abstract guiding ideas for self-realisation. This means that the way is now opened up for a serious cultural struggle over what contributions are particularly valuable in a society. The classic sociological tradition (Durkheim, Weber, Mead, Marx) posited that participation in the division of labour (each segment contributing to the whole) would provide sufficient grounds to generate self-esteem. Paid work is still a powerful arena for developing self-esteem. But post-1960s feminism deemed the Marxian notion of class as inadequate to account for the full range of women's exploitation, oppression and yearning for recognition. Maggie Benston (1969) insisted that women's unpaid domestic labour was crucial to the reproduction of capital, and many thousands of words were expended in learned journals about whether Marx's notion of reproduction included the caring for children (Dinnerstein, 1976; Balbus, 1982). Hart (1995) argued that the masculinist construction of work and the normalisation of the monolithic family obscured the misery of women's lives and continued to degrade their work of nurturing. She urged us to re-frame the meaning of productivity away from its present connotation as learning for earning toward a reconstituted notion of productivity as the enhancement of life itself. The woman's movement can be understood primarily, I think, as a struggle for self-respect and self-esteem. They know that self-esteem is not handed to them on silver platters.

The struggle to have one's abilities recognised is a salient social learning dynamic. When certain groups 'raise the value of the abilities associated with their way of life' (Honneth, 1995, p. 127), other groups are forced to pay attention and wedge open their understanding of the ways of realising one's self. For instance, in Canadian society, the Special Olympic games are an important learning moment. Here we see men and women with different kinds of mental and physical incapacities playing sports and exulting in their accomplishments. This deepens our sense of solidarity with them as fellow and sister Canadians. We learn that identity has many different faces and body shapes.

Honneth's three patterns of recognition provide the key to conceptualise disrespect. The first type of disrespect affects a person at the level of physical integrity when individuals are denied the opportunity to dispose freely of their own bodies. Torture, rape and pain are imposed upon a being who is defenceless and at the mercy of another subject. The autonomy of the person is radically violated; the moral relationship of mutuality severed. People are objectified, denied voice, their identities hooded. 'Physical abuse', Honneth informs us, 'does lasting damage to one's basic confidence (learned through love) that one can autonomously co-ordinate one's own body' (p. 102). Confirming this insight, Johanna Meehan (1995b) observes that incest survivors report experiencing their subjectivity as 'disturbingly discontinuous and empty' (p. 243). They were disassociated from their bodies. Victims of childhood incest lacked trust in others and were unable to believe they were worthy of respect from others (Herman, 1978; Blume, 1990).

The second form of denigration affects a person's 'moral self-respect' by subjugating the individual through structurally excluding them from the 'possession of certain rights within a society' (Honneth, 1995, p. 133). For example, excluding some people from the right to vote (Asians, women and First Nations in Canadian history), signifies a 'violation of the intersubjective expectation to be recognized as a subject capable of forming judgments' (pp. 133–4). This second type of disrespect is to be 'set off from a third type of degradation, one that entails negative consequences for the social value of individuals and groups' (p. 134). Honneth names these the 'evaluative degradation of certain patterns of self-respect so that they cannot relate to the their mode of life as something of positive significance within their community' (p. 134). Thus social devaluation leads to a loss of personal self-esteem. The 'experience of being socially denigrated or humiliated', Honneth argues, 'endangers the identity of human beings' (p. 135). The 'affective sensations' of being humiliated – the experience of shame – 'consists, to begin with, in a kind of lowering of one's own feeling of self-worth' (p. 137). Honneth believes that, 'It is only because human subjects are incapable of reacting in emotionally neutral ways to social injuries – as exemplified by physical abuse, the denial of rights, and denigration – that the normative patterns of mutual recognition found in the social lifeworld have any chance of being realized' (p. 138).

Feminist theorist Nancy Fraser (2000) acknowledges that '(r)ecognition from others is thus essential to the development of a sense of self. To be denied recognition – or to be "misrecognized" – is to suffer both a distortion of one's relation to one's self and an injury to one's identity' (p. 2). But theoretical and political problems arise when we transpose the struggle for recognition from the individual person to groups. Equating the politics of recognition with identity politics enables stigmatised groups to reify their identities, fixing them into something hard, unbending and impermeable. Since identity politics places such a strong emphasis on collective identity, the way is opened up for groups to discourage internal learning processes that scrutinise, say, 'patriarchal strands within a subordinated culture' (p. 4). Struggles within the group for the authority to represent it can easily be repressed. Another serious problem is that identity politics encourages groups to simply demand that others accept their claims as authentic. This separatist attitude seeks to 'exempt "authentic" collective self-representation from all possible challenges in the public sphere' and 'scarcely fosters social interaction across differences' (p. 5). Fraser argues that 'what requires recognition is not group-specific identity but the status of individual group members as full partners in social interactions' (p. 5). This status-based model assumes that 'misrecognition is neither a psychic deformation nor a free-standing cultural harm but an institutionalized relation of social subordination' (p. 5). Misrecognition is perpetrated through 'institutionalized patterns' such as marriage law that excludes same-sex partnerships. All individuals ought to be embraced as peers. Thus, the overcoming of misrecognition requires the overcoming of the denial of full status to individuals and not the valorisation of group identity.

The just learning society paradigm calls out for the putting in place of minimal economic, social, cultural and political conditions to fracture the them-versus-us dichotomy plaguing the world – 'two armies in battle order preparing for the next confrontation, the next revenge match' (Maalouf, 2000, p. 31). Maalouf rightfully insists that we must 'reconcile [our] need for identity with an open and unprejudicial tolerance of other cultures . . .' (p. 35). One might imagine the gradual emergence of a global cosmopolitan order wherein all peoples of the world could find themselves mirrored in the new hybrid and imaginative cultural forms appearing out of the mix and clash of civilisations. Perhaps, but I am more comfortable with imagining that small, good places (that have legal guarantees of rights and wide scope for human self-realisation) must carry the burden of affirming the self-worth of everyone. It is in the daily life in specific cultural places and ecoscapes that nurture care and respect. The little girl helps grandmother carry some water to her house. Boys help their fathers tend the olive trees. Families gather with friends to drink wine and laugh and gossip. People feel esteemed because their small, good place values their contributions. But we are a long way from the fulfilment of this fantasy.

A realistic utopia for the twenty-first century

Today the discourse of lifelong learning, the learning organisation, learning economy, knowledge-enabled corporations, and learning democracy permeates discussions in Europe and, increasingly, in many parts of the globe. Adult learning, we are told, holds the 'key to the twenty-first century.' Our critical inquiry has exposed, however, the gap between the inspiring rhetoric of the learning society and the grim realities of wasted human potential littering the global landscape. This tour through the contemporary intellectual world reveals the impossibility of thinking about a just learning society apart from the power, greed, and privilege of those who hoard the goods and skew the learning processes in the service of the money-code. The Canadian sociologist of work and education, David Livingstone (2000), claims that the knowledge society is alive and well. Adults are engaged in an unprecedented high level of formal schooling, continuing education and non-formal learning. But he maintains that the knowledge economy is still illusory. His core idea is that current workplaces seriously under-employ people's learning capacities and competencies. This under-employment has several dimensions: the talent use gap; structural unemployment; involuntary reduced employment; the credential gap; the performance gap; and subjective underemployment. Livingstone thinks that recommendations for the growing need for lifelong learning miss the point. The primary emphasis should be on reorganising work to enable more people to apply in legitimate and sustainable ways the knowledge and skills they already possess.

Our modestly resilient hope that a just learning society is a realistic utopia (and not a mere myth or delusion of tender-hearted romantics) lies with the recognition that human beings have the capacity for self-determination and self-expression. But the contexts within which we make our living, live our lives as citizens and express our uniqueness enables or constrains possible courses of action and ways of interacting with others. All interactions are not learning encounters. Indeed, the context of the interaction – let us say a workplace rife with hazards – must not foreclose the possibility that workers could become more knowledgeable about the health conditions of the workplace. The communicative infrastructure of the institution, association or interaction must be consciously designed to foster knowledgeability and not ignorance, a co-operative spirit rather than cynicism in the face of the power. Can we not imagine human beings as unique persons, as workers and citizens unfolding their potentialities as they move through the lifespan and the multiple worlds of the system and the lifeworld?

Formidable roadblocks confront us along the learning journey. A historical understanding of the capitalist organisation and design of work breeds deep scepticism about the developmental potential of the workplace for most human beings forced to labour for wages in our age of insecurity. Braverman (1974) argued compellingly that twentieth-century capitalist work design dissolved the unity of thought and action, conception and execution, hand and mind embodied in pre-industrial craft. Little by little, battle after battle, the production process forced dependent wage-earners to surrender their occupational and social competence and the shaping of their own work. If Braverman is correct, then the impelling logic of the capitalist organisation challenges directly the achievement of a developmental, learner-centred and participatory democratic workplace for most people.

The learning organisation represents a potent conceptual advance from the old, individualistic andragogical model of adult learning. It is the architecture of the job design itself that serves as a benchmark for developmental work. The central job characteristics of skill variety, task identity and significance affect work's purposefulness, worker autonomy influences feelings of responsibility, and feedback permits workers to know the actual effects of their work. These critical psychological experiences are structurally induced; and these internal states, in turn, influence work satisfaction and commitment to the work community. Good work is designed, it does not just naturally occur. Truly meaningful learning can only occur if the workplace provides, in its everyday functioning, opportunities for all workers to develop their capacities. We have argued forcefully that the empowered worker requires concrete, practicable opportunities to exercise her capacity for self-determination. The job design is the point at which developmental humanism faces its biggest challenge: the logic of instrumentality and efficiency cares little for the flowering of the person. We are excruciatingly aware, as we survey the dispiriting jobs in dispiriting workplaces, of how far removed these places are from our normative ideal. We also acknowledge that many women prefer to channel considerable energy in developing their knowledge and skills in caring for children and running the household rather than pursuing full-blown careers (Hakim, 2000).

Our argument is that a strong case for worker empowerment as a moral demand is normatively anchored in the Kantian categorical imperative. It is also based on the affirmation that the business enterprise must be a social good. The learning dynamics emerging from private biographies and social movement actions, on behalf of besieged ecosystems and millions of poverty-stricken people throughout our world, press the big corporations of the globe to open their doors to communicative logic to hear the agonies of the suffering. Organisation learning theorists and practitioners cannot ignore the persistent reality of capitalist class ownership of the means of production (capitalism's basic value programme). We can, I think, avoid the despair that this bitter truth might induce within us. For one thing, some companies have, in fact, begun to learn how to restructure themselves as ethical business enterprises. There are also countless small signposts springing up throughout the globe pointing the way to new, green, sustainable ways of working the land and producing goods (Milani, 2000). For another, Bird's calibration of the different degrees (and kinds) of power – from scant to governance – adds a valuable conceptual frame permitting adult educators, as architects of learning environments, to have benchmarks for their work, even in unwelcoming environments. It is better to achieve some degree of power than to have no power at all. Better still, adult educators may, if the circumstances are right, help working people to imagine that they could be co-legislators in their workplaces. Finally, our discussion of inhibitors to learning in business organisations points to the irrepressible power of communicative action. When organisational silence is maintained, either as a conscious, maleficent design, or as the by-product of organisational bumbling, workers are aware that their capacity for speech and action is not being heeded. The psychological consequences for individual workers is devastating. The organisation

212

itself loses valuable knowledge and perspectives on how to run a moral and ethical business enterprise.

We have argued that the idea of active citizenship is an integral component of the developmental humanist perspective. In fact, developmental humanists value civil society and the public spheres as pre-eminent domains for the unfolding and expression of capacities for speech and action. For Aristotle, the good life was not something one possessed; one became good through the exercising of these uniquely human capacities. Freed from the exigencies of the realm of necessity, citizens entered the public sphere where they could live and talk together. Within this free public space, citizens could then recognise their commonality with others and individuate themselves. Citizens can only 'develop and exercise' practical wisdom through 'deliberation within the context of particular problems and action situations' (Keane, 1984, p. 117). Like the workplace, it is possible that the existing power and interest dynamics will either distort the communicative processes or actively disenable the development of practical political wisdom and know-how.

Many thinkers in Europe and North America are deeply worried about the actually existing state of civic and political participation in their countries. Jurgen Habermas's justly famous analysis of the degradation of the public sphere in the late 1950s and early 1960s signalled big trouble in the Western-liberal democracies (Habermas, 1962). One of the fundamental questions facing the developmental humanist tradition of adult education research and practice is: What precisely are the enabling conditions for strong democracy in our networked world? This, of course, is a complex question. We have to have our wits about us because the beautiful dreamers of cyber-democracy believe that network technology is conjuring in a new age of democracy! An iconoclastic social critic like Zygmunt Bauman startles us when he proclaims that democracy is 'becoming increasingly toothless and impotent to guard or adjust the conditions vital for the life of citizens . . .' (1999, p. 169). But Bauman's despairing outlook fails to account for the persistence of citizen action, talking, and contending in various communicative spaces within civil society. In *Between Facts and Norms* (1996), Habermas defends the lifeworld and civil society as a pre-eminent learning domain for deliberative democracy. We should neither capitulate to a cynical view of politics nor rest complacently about the future of developmental citizenship. The market looks after itself; civil

213

society left on its own, falls apart. And when civil society is degraded and the lifeworld corroded, the spiritual and moral foundations for citizen engagement dissipate. If we do not trust each other and think only of maximising our self-interest, the deliberation falls out of democracy and we face off against each other as competitors and strangers. Our research reveals, as well, that adult educators must awaken to the actual way the learning dynamics within civil society work. Civil society must become more conscious of itself as a social learning infrastructure. Understanding this, Nova Scotian Guy Henson believed that adult education would not fulfil its task unless it played 'its full part in enabling people to use their intelligence, their skill and their finest qualities for economic and social progress and for achieving a richer and happier life' (1946, p. 10).

The beautiful dream of the learning society – societies mobilising their learning resources, lifelong and lifewide, in the service of the good society – requires well-furnished stocks of social capital and the structured spaces for life in civil society to flourish. In *Bowling Alone: The Collapse and Revival of American Community* (2000), Robert Putnam focuses our thinking on the relationship between democratic self-government and an actively engaged citizenry. That democratic self-government actually requires an active, well-informed citizenry has been an American axiom for centuries. As well, European and Canadian adult education researchers have believed strongly the claim that the 'health of our public institutions depends, at least in part, on widespread participation in private voluntary groups – these networks of civic engagement that embody social capital' (p. 336).

Putnam argues that healthy civil society associations shape active citizenship in four ways. First, civil society associations permit individuals to express their interests and demands on government; political learning flows through these networks, and in these networks public life is discussed. Second, associations multiply or amplify citizen voices. Third, associations and less formal networks of civic engagement (learning and action) may instil 'habits of co-operation' and 'public-spiritedness' and enable citizens to acquire the 'practical skills necessary to partake in public life' (p. 336). Fourth, voluntary associations are potential 'schools of democracy' where citizens learn to run meetings, speak in public, take responsibility for common matters. One can easily see the important role that European and North American adult education institutions, folk high schools, workers' education circles, and community centres have played

214

historically in fostering the acquisition of knowledge, skills and attitudes for active citizenship (Johnston, 1999; Forrester, 1998; *International Journal of Lifelong Education*, 2003).

Putnam's developmental humanist vision is, however, in his view, deeply threatened by major trends in American society. In his original, and much celebrated article, 'Bowling Alone', Putnam found that increasing numbers of Americans bowl not in leagues but by themselves. When he expanded this article into a massive synthesis of empirical studies of participation, Putnam discovered evidence of a major crisis percolating in America. 'Voluntary associations where citizens affiliate with one another freely, collectively solve community problems and build networks of social trust – have declined. Participation in public life is plummeting. Americans, Putnam and his supporters argue, no longer practice self-government or democracy' (Mattson, 1999). Americans are more individualised, more socially isolated, less participatory than they have ever been in their history. The citizen role has been deflated and the consumer role inflated. Indeed, our investigation of the consumer paradise imaginary reveals that ordinary people face inordinate pressure people to abandon self-determination for self-fulfilment in the act of consuming.

But Internet enthusiasts tell us not to worry too much because the 'democratic deficits' of an eroding civil and political participatory culture are being replaced by a mobile information society. As Peter Kollock and Marc Smith observe in their essay, 'Communities in cyberspace', 'It is widely believed and hoped that the ease of communicating and interacting on line will lead to a flourishing of democratic institutions, heralding a new and vital arena of public discourse' (cited, Putnam, 2000, p. 173). Can we speak of electronically enhanced strong democracy? At first sight, the vision of cyberspace as the new frontier of direct democracy seems like a dream come true. Citizens engaging each other in point-to-point interaction beyond the supervision and censorship of hierarchical governments and corporations. However, with several exceptions, the Internet reflects little use that can be called civic or political at all. Unless linked with body-to-body interaction in public spaces, cyber-democracy, by itself, is rarely democratic in the strong, interactive, participatory sense. Still, there is room for debate and experimentation by adult educators and activists intent on widening the conversational net. Currently, the bloggers on the Internet may play a key role in keeping alive what the mainstream media represses. One has to sift information through a critical strainer, but gems of insight are caught.

In our mobile information age, good citizenship presupposes that the democratic ordering of government enables citizens to enjoy an equal ability to participate meaningfully in the decisions that closely affect their lives as individuals in communities. This developmental humanist vision, however, faces at least three serious challenges to the dream that computer-mediated communication will breed new and improved virtual communities able to stand in for the old, face-to-face ones. First, the problem of the digital divide. Access to cyberspace is not equitably distributed throughout the population. We confront the spectre of a kind of cyber-apartheid, with bridging forms of social capital diminished as elite networks become less accessible to have-nots. Nor has the Internet mobilised those previously inactive groups. Second, computer-mediated communication transmits much less non-verbal information than face-to-face communication. For Putnam, the poverty of social cues in computer-mediated communication inhibits inter-personal collaboration and trust, especially when the interaction is anonymous and not nested in a wider context. He thinks that social capital may turn out to be a prerequisite for, rather than a consequence of, effective computer-mediated communication. Third, the Internet makes it very easy for us, as persons and as privileged inhabitants of the North, to confine our communication to people who share precisely our interests. Moreover, the 'commercial incentives that currently govern Internet development seem destined to emphasize individual entertainment and commerce rather than community engagement' (Putnam, 2000, p. 179).

The best of adult education research traditions affirms that human individuation requires structures that permit human beings to express their many-sided potentials. Without good work and active citizenship, infused by a sense that life is worth embracing, life goes sour and the pathological consequences reverberate in and out of the lifeworld. The actually existing structures of work in a just learning economy must permit us to do and create useful things and services for others. And civil society is still a fundamental training ground for adults to unfold and express their capacities as authentic speakers and decision makers. If our learning age blocks meaningful work and active citizenship, offering ersatz fulfilment in its stead, what happens, in effect, is the creation of a powerful dam within the lifeworld. The dam will eventually burst its walls.

Our critical inquiry into the pathologies and possibilities of the lifeworld reveals clearly that the primary socialising agencies of the family, formal schools and community surround must create the conditions for children to develop a strong sense of self-confidence and deep respect for others. Caring for children must be publicly recognised as a fundamental act of citizenship. Without adequate financial and cultural support, lifeworlds are easily pathologised. These damaged lifeworlds produce personalities who lack the self-confidence and interest in understanding the world they inhabit, or, perhaps more controversially, lack the linguistic competencies necessary to engage the world reflectively (Mueller, 1973; Bernstein, 1975). Italian revolutionary Antonio Gramsci certainly thought the oppressed Sardinian peasantry had to acquire, through disciplined study, the ability to think abstractly. They had to be able to assess their concrete situations from universal vantage points. If not, they would remain trapped within fatalistic world-views (Welton, 1982).

Carol Gould (*Rethinking Democracy: Freedom and Social Cooperation in Politics, Economy and Society* (1988)) believes that there is a personality structure 'appropriate to participation in democratic institutions . . .' (p. 284). For her, democratic agency is 'not the agency of an isolated individual considered outside of any social context, but is rather the exercise of this power in free association with the agency of others' (p. 289). She insists that the agential right to co-determine actions pertains to 'contexts of economic, cultural, and social organizations' as well as to the 'domain of political democracy' (p. 289). What traits of character are needed in such contexts? First, individuals need initiative, the 'quality of activity against passivity' (p. 289). They must be able to freely enter into any structure of participation. But entering into dialogic relationships requires self-understanding: 'awareness of the relation of one's own interests or needs to the common interests of the group' (p. 290). The second basic character trait is the disposition to reciprocity. A relational character trait, reciprocity is realised 'only in a situation of social interaction' (p. 290). This disposition, the centrepiece of the democratic personality, places a premium on granting equivalency to the other's perspective and demands the skills of listening and heeding the other. This openness to the other catalyses the learning process and makes possible the establishment of a 'shared point of view' and an 'explicit understanding of differences in point of view' (p. 291). Without openness to 'alternative arguments and views' (p. 291), conflict resolution easily

217

slips into coercion. Gould maintains that recognition of the other as equal agent is a fundamental feature of the disposition to reciprocity. This includes respecting their rights. 'Without this recognition of the equal rights of others', Gould says, 'and an appreciation of their interests and needs, democracy can become simply a contest of wills and power, and tends toward tyranny of the majority' (p. 291). This disposition to reciprocity also requires agreement on the pedagogical procedures necessary to 'forming an association and to its ongoing functioning' (p. 291). It also requires the practice of listening. 'By not listening we deny ourselves the insight, vision, compassion, and ordinary meaning of others. We deny ourselves possibilities of learning, growth, understanding who we are – collectively and individually' (Forester, 1980, p. 221).

For many democratic theorists the most prominent trait is tolerance. This trait, Gould argues, suggests that 'each agent should reciprocally accept differences in the other and not require conformity ... to any give set of beliefs or modes of behavior' (1988, p. 292). This trait focuses attention on very contentious philosophical and practical issues. Deep scepticism about establishing firm foundations that would permit us to achieve consensus or approximate commensurability pervades contemporary intellectual cultural and everyday life (Bernstein, 1992). What needs to be heard at the extremities of this debate? Is not the answer that autonomous public life ought not repress irreducible differences among human actors? That it is possible to recognise the partiality of one's initial views and develop a more considered standpoint? Within our institutional life, our interactions ought to mutually enhance each other's needs and self-development. Both Gadamer (1975) and Habermas insist that difference, otherness and mutuality are constitutive of our humanness. We can both respect difference and struggle with one another to find the common ground of human solidarity. Our horizons both fuse and remain open to the future. Even if one accepts the arguments of radical pluralists (Mouffe, 1993), commensurable norms and pedagogical procedures are required to ensure that difference will be respected and expressible in our institutional life. Ben Agger says that 'we speak to each other in hope of sharing our common humanity, however buried or distorted, and of buffering our mortal aloneness' (1981, p. 14).

Gould also believes that the character traits of flexibility and open-mindedness are corollaries to the others. She thinks that flexibility and open-mindedness require rationality, that is, we must be able to comprehend 'alternative views and frameworks' (1988, p. 293). This

218

'quality of mind' is necessarily an educated mind, recalling John Dewey's call to construct an educative democracy in the US (Dewey, 1927). Commitment and responsibility are, moreover, pertinent to the formation of the democratic personality. 'Responsibility to abide by the decisions in which one has participated and to act in accordance with such decisions is likewise a precondition for the viability of any democratic institution' (Gould, 1988, p. 293).

Finally, Gould considers several character traits, often identified with women's culture, supportiveness, sharing and communicativeness, as clearly relevant to the democratic personality. She does not think that they are 'exclusively women's traits' (pp. 293–4). However, like Patemen (1989), Gould argues that these traits have often been excluded from the political and economic domains marked by 'egoistic pursuit of self-interest in competition with others, and by authoritarian or hierarchical models of social relations in which the emphasis is on individual power or control over others' (p. 294). Gould holds out the promise that if the 'alternative character traits historically association with women' were allowed into play in the public domain, changes in the 'procedures and structures of democratic decision-making' (p. 294) would occur. This would open up the 'options for democratic decision-making to modes derived from the experience and character formation historically associated with women, as well as those typically identified with men' (p. 294). Gould offers her account of democratic traits as specifying only the enabling personality conditions for participation in decision making. She does believe, though, that people will 'choose positively to participate', given their 'interest in freedom and in expressing their autonomy' (p. 298).

The just learning society paradigm is offered, then, as a counter-utopia to the commodity paradise utopia of globalising capitalism. We end with the modest hope that human beings have the intellectual and spiritual resources to create another world, one anchored in the ingenious learning capacity of our species. Our yearning for a vibrant, colourful, tolerant and artful learning society has a 'stubbornly transcending power, because it is renewed with each act of unconstrained understanding, with each moment of living together in solidarity, of successful individuation, and of saving emancipation' (Habermas, 1982, p. 221). Habermas has the last word.

References

Abrahamsson, L. (2001). 'Gender-based learning dilemmas in work organizations'. In: *Proceedings, Second International Conference on Researching Work and Learning.* Calgary, 26–28 July, pp. 106–13.

Acker, J. (1991). 'Hierarchies, jobs, bodies: a theory of gendered organization', in N. Jackson (ed.) *Skills Formation and Gender Relations: The Politics of Who Knows What.* Geelong: Deakin University Press.

Adachi, K. (1976). *The Enemy That Never Was: A History of the Japanese Canadians.* Toronto: McClelland and Stewart.

Adbusters (2004). No. 51, January–February.

Agger, B. (1981). 'A critical theory of dialogue', *Humanities in Society*, 4(1): 7–30.

Alvesson, M. and Willmott, H. (1992). 'On the idea of emancipation in management and organization studies', *Academy of Management Review* 17(3): 432–64.

Anderson, J. (1996). Translator's note to *The Struggle for Recognition: The Moral Grammar of Social Conflicts.* Cambridge: The MIT Press.

Andrew, E. (1981). *Closing the Iron Cage: The Scientific Management of Work and Leisure.* Montreal: Black Rose Books.

Argyris, C. (1957). *Personality and Organization.* New York: HarperCollins.

Argyris, C. (1978). *Organizational Learning: A Theory-of-Action Perspective.* Reading, MA: Addison-Wesley Publishing Co.

Argyris, C. (1993). 'Ineffective learning in organizations'. In: *Knowledge for Action: A Guide to Overcoming Barriers to Organizational Change.* San Francisco: Jossey-Bass, pp. 15–48.

Armstrong, K. (2000). *The Battle for God.* New York: Alfred A. Knopf.

Armstrong, K. (2001). *Buddha.* New York: Penguin Books.

Aronowitz, S. (1975). *False Promises: The Shaping of American Working Class Consciousness. New York: McGraw-Hill.*

Ashforth, B.E. (1985). 'Climate formation: issues and extensions', *Academy of Management Review*, 10: 837–47.

Bahour, S. (2002). 'Corporate America and Israeli occupation', Media Monitors Network. Online at: http://www.mediamonitors.net/sambahour26.html

Balbus, I. (1982). *Marxism and Domination*. Princeton: Princeton University Press.

Baldry, C. *et al.* (1998). 'Bright satanic offices: intensification, control and team taylorism'. In: C. Warhurst and P. Thompson (eds) *Workplaces of the Future*. London: Macmillan Press.

Bandura, A. (1977). 'Self-efficacy: Toward a unifying theory of behavioural change', *Psychological Review*, 84: 191–215.

Barber, B. (1995). *Jihad vs. McWorld*. New York: Ballantine Books.

Barney, D. (2000). *Prometheus Wired: The Hope for Democracy in the Age of Network Technology*. Vancouver: UBC Press.

Batchelor, S. (1983). *Alone with Others: An Existential Approach to Buddhism*. New York: Grove Press.

Baudrillard, J. (1983). *Simulations*. New York: Semiotext(e).

Bauman, Z. (1993). *Postmodern Ethics*. Oxford: Blackwell Publishing.

Bauman, Z. (1999). *In Search of Politics*. Cambridge, UK: Polity Press.

Beck, U. (1994). 'The reinvention of politics: towards a theory of reflexive modernization'. In: U. Beck, A. Giddens and S. Lash. *Reflexive Modernization: Politics, Tradition and Aesthetics in Modern Social Order*. Cambridge, UK: Polity Press.

Bell, D. (1973). *The Coming of Post-Industrial Society: A Venture in Social Forecasting*. New York: Basic Books.

Benhabib, S. (1987). 'The generalized and the concrete other: the Kohlberg-Gilligan controversy and feminist theory'. In: S. Benhabib and D. Cornell (eds) *Feminist as Critique*. Minneapolis: University of Minnesota Press, pp. 77–95.

Benhabib, S. (1992). *Situating the Self: Gender, Community, and Postmodernism in Contemporary Ethics*. New York: Routledge.

Benhabib, S. (1995). 'The debate over women and moral theory revisited'. In: J. Meehan (ed.) *Feminists Read Habermas: Gendering the Subject of Discourse*. New York: Routledge, pp. 181–203.

Bennett, O. (2001). *Cultural Pessimism: Narratives of Decline in the Postmodern World*. Edinburgh: Edinburgh University Press.

Bennis, W. (1966). *Changing Organizations: Essays on the Development and Evolution of Human Organization*. New York: McGraw-Hill.

Benston, M. (1969). 'The political economy of women's liberation', *Monthly Review,* 21(4): 13–27.

Berger, P., Berger, B. and Kellner, H. (1974) *The Homeless Mind: Modernization and Consciousness.* New York: Random House.

Berger, P.L. and Luckman, T. (1967). *The Social Construction of Reality.* New York: Doubleday.

Bernays, E. (1955). *The Engineering of Consent.* Norman: University of Oklahoma Press.

Bernstein, B. (1975). *Class, Codes and Control.* London: Routledge and Kegan Paul.

Bernstein, R. J. (1992). *The New Constellation: The Ethical-Political Horizons of Modernity/Postmodernity.* Cambridge, MA: The MIT Press.

Berringer, B. (2002). 'Defensive routines: inhibitors of the learning organization', paper presented to CASAE regional conference, 11 May.

Bies, R. J. and Tripp, T.M. (1999). 'Two faces of the powerless: coping with tyranny'. In: R.M. Kramer and M. Neale (eds) *Power and Influence in Organizations.* Thousand Oaks, California: Sage, pp. 203–19.

Bird, F. (1996). *The Muted Conscience: Moral Silence and the Practice of Ethics in Business.* London: Quorum Books.

Bird, F. (1999). 'Empowerment and justice'. In: J. Quinn and P.W.F. Davies (eds) *Ethics and Empowerment.* London: Macmillan Press.

Blauner, R. (1964). *Alienation and Freedom: The Factory Worker and His Industry.* Chicago: University of Chicago Press.

Blume, S. (1990). *Secret Survivors: Uncovering Incest and its After Effects in Women.* New York: John Wiley and Sons.

Blumenberg, H. (1985). *The Legitimacy of the Modern Age.* Cambridge, MA: The MIT Press.

Bonhoeffer, D. (1962). *Letters from Prison.* E. Bethge (ed.). New York: Macmillan.

Bramel, D. and Friend, R. (1981). 'Hawthorne, the myth of the docile worker, and class bias in psychology', *American Psychologist* 36(8): 867–78.

Braverman, H. (1974). *Labor and Monopoly Capitalism: The Degradation of Work in the Twentieth Century.* New York: Monthly Review Press.

Briggs, A. (1959). *The Age of Improvement 1783–1867.* London: Longman Group Ltd.

Brown, L. and Flavin, C. (1999). *State of the World*. New York: W.W. Norton.

Buber, M. (1923). *I and Thou*. New York: Scribner [1970].

Burawoy, M. (1985). *The Politics of Production*. London: Verso.

Burke, P. (2000). *A Social History of Knowledge: From Gutenberg to Diderot*. Cambridge, UK: Polity Press.

Burrell, G. and Morgan, G. (1979). *Sociological Paradigms and Organizational Analysis*. London: Heinemann.

Butler, J. (1992). 'Contingent foundations: feminism and the question of postmodernism'. In: J. Butler and J. Scott (eds) *Feminists Theorize the Political*. New York: Routledge.

CAAE (1942). *Report of the Proceedings of a Special Programme Committee of the Canadian Association for Adult Education*, 27–31 December, Toronto: CAAE.

Carey, A. (1967). 'The Hawthorne studies: a radical criticism', *American Sociological Review*, 32: 403–16.

Carlyle, T. (1829). 'Signs of the times'. In: (1853) *The Collected Works of Thomas Carlyle*, 16 vols. London: Chapman and Hall.

Castells, M. (1997). *The Power of Identity*. Oxford: Blackwell Publishers.

Chambers, S. (1995). 'Feminist discourse/practical discourse'. In: J. Meehan (ed.) *Feminists Read Habermas: Gendering the Subject of Discourse*. New York: Routledge, pp. 163–79.

Chodorow, N. (1978). *The Reproduction of Mothering: Psychoanalysis and the Sociology of Gender*. Berkeley: University of California Press.

Cloward, R. and Piven, F. (1977). *Poor People's Movements: Why They Succeed, How They Fail*. New York: Pantheon Books.

Coady, M. (1939). *Masters of Their Own Destiny*. New York: Harper and Row.

Conger, J.A. and Kanungo, R. (1988). 'The empowerment process: integrating theory and practice', *Academy of Management Review*, 13(3): 471–82.

Cook, D. (2001). 'The talking cure in Habermas's republic', *New Left Review*, 12, November–December: 135–51.

Cooke, M. (1999). 'Habermas, feminism and the question of autonomy'. In: P. Dews (ed.) *Habermas: A Critical Reader*. Oxford: Blackwell Publishers.

Cox, T. (1993). *Cultural Diversity in Organizations: Theory, Research, and Practice*. San Francisco: Berrett-Koehler.

Crompton, R. and Jones, G. (1984). *White Collar Proletariat: Deskilling and*

223

Gender in Clerical Work. Philadelphia: Temple University Press.

Csikszentmihalyi, M. (1997). *Finding Flow.* New York: Basic Books.

Cusac, A. (2003). 'Brazen bosses', *The Progressive,* February, pp. 23–9.

Cyert, R. and March, J. (1963). *A Behavioral Theory of the Firm.* Engelwood Cliffs, NJ: Prentice Hall.

Davies, P. and Mills, A. (1999). 'Ethics, empowerment and ownership'. In: J. Quinn and P.W.F. Davies (eds) *Ethics and Empowerment.* London: Macmillan Press.

Delors, J. (1996). *Learning: The Treasure Within. Report to UNESCO of the International Commission on Education for the Twenty-first Century.* Paris: UNESCO.

Dewey, J. (1927). *The Public and its Problems.* London: Allen and Unwin.

Dews, P. (1992). *Autonomy and Solidarity: Interviews with Jurgen Habermas.* London: Verso.

Dews, P. (1999). *Habermas: A Critical Reader.* Oxford: Blackwell Publishers.

Dinnerstein, D. (1976). *The Mermaid and the Minotaur: Sexual Arrangements and Human Malaise.* New York: Harper and Row.

Dixon, N. (1999). *The Organizational Learning Cycle.* Hampshire: Gower Publishing.

Dobell, R. (1995). 'Environmental degradation and the religion of the market'. In: H. Coward (ed.) *Population, Consumption, and the Environment.* Albany: SUNY Press.

Dohrn, S. (1988). 'Pioneers in a dead-end profession: The first women clerks in bank and insurance companies'. In: G. Anderson (ed.) *The White-Blouse Revolution: Female Office Workers Since 1870.* Manchester: Manchester University Press.

Donald, M. (2001). *A Mind So Rare: The Evolution of Human Consciousness.* New York: W.W. Norton and Company.

Drucker, P. (1994). 'The age of social transformation', *The Atlantic Monthly,* 274(5): 53–80.

Dubeck, P. (1979). 'Sexism in recruiting management personnel for a manufacturing firm'. In: R. Alvarez *et al., Discrimination in Organizations.* San Francisco: Jossey-Bass.

Duncan, R. and Weiss, A. (1979). 'Organizational learning: implications for organizational design'. In: B.M. Shaw (ed.) *Research in Organizational Behavior,* vol. I. Greenwich, Ct.: JAI Press, pp. 75–123.

Dyer-Witheford, N. (1999). *Cyber-Marx: Cycles and Circuits in High-*

Technology Capitalism. Urbana: University of Illinois Press.

Ehrlich, P. (1968). *The Population Bomb.* New York: Ballantine Books.

Eley, G. (1992). 'Nations, publics, and political cultures: placing Habermas in the nineteenth century'. In: C. Calhoun (ed.) *Habermas and the Public Sphere*. Cambridge, MA: The MIT Press, pp. 289–339.

Elliot, L. (2002). 'All talk, no substance', *The Guardian Weekly*, 21–27 November.

Engel, M. (2003). 'Road to ruin', *The Guardian Weekly*, 6–12 November 2003.

Ewen, S. (1976). *Captains of Consciousness: Advertising and the Social Roots of the Consumer Culture.* New York: McGraw Hill.

Fahey, J. (2002). Quoted in '87 percent of young Americans can't find Iraq on map', *St. Louis Post-Dispatch*, 21 November.

Faure, E. *et al.* (1972). *Learning To Be.* London: Harrap Publishers.

Fay, B. (1987). *Critical Social Science: Liberation and its Limits.* Ithaca, New York: Cornell University Press.

Festinger, L. (1957). *A Theory of Cognitive Dissonance.* Stanford: Stanford University Press.

Flax, J. (1993). *Disputed Subjects.* New York: Routledge.

Fleming, M. (1997). *Emancipation and Illusion: Rationality and Gender in Habermas's Theory of Modernity.* University Park: The Pennsylvania State University Press, pp. 13–34.

Foegen, J.H. (1999). 'Why not empowerment?', *Business and Economic Review*, 45(3): 31–3.

Follett, M.P. (1925). 'Power'. In: H. Metcalf and L. Urwick (eds) (1942), *Dynamic Administration: The Selected Papers of Mary Parker Follett.* New York: Harper and Row.

Forester, J. (1980). 'Listening: the social policy of everyday life (Critical theory and hermeneutics in practice)', *Social Praxis*, 7: 219–32.

Forrester, K. (1998). 'Adult learning: "A key for the twenty-first century" Reflections on the UNESCO fifth international conference 1997', *International Journal of Lifelong Education,* 17(6): 423–34.

Fraser, N. (1989). 'What's so critical about critical theory? The case of Habermas and gender'. In: N. Fraser, *Unruly Practices: Power, Discourse, and Gender in Contemporary Social Theory*. Minneapolis: University of Minnesota Press.

Fraser, N. (1992). 'Re-thinking the public sphere: A contribution to the critique of actually existing democracy'. In: C. Calhoun (ed.) *Habermas and the Public Sphere*. Cambridge, MA: The MIT Press.

225

Fraser, N. (2000) 'Rethinking recognition', *New Left Review*, 3, May–June. Online at: www.newleftreview.net/NLR23707

Freire, P. (1972). *Pedagogy of the Oppressed*. New York: Herder and Herder.

Friedman, J. (1987). *Planning in the Public Domain: From Knowledge to Action*. Princeton: Princeton University Press.

Fromm, E. (1955). *The Sane Society*. New York: Rinehart.

Fromm, E. (1976). *To Have Or To Be?* New York: Harper and Row.

Fukuyama, F. (1992). *The End of History and the Last Man*. Toronto: Maxwell Macmillan.

Furedi, F. (2002). *Cultures of Fear: Risk-Taking and the Morality of Low Expectation*. New York: Continuum.

Furedi, F. (2004). *Therapy Culture: Cultivating Vulnerability in an Uncertain Age*. London: Routledge.

Gadamer, H. (1975). *Truth and Method*. New York: Continuum.

Garrahan, P. and Stewart, P. (1992). *The Nissan Enigma: Flexibility at Work in a Local Economy*. London: Manswell Publishing.

Gaskel, J. and MacLaren, A. (eds) (1987). *Women and Education*. Calgary: Detselig Press.

Gaventa, J. (1980). *Power and Powerlessness: Quiescence and Rebellion in an Appalachian Valley*. Urbana: University of Illinois Press.

Gaventa, J. and Jones, E. (c.2002). *Concepts of Citizenship: A Review*. Institute of Development Studies: Sussex University.

Ghoshal, S. and Moran, P. (1996). 'Bad for practice: a critique of the transaction cost theory', *Academy of Management Journal*, 21: 13–47.

Giddens, A. (1991). *Modernity and Self-Identity*. Stanford: Stanford University Press.

Gilligan, C. (1982). *In a Different Voice: Psychological Theory and Women's Development*. Cambridge, MA: Harvard University Press.

Ginzberg. E. (ed.) (1964). *Technology and Social Change*. New York: Columbia University Press.

Gladwell, M. (2002). 'The talent myth', *The New Yorker*, 22 July, pp. 28–33.

Gold, M. (1999). *The Complete Social Scientist: A Kurt Lewin Reader*. Washington, DC: American Psychological Association.

Goleman, D. (1995). *Emotional Intelligence*. New York: Bantam Books.

Gorz, A. (1985). *Paths to Paradise: On the Liberation from Work*. London: Pluto Press.

Gould, C. (1988). *Rethinking Democracy: Freedom and Social Cooperation in*

Politics, Economy, and Society. Cambridge, UK: Cambridge University Press.

Gouthro, P. (1999). 'The homeplace-not the marketplace: developing a critical feminist approach to adult education', *Proceedings of the 40th annual Adult Education Research Conference*. Dekalb: Northern Illinois University, pp. 121–5.

Gouthro, P. (2002). 'What counts? examining academic values and women's life experiences from a critical feminist perspective', *The Canadian Journal for the Study of Adult Education*, 16(1): 1–19.

Greenberger, D.B. and Strasser, S. (1986). 'The development and application of a model of personal control in organizations', *Academy of Management Review*, 11: 164–77.

Gross, P. and Levitt, N. (1998). *Higher Superstition: The Academic Left and its Quarrels with Science*. Baltimore/London: The Johns Hopkins University Press.

Guehenno, J. (1995). *The End of the Nation-State*. Minneapolis: University of Minnesota Press.

Habermas, J. (1962). *The Structural Transformation of the Public Sphere: An Inquiry into a Category of Bourgeois Society*. Cambridge, MA: The MIT Press.

Habermas, J. (1970). *Toward a Rational Society*. Boston: Beacon Press.

Habermas, J. (1979). *Communication and the Evolution of Society*. Boston: Beacon Press.

Habermas, J. (1982). 'A reply to my critics'. In: J.B. Thompson and D. Held (eds) *Habermas: Critical Debates*. Cambridge, MA: The MIT Press.

Habermas, J. (1984, 1987). *Theory of Communicative Action*. Boston: Beacon Press.

Habermas, J. (1990). 'Hannah Arendt: on the concept of power'. In: J. Habermas, *Philosophical-Political Profiles*. Cambridge, MA: The MIT Press, pp. 173–89.

Habermas, J. (1992). 'Further reflections on the public sphere'. In: C. Calhoun (ed.) *Habermas and the Public Sphere*. Cambridge, MA: The MIT Press, pp. 421–61.

Habermas, J. (1996). *Between Facts and Norms*. Cambridge, MA: The MIT Press.

Habermas, J. (2001). *The Post-National Constellation: Political Essays*. Cambridge, MA: The MIT Press.

Habermas, J. (2003). *The Future of Human Nature*. Cambridge, UK: Polity Press.

Hakim, C. (2000). *Work-Lifestyle Choices in the 21st Century.* Oxford: Oxford University Press.

Hall, E.M. and Dennis, L.A. (1968). *Living and Learning: The Report of the Provincial Committee on Aims and Objectives of Education in the Schools of Ontario.* Ontario: Ontario Department of Education.

Hammonds, K., Kelly, K. and Thurston, K. (1994). 'The new world of work: beyond the buzzwords in a radical redefinition of labor', *Business Week,* 17 October.

Handy, C. (1996). *Beyond Certainty: The Changing World of Organizations.* Boston: Harvard Business School Press.

Hart, M. (1995). 'Motherwork: a radical proposal to rethink work and education'. In: M. Welton (ed.) *In Defense of the Lifeworld: Critical Perspectives on Adult Learning.* Albany: SUNY Press.

Harvey, D. (1989). *The Condition of Postmodernity.* Oxford: Oxford University Press.

Harvey, D. (2000). *Spaces of Hope.* Berkeley: University of California Press.

Havel, V. (1990). *Disturbing the Peace.* New York: Random House.

Heaman, E. (1998). *The Inglorious Arts of Peace: Exhibitions in Canadian Society During the Nineteenth Century.* Toronto: University of Toronto Press.

Hecht, J. (2003). *Doubt: A History.* San Francisco: HarperCollins.

Hedberg, B. (1981). 'How organizations learn and unlearn'. In: P. Nystrom and W. Starbuck (eds) *Handbook of Organizational Design: Adapting Organizations to Their Environment.* Oxford: Oxford University Press.

Hendley, S. (2000). *From Communicative Action to the Face of the Other: Levinas and Habermas on Language, Obligation, and Community.* Oxford: Lexington Books.

Henson, G. (1946). *A Report on Provincial Support of Adult Education in Nova Scotia.* Halifax: Nova Scotia.

Herman, J. (1978). *Father-Daughter Incest.* Cambridge, MA: Harvard University Press.

Hobsbawm, E. (1994). *The Age of Extremes: The Short Twentieth Century 1914–1991.* London: Abacus Books.

Holmes, S. (2002). 'Looking away', *London Review of Books,* 14 November.

Homer-Dixon, T. (2000). *The Ingenuity Gap.* New York: Alfred A. Knopf.

Honneth, A. (1995). *The Struggle for Recognition: The Moral Grammar of Social Conflicts.* Oxford: Polity Press.

Hunnius, G., Garson. D., and Case, J. (1973). *Workers' Control: A Reader on Labor and Social Change.* New York: Vintage Books.

Ihde, D. (1990). *Technology and the Lifeworld: From Garden to Earth.* Bloomington: Indiana University Press.

International Journal of Lifelong Education (2003). Special issue: 'Citizenship, democracy and lifelong learning', 22(6).

Isaac, J. (1992). *Arendt, Camus, and Modern Rebellion.* New York: Yale University Press.

Jaffe, D., Scott, C., and Tobe, G. (1994). *Rekindling Commitment.* San Francisco: Jossey-Bass.

Jaspers, K. (1962). *The Great Philosophers: The Foundations.* New York: Harcourt, Brace and World.

Johnston, R. (1999). 'Adult learning for citizenship: Towards a reconstruction of the social purpose tradition', *International Journal of Lifelong Education,* 18(3): 175–90.

Kant, I. (1793). *Religion Within the Limits of Reason Alone.* New York: Harper and Row [1960].

Kariel, H. (1956). 'Democracy unlimited: Kurt Lewin's field theory', *The American Journal of Sociology* LXII: 280–9.

Kasser, T.M. (2002). *The High Price of Materialism.* Cambridge, MA: The MIT Press.

Keane, J. (1984). *Public Life and Late Capitalism: Toward a Socialist Theory of Democracy.* Cambridge, UK: Cambridge University Press.

Keane, J. (2000). *Vaclav Havel: A Political Tragedy in Six Acts.* New York: Basic Books.

Keichel, W. (1989). 'How important is morale, really?', *Fortune,* 22 March, pp. 121–2.

Kelly, G. A. (1955). *The Psychology of Personal Constructs.* New York: Norton.

Kersten, G. (2001). 'Knowledge workers feed an organization', *The Financial Times,* 18 September, p. M6.

Kidd, J. R. (1974). *A Tale of Three Cities: Elsinore-Montreal-Tokyo.* Syracuse: Syracuse Publications in Continuing Education.

Klein, N. (2000). *No Logo: Taking Aim at the Brand Bullies.* Toronto: Alfred A. Knopf Canada.

Knights, D. and Wilmott, H. (1986). *Gender and the Labour Process.* Aldershot: Gower.

Knowles, M. (1980). *The Modern Practice of Adult Education: From Pedagogy to Andragogy.* New York: The Adult Education Co.

Lasch, C. (1979). *The Culture of Narcissism. American Life in An Age of Diminishing Expectations.* New York: Norton.

Lasch, C. (1984). *The Minimal Self: Psychic Survival in Troubled Times.* New York: W.W. Norton.

Legge, K. (1995). *Human Resource Management: Rhetoric and Realities.* London: Macmillan Press.

Leiss, W. (1976). *The Limits to Satisfaction: An Essay on the Problem of Needs and Commodities.* Toronto: University of Toronto Press.

Levinas, E. (1969). *Totaliity and Infinity.* Pittsburgh: Duquesne University Press.

Likert, R. (1961). *New Patterns of Management.* New York: McGraw-Hill.

Lind, E.A. and Tyler, T.R. (1988). *The Social Psychology of Procedural Justice.* New York: Plenum.

van der Linden, H. (1998). 'A Kantian defense of enterprise democracy'. In: J. Kneller and S. Axinn (eds) *Autonomy and Community: Readings in Contemporary Kantian Social Philosophy.* Albany: SUNY Press, pp. 213–37.

Livingstone, D. (2000). 'Lifelong learning and underemployment in the knowledge society', *Comparative Education,* 35(2): 163–86.

Lowe, G. (2000). *The Quality of Work.* Toronto: Oxford University Press.

Loy, D. (2002). *A Buddhist History of the West: Studies in Lack.* New York: SUNY Press.

Lukes, S. (1974). *Power: A Radical View.* London: Macmillan Press.

Maalouf, A. (2000). *In the Name of Identity.* New York: Penguin Books.

Machlup, F. (1962). *The Production and Distribution of Knowledge in the United States.* Princeton: Princeton University Press.

March, J. and Olsen, J.P. (1976). *Ambiguity and Choice in Organizations.* Bergen: Universitetsforlaget.

Marrow, A.J. (1969). *The Practical Theorist: The Life and Work of Kurt Lewin.* New York: Basic Books.

Marshall, T.H. (1965). *Class, Citizenship and Social Development.* New York: Basic Books.

Marx, K. (1867). *Capital. Volume I.* Moscow: Progress Publishers [n.d.].

Mattson, K. (1999). 'State of the union', *In These Times,* 21 February, pp. 22–23.

Mayo, E. (1933). *The Human Problems of an Industrial Civilization.* Cambridge, MA: Harvard University Press.

Mayo, E. (1945). *The Social Problems of an Industrial Civilization.*

Cambridge, MA: Harvard University, Graduate School of Business Administration.

McCarthy, T. (1991). *Ideals and Illusions: On Reconstruction and Deconstruction in Contemporary Critical Theory*. Cambridge, MA: The MIT Press.

McGregor, D. (1960). *The Human Side of Enterprise*. New York: McGraw-Hill.

McKibben, B. (2003). *Enough: Staying Human in an Engineered Age*. New York: Times Books.

McKinnon, C. and Hampsher-Mon, I. (eds) (2000). *The Demands of Citizenship*. London: Continuum.

McLellan, D. (1977). *Selected Writings: Karl Marx*. Oxford: Oxford University Press.

McMurtry, J. (1999). *The Cancer Stage of Capitalism*. London: Pluto Press.

Meadows, D. *et al.* (1974). *The Limits to Growth: A Report for the Club of Rome's Project on the Predicament of Mankind*. New York: Universe Books.

Meehan, J. (ed.) (1995a). *Feminists Read Habermas: Gendering the Subject of Discourse*. New York: Routledge.

Meehan, J. (1995b). 'Autonomy, recognition, and respect: Habermas, Benjamin, and Honneth'. In: J. Meehan (ed.) *Feminists Read Habermas: Gendering the Subject of Discourse*. New York: Routledge.

Milani, B. (2000). *Designing the Green Economy: The Postindustrial Alternative to Corporate Globalization*. New York: Rowman and Littlefield.

Milkman, R. (1998). 'The new American workplace: High road or low road? In: P. Thompson and C. Warhurst (eds) *Workplaces of the Future*. London: Macmillan Press.

Miller, D. and Slater, D. (2000). *The Internet: An Ethnographic Approach*. Oxford: Berg.

Mills, A. (1988). 'Organization, gender and culture', *Organization Studies* 9(3): 351–69.

Mills, C.W. (1959). *The Sociological Imagination*. New York: Oxford University Press.

Mishra, P. (2004). *An End to Suffering: The Buddha in the Modern World*. New York: Farrar, Straus and Giroux.

Mokhiber, R. and Weissman, R. (2002). 'Bad apples in a rotten system: the ten worst corporations of 2002', *Multinational Monitor*, 23(12), December.

Moon, C. and Stanworth, C. (1999). 'Ethics and empowerment: managerial discourse and the case of teleworking'. In: J. Quinn and P.W.F. Davies (eds) *Ethics and Empowerment*. London: Macmillan Press.

Moore, B. (1973). *Reflections on the Causes of Human Misery and Upon Certain Proposals to Eliminate Them*. Boston: Beacon Press.

Moravec, H. (1988). *Mind Children: The Future of Robot and Human Intelligence*. Cambridge, MA: Harvard University Press.

Morris, J.A. and Feldman, D.C. (1996). 'The dimensions, antecedents, and consequences of emotional labour', *Academy of Management Review*, 21: 986–1010.

Morrison, E. and Milliken, F.J. (2000). 'Organizational silence: a barrier to changes and development in a pluralistic world', *Academy of Management Review*, 25(4): 706–25.

Mouffe, C. (1993). *The Return of the Political*. London: Verso.

Mueller, C. (1973). *The Politics of Communication: A Study in the Political Sociology of Language, Socialization, and Legitimation*. New York: Oxford University Press.

N.T. (2002). 'Gender-based organizational barriers: inhibitors of the learning organization'. Paper presented to the CASAE regional conference, 11 May.

Naisbitt, J. (1984). *Megatrends: Ten New Directions Transforming Our Lives*. New York: Warner Books.

Negt, O. (2000). 'Chances of a civil society in learning', *Lifelong Learning in Europe*, 1: 8–15.

Nemeth, C.J. (1997). 'Managing innovation: when less is more', *California Management Review*, 40(1): 59–74.

Nemeth, C.J. and Wachter, J. (1983). 'Creative problem solving as a result of majority versus minority influence', *European Journal of Social Psychology*, 13: 45–55.

Niedzviecki, H. (2004). *Hello I'm special: How Individuality Became the New Conformity*. Toronto: Penguin Canada.

Nisbet, R. (1980). *History of the Idea of Progress*. New York: Basic Books.

Nkomo, S. (1992). 'The emperor has no clothes: rewriting "race in organizations"', *Academy of Management Review*, 17(3): 487–513.

Noble, D. (1977). *American By Design: Science, Technology, and the Rise of Corporate Capitalism*. New York: Alfred A. Knopf.

Noble, D. (1998). *The Religion of Technology*. New York: Alfred A. Knopf.

Olsson, K. (2003). 'Up against Wal-Mart', *Mother Jones on-line,* March/April, pp. 1–3.

Parker, L.E. (1993). 'When to fix it and when to leave: the relationship among perceived control, self-efficacy, dissent and exit', *Journal of Applied Psychology,* 78: 949–59.

Parkin, A. (1996). 'Building civil society "from the ground up": the Halifax People's Summit'. Paper presented to the Centre for Studies in Democratization, 16–17 February.

Pateman, C. (1989). *The Disorder of Women: Democracy, Feminism and Political Theory.* Stanford: Stanford University Press.

Pentland, H.C. (1981). *Labour and Capital in Canada 1650–1860.* Toronto: James Lorimer.

Peters, T. (1982). *Thriving on Chaos.* New York: Alfred A. Knopf.

Pfeffer, J. (1997). *New Directions for Organization Theory.* New York: Oxford University Press.

Philippe, C. (2000). Personal communication.

Phillips, A. and Taylor, B. (1980). 'Sex and skill: notes towards a feminist economics', *Feminist Review,* 6: 79–88.

Pinker, S. (1997). *How the Mind Works.* New York: W.W. Norton and Co.

Pinker, S. (2003). *The Blank Slate: The Modern Denial of Human Nature.* New York: Penguin Books.

Polyani, K. (1944). *The Great Transformation.* Boston: Beacon Press [1957].

Porat, M.U. (1977). *The Information Economy: Definition and Measurement.* Washington, DC: US Department of Commerce, Office of Telecommunications.

Porat, M.U. (1978). 'Communication policy in an information society'. In: G. Robinson (ed.) *Communications for Tomorrow: Policy Perspectives for the 1980s.* New York: Praeger.

Poster, M. (1990). *The Mode of Information: Poststructuralism and Social Context.* Cambridge, UK: Polity.

Potterfield, T. (1999). *The Business of Employee Empowerment: Democracy and Ideology in the Workplace.* London: Quorum Books.

Power, S, (2002). '*A Problem from Hell*': America and the Age of Genocide. New York: HarperCollins.

Putnam, R. (2000). *Bowling Alone: The Collapse and Revival of American Community.* New York: Simon and Schuster.

Quinn, J. (1999). 'Is empowerment ethical? Why ask the question?'. In: J. Quinn and P.W.F. Davies (eds) *Ethics and Empowerment.* London: Macmillan Press, pp. 23–37.

Quinn, J. and Davies, P.W.F. (eds) (1999). *Ethics and Empowerment.* London: Macmillan Press.

Ramonet, I. (2003). 'Set the media free', *Le Monde Diplomatique,* October.

Rappaport, J., Swift, C. and Hess, R. (1987). *Studies in Empowerment: Steps Toward Understanding and Action.* New York: Haworth Press.

Rieff, P. (1966). *The Triumph of the Therapeutic: Uses of Faith after Freud.* New York: Harper and Row.

Roethlisberger, F. and Dickson, W. (1939). *Management and the Worker.* Cambridge, MA: Harvard University Press.

Rutherford, P. (2000). *Endless Propaganda: The Advertising of Public Goods.* Toronto: University of Toronto Press.

Ryan, M. (1992). 'Gender and public access: women's politics in nineteenth-century America'. In: C. Calhoun (ed.) *Habermas and the Public Sphere.* Cambridge, MA: The MIT Press, pp. 259–88.

Schell, J. (1982). *The Fate of the Earth.* New York: Alfred A. Knopf.

Scheuermann, W.E. (1999). 'Between radicalism and resignation: democratic theory in Habermas's *Between facts and norms*'. In: P. Dews (ed.) *Habermas: A Critical Reader.* Oxford: Blackwell Publishers, pp. 155–77.

Schied, F. *et al.* (1998). 'Complicity and control in the workplace: a critical case study of TQM, learning, and the management of knowledge', *International Journal of Lifelong Education,* 17(3): 157–72.

Schienstock, G. and Kuusi, O. (eds) *Transformation Towards a Learning Economy.* Helsinki: Sitra.

Schiller, H. (1989). *Culture Inc.: The Corporate Take-Over of Public Expression.* New York: Oxford University Press.

Selman, G. (1989). '1972 – year of affirmation for adult education', *The Canadian Journal for the Study of Adult Education,* III(1): 33–45.

Senge, P. (1990). *The Fifth Discipline: The Art and Practice of the Learning Organization.* New York: Doubleday.

Sennett, R. (1976). *The Fall of Public Man.* New York: Alfred Knopf.

Sennett, R. (1998). *The Corrosion of Character: The Personal Consequences of Work in the New Capitalism.* New York: Norton.

Serafini, S. and Andrieu, M. (1981). *The Information Revolution and its Implications for Canada.* Ottawa: Government of Canada.

Sewell, G. and Wilkinson, B. (1993). 'Human resource management in "surveillance" companies'. In: J. Clark (ed.) *Human Resource Management and Technical Change.* London: Sage.

Shaw, M.E. (1981). *Group Dynamics: The Psychology of Small Group Behavior.* New York: McGraw-Hill.

Smith, A. (1976). *The Theory of Moral Sentiments.* D.D. Raphael and A.L. Macfie (eds). Oxford: Clarendon Press.

Solomon, B.B. (1976). *Black Empowerment.* New York: Columbia University Press.

Stalker, J. (1998). 'Women in the history of adult education: misogynist responses to our participation.' In: S. Scott, B. Spencer and A. Thomas (eds) *Learning for Life.* Toronto: Thompson Educational Publishers.

Stiglitz, J. (2002). 'The roaring nineties', *The Atlantic Monthly*, October 2002, pp. 75–88.

Sunahara, A. (1981). *The Politics of Racism: The Uprooting of Japanese Canadians During the Second World War.* Toronto: James Lorimer.

Talbot, S. (1995). *The Future Does Not Compute: Transcending the Machines in Our Midst.* Sebastopool, California: O'Reilly and Associates.

Tallis, R. (1997). *Enemies of Hope: A Critique of Contemporary Pessimism.* New York: St. Martin's Press.

Tawney, R. (1926). *Religion and the Rise of Capitalism.* New York: Harcourt, Brace.

Taylor, C. (1991). *The Malaise of Modernity.* Concord, Ontario: Anansi Press.

Taylor, C. (1992). 'The politics of recognition'. In: A. Gutman (ed.) *Multiculturalism and the 'Politics of Recognition': An Essay by Charles Taylor.* Princeton: Princeton University Press, pp. 25–73.

Thomas, A. (1991). *Beyond Education: A New Perspective on Society's Management of Learning.* San Francisco: Jossey-Bass.

Thompson, E. P. (1963). *The Making of the English Working Class.* New York: Pantheon Books.

Thompson, P. and Warhurst, C. (1998). 'Hands, hearts and minds: changing work and workers at the end of the century'. In: P. Thompson and C. Warhurst (eds), *Workplaces of the Future.* London: Macmillan Press.

Thomson, W. (1944). *Adult Education: Theory and Policy.* Division of Adult Education Papers, Saskatchewan Archives, Regina, Saskatchewan.

Toffler, A. (1980). *The Third Wave.* London: Collins.

Toffler, A. (1990). *Powershift: Knowledge, Wealth and Violence at the Edge of the Twenty-First Century.* New York: Bantam Books.

Toulmin, S. (2001). *Return to Reason.* Cambridge, MA: Harvard University Press.

Townley, B. (1994). *Reframing Human Resource Management: Power, Ethics and the Subject at Work.* London: Sage.

UNESCO (1997). *Adult Education: The Hamburg Declaration. The Agenda for the Future.* Fifth international conference on adult education, 14–18 July 1997. UNESCO.

Waller, R.D. (ed.) (1956) *A Design for Democracy.* London: Max Parrish.

Walsh, N. (2004). 'Russia dumps its children on the streets', *The Guardian Weekly,* 6–12 May.

Ward, P.W. (1978). *White Canada Forever: Popular Attitudes and Public Policy Toward Orientals in British Columbia.* Montreal: McGill-Queen's University Press.

Waterman, R., Waterman, R.J. and Collard, B. (1994). 'Toward a career resilient workforce', *Harvard Business Review,* July–August, pp. 87–95.

Weber, M. (1946). *From Max Weber: Essays in Sociology,* ed. and trans. H. Gerth and C. W. Mills. New York: Oxford University Press.

Weber, M. (1948). 'Science as vocation', in M. Weber, *From Max Weber: Essays in Sociology* (trans. by H.H. Gerth and C. Wright Mills). London: Routledge and Kegan Paul, pp. 129–56.

Webster, F. (1995). *Theories of the Information Society.* London: Routledge.

Weick, K. (1995). *Sensemaking in Organizations.* Thousand Oaks: Sage.

Welton, M. (1982). 'Gramsci's contribution to the analysis of public education knowledge', *Journal of Educational Thought,* December, pp. 140–9.

Welton, M. (1986a). 'Mobilizing the people for socialism: Watson Thomson and the Cold War politics of adult education in Saskatchewan, 1944–6', *Labour/Le Travail,* 18(Fall): 111–38.

Welton, M. (1986b). '"An authentic instrument of the democratic process": the intellectual origins of the Canadian Citizens' Forum', *Studies in the Education of Adults,* 18(1): 35–49.

Welton, M. (1991). *Toward Development Work: The Workplace as a Learning Environment.* Geelong: Deakin University Press.

Welton, M. (ed.) (1995). *In Defense of the Lifeworld: Critical Perspectives on Adult Learning.* Albany: SUNY Press.

Welton, M. (2001). *Little Mosie from the Margaree: A Biography of Moses Michael Coady.* Toronto: Thompson Educational Publishers.

Welton, M. and Lecky, J. (1997). 'Volunteerism as the seedbed of democracy: the educational thought and practice of Guy Henson of Nova Scotia', *Studies in the Education of Adults,* 29(1): 25–38.

Wernick, A. (1991). *Promotional Culture: Advertising, Ideology, and Symbolic Expression.* London: Sage.

White, S. (1988). *The Recent Work of Jurgen Habermas: Reason, Justice and Modernity.* Cambridge, UK: Cambridge University Press.

Winnicott, D.W. (1965). *The Maturational Process and the Facilitating Environment.* London: Hogarth Press.

Wortman, C.B. and Brehm, J.W. (1975). 'Responses to uncontrollable outcomes: an integration of reactance theory and the learned helplessness model'. In: L. Berkowitz (ed.) *Advances in Experimental Social Psychology.* New York: Academic Press, pp. 277–336.

Young, J. (1822). *Letters of Agricola.* Halifax: Holland Publishers.

Zuboff, S. (1988). *In the Age of the Smart Machine.* New York: Basic Books.

Index

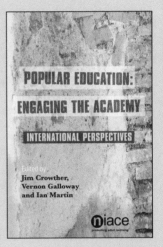